KEITH A.P. SANDIFORD is an associate professor of history at the University of Manitoba, Winnipeg, Manitoba.

This book closes an obvious gap in nineteenth-century historiography by carefully analysing British policy and public opinion with regard to the Schleswig-Holstein problem from 1848 to 1864. Solidly based on a study of private and public correspondence, memoirs, biographies, newspapers, periodicals, sessional papers, foreign office documents, and parliamentary debates, it argues that the failure of British policy was due to division and uncertainty of opinion: Britain vacillated between a pliant and a defiant course and eventually chose the worst features of both. Professor Sandiford demonstrates that the failure of Russell's Schleswig-Holstein diplomacy in 1864 was largely the result of a long sequence of British miscalculations dating back at least to 1848. He also shows that the general bewilderment, both within and outside the British Parliament, permitted the queen and a handful of her ministers to exert more influence on Britain's policy in 1863-4 than has previously been supposed.

SANDIFORD, Keith A. P.   Great Britain and the Schleswig-Holstein question, 1848–64: a study in diplomacy, politics, and public opinion. University of Toronto, 1975.   204p   map   bibl   75-16373.   15.00. ISBN 0-8020-5334-3. C.I.P.
Sandiford subjects the diplomatic crisis preceding the Dano-German war of 1864 to detailed narrative treatment, concentrating on the policies and attitudes of the cabinet and court, the press and Parliament. It is a sorry chronicle of divided counsels, diplomatic and military impotence, and deflated pretentions. The treatment is scholarly, methodical, but often limited in perspective. The work, however, is well integrated with that of other writers, chiefly biographers and diplomatic historians, and it succeeds in representing the crisis as marking a cataclysm in the British public's understanding of its influence and role in European affairs. It put an end to "Palmerstonianism" and inaugurated a period of "relative isolation." The theme is important, but the book is suitable only to highly specialised collections.

KEITH A. P. SANDIFORD

Great Britain and the Schleswig-Holstein Question 1848-64: a study in diplomacy, politics, and public opinion

UNIVERSITY OF TORONTO PRESS
Toronto and Buffalo

© University of Toronto Press 1975
Toronto and Buffalo
Printed in Canada

Library of Congress Cataloging in Publication Data

Sandiford, Keith A   P   1936-
    Great Britain and the Schleswig-Holstein question,
    1848-64.

    Bibliography: p.
    Includes index.
    1. Schleswig-Holstein question.   2. Great Britain
    – Foreign relations – 1837-1901.   3. Schleswig-Holstein
    War, 1864.   I. Title.
    DD491.s68s255   327.41'0489   75-16373
    ISBN 0-8020-5334-3

To Lorraine, Garfield, and Shelley

Acknowledgments

The author wishes to acknowledge his indebtedness to the editors of *History* and the *Canadian Journal of History* for permission to reprint material first published in their respective journals. Grateful acknowledgments are also due to Edwin Arnold Ltd, Cambridge University Press, and Manchester University Press for permission to reproduce maps previously published by them.

Contents

Preface

It is not the purpose of this book to treat the Schleswig-Holstein question as a problem in international politics. This has already been done by a host of European scholars as well as by Professor L.D. Steefel, a brilliant American historian. The present study is concerned primarily with the immediate British reaction to the Schleswig-Holstein crisis of 1863–4. It is an attempt to examine royal, ministerial, ambassadorial, parliamentary, press, and public opinion; to demonstrate the interconnection among these bodies of thought; to estimate their effect on British policy in the Dano-German conflict; to submit this policy to a critical analysis; and to assess, very briefly, its overall influence on the subsequent role of Britain in Europe. The first chapter establishes the need for this work by looking at the curious fashion in which British historians have generally side-stepped the issue; while the second, third, and fourth chapters are meant to illuminate a segment of British diplomacy that has previously been much neglected. Even the biographers of Palmerston and Russell have ignored the development of the Schleswig-Holstein dispute in the interval between the London Treaty of 1852 and the occupation of Holstein in 1863.

This close study of the diplomatic records, private correspondence, and public opinion has tended on the whole to support many of the better known generalizations that traditionally have been made on the Schleswig-Holstein question – although, from the purely British standpoint, it provides a more detailed treatment of the subject than has hitherto been attempted. The reader will notice, however, that in some important respects it differs from orthodox interpretations: the work shows, for instance, how ambivalent was the attitude of Palmerston during the first six months of 1864 in his treatment of the Danish crisis; it illustrates that British public opinion on the Dano-German war was far more divided than has been suggested previously; it places more than the usual stress on royal and ministerial influence over British policy in this matter; and it demonstrates that the failure of Russell's Schleswig-Holstein diplomacy in 1864 was largely the result of a long sequence of British miscalculations dating back at least to 1848.

This monograph has grown out of my doctoral thesis presented in 1966 at the University of Toronto. The study was initiated there under the direction of Professor J.B. Conacher who has maintained a lively interest in the project from the beginning. He carefully read the rough draft of the manuscript and made several useful suggestions. Professors John L. Finlay, Richard A. Lebrun, and Thomas E. Vadney of the University of Manitoba have critically examined some of the chapters and offered judicious counsel. A research grant from the Canada Council provided assistance of a more material sort. From the staff of the British Museum, the Historical Manuscripts Commission, the Institute of Historical Research, and the Public Record Office (London), and the libraries of the University of London, the University of Manitoba, and the University of Toronto, I have also received considerable help. To all these persons and institutions I cannot but be grateful. I must also acknowledge a special debt to my wife, Lorraine, who has offered vital encouragement at crucial stages, and to our departmental secretary, Miss Blanche Miller, who has cheerfully performed all the miscellaneous tasks involved in the preparation of a typescript.

The book has been published with the help of a grant from the Social Science Research Council of Canada, using funds provided by the Canada Council, and a grant from the Andrew W. Mellon Foundation to the University of Toronto Press.

GREAT BRITAIN AND THE SCHLESWIG-HOLSTEIN
QUESTION 1848-64

Map I Denmark and the Elbe Duchies (note Danish version of places north of the Eider). Reprinted from Toyne: *The Scandinavians in History*, by permission of Edward Arnold Ltd.

1
British historians and
the Schleswig-Holstein crisis

The Schleswig-Holstein crisis of 1863–4 was one of the important turning-points in the history of British foreign policy. It produced the most emphatic diplomatic defeat suffered by the Victorians and it precipitated their eclipse in Europe during the Bismarckian age. But despite its historical significance, it has not yet received adequate attention from British historians.

It is tempting to attribute this to psychological causes: to say that historians are naturally patriotic and prefer to deal with national triumph rather than with catastrophe. This explanation cannot suffice, however, for Danish historians have been discussing their country's tragedy from that day to this. Indeed, within twenty-five years of the loss of the Danish duchies, Alexander Thorsøe had produced his solid account of Frederick VII's reign, and by 1901 Kristian Erslev had published his thesis which many still consider the definitive work on the Augustenburg claims. In 1906 Niels Neergaard completed his classic history of Denmark from 1848 to 1866. Between the World Wars, Danish scholars like Erik Arup, Aage Friis, and Erik Møller continued to examine various aspects of the Schleswig-Holstein question; and during the period 1923–66, Holger Hjelholt wrote several studies on the Dano-German dispute.

There is indeed a substantial volume of European literature on the question of Schleswig-Holstein, and the formation of British policy during the crisis has sometimes been critically examined from continental vantage-points. But strangely enough, British historians have generally displayed no similar enthusiasm for this kind of discussion. As a result, the immediate British response to the Schleswig-Holstein crisis has not yet been thoroughly analysed. In partial explanation of this oddity, it must be noted that for many years, even after World War I, the

Foreign Office papers dealing with the 1860s were not open to students except by special permit. It was not in fact until the early 1930s that the opening of the archives was extended and the British government removed the restrictions governing the use of the Foreign Office documents after 1861. Even so, it is clear that a British historian of repute would not have been denied access to the Schleswig-Holstein materials had he applied for special permission to consult them. It is also true that many British historians sought and received permission to use similar papers on other contemporary issues long before the formal waiving of the official restrictions.

In fact, only four English-speaking historians have thus far attempted a detailed treatment of the Schleswig-Holstein question as a problem in European politics, and two of these – Chester W. Clark and Lawrence D. Steefel – are actually Americans. The other two are Werner E. Mosse and Sir Adolphus William Ward. A detailed study of British policy in Schleswig-Holstein has to date been attempted only by Mosse, Steefel, and Ward. Clark, in his *Franz Joseph and Bismarck before 1866* (Harvard, 1934), displayed only a secondary interest in the British role. His primary concern was to combat the popular 'Prussian' account of German history in the 1860s by making more effective use of Austrian sources than had hitherto been done. By focusing so carefully on Austria's motives and schemes, he developed a keen appreciation of her difficulties and thus partially succeeded in rehabilitating Count Johann von Rechberg, the much maligned Austrian minister.

Steefel's excellent monograph, *The Schleswig-Holstein Question* (Harvard, 1932), is still the definitive exposition of the subject in English. His industrious research in the archives of the main European capitals resulted in a brilliant synthesis of the Austrian, British, French, Hanoverian, Prussian, and Scandinavian materials then at his disposal. His treatment of Russian diplomacy was somewhat cavalier, and there were Austrian sources (later used by Clark) that Steefel did not consult, but his analysis is well-balanced and most of his judgments are sound. Steefel succeeded in placing the complicated Elbe riddle quite squarely in its local and international contexts. On the British side, he looked carefully at the parliamentary papers, some of the Foreign Office despatches, the most important parliamentary debates, the files of *The Times* and the *Morning Post*, and some of the private correspondence of Earl Russell, the foreign secretary, and A.H. Layard, the under-secretary for foreign affairs. Steefel is justifiably critical of British policy in Schleswig-Holstein although he does not suggest alternative courses that Britain might possibly have pursued with greater success or dignity.

Sir A.W. Ward, in *Germany: 1815-90* (Cambridge, 1917), made considerable use of the available printed materials in English, French and German, but his treatment of the Schleswig-Holstein question suffered from inadequate research on Austrian, Danish, and Russian sources. Like his father, who was the British consul at Hamburg in the 1860s, Ward sympathized with the German claims and therefore viewed critically the policy of Britain and Denmark in the duchies. He examined British policy at greater length in the chapter entitled 'The Schleswig-Holstein Question, 1852-1866' in the second volume of the *Cambridge History of British Foreign Policy: 1815-1866* (1922). Here Ward condemns the London Treaty of 1852 and throws much light on the development of the Schleswig-Holstein crisis after the Danish king Christian VIII's publication of the notorious 'Open Letter' in 1846. He deals more patiently with Russell's various Schleswig-Holstein proposals between 1859 and 1865 than is normally done even by Russell's biographers. Ward's narrative, however, is based almost entirely on the papers presented to Parliament and there are therefore substantial gaps in his research. He made little use of the Foreign Office documents (which he would surely have been permitted to use for this purpose), the parliamentary debates, or the private correspondence relating to the topic. Nor did he display much interest in press and public opinion. The queen played an important role in determining British policy in the Danish crisis, and the cabinet consistently prevented Russell from pursuing the line of his choice, but these factors are neglected by Ward. Even though he seriously criticizes Russell's program in the duchies, he never seems conscious of the difficulties facing the foreign secretary and he does not try to indicate what the British government could actually have done to avoid embarrassment in 1864.

The majority of the defects in Ward's work have been corrected by Mosse, who has succeeded in making a valuable contribution to historical knowledge, largely by exploring the Royal Archives in Windsor Castle with commendable assiduity. His great work, *The European Powers and the German Question, 1848-71* (Cambridge, 1958), is particularly concerned with explaining the attitudes of Britain and Russia towards the development of German unification. Here Mosse demonstrates intelligently how and why domestic as well as diplomatic circumstances conspired to prevent Russia and Britain from pursuing, in central Europe, a policy of active interference that would clearly have thwarted Bismarck's plans. His research on primary British and Russian sources is honest and thorough, and his work therefore supplements that of countless Europeans who had previously been dealing with the Bismarckian miracle chiefly from French and Prussian points of view. Mosse's analysis of the impact of the Schleswig-Holstein question on European politics is shrewd. He rightly stresses the Anglo-Russian mistrust of Napoleon III as the key to an understanding of 1864, and thereby also shows why it was hardly possible for France to pursue a bolder course in the Danish crisis. He takes a favourable view of Napoleon's masterly inaction, but concludes (p. 211) that the British policy was 'conducted with an incredible lack of skill and consistency.'

Mosse himself did much to explain this British lack of resolution in the Danish crisis when he produced his scholarly essay, 'Queen Victoria and her Ministers in the Schleswig-Holstein Crisis, 1863–64,' which appeared in Volume LXXVIII of the *English Historical Review* (April 1963). By focusing largely on the court, he emerged with a careful assessment of the queen's role in the shaping of British policy in the Dano-German dispute. His argument here (pp. 263–83) is that the queen played a very effective part in preventing Russell from pursuing a violent anti-German policy. He shows how often the queen, by allying herself with the peace-party within the cabinet, compelled the foreign secretary to alter and even to withdraw despatches that he was proposing to send to European courts. Mosse observes that the queen occasionally stretched her constitutional rights to their limit, and concludes (perhaps too cautiously in view of his abundant evidence) that her influence was 'subtle' and 'intangible,' and that she might well have affected Britain's Schleswig-Holstein diplomacy 'in detail rather than substance.'

Altogether Mosse's treatment of British policy in the Schleswig-Holstein affair is much more comprehensive than Steefel's or Ward's. Not only is the base of his British research broader than theirs but he is addressing himself to a wider range of questions. Thus he is able to stress the importance of ministerial discord, to comment briefly on press and public opinion, to examine the role of Parliament in 1864, and to emphasize the involvement of the court. He seems less sound when dealing with the Dano-German crisis of 1848-52, but he is clearly on top of his material in the 1860s – especially when commenting on the relationship between the Polish revolt and the Danish crisis.

Mosse is also much more reliable than the host of British historians who have touched briefly on Schleswig-Holstein as a problem in nineteenth-century British foreign policy. Apart from a few of the biographers of Palmerston and Russell, the British historians who have perhaps managed most effectively to unravel the Schleswig-Holstein puzzle are K. Bourne, R.W. Seton-Watson, and Sir E.L. Woodward.

In *Britain in Europe, 1789-1914* (Cambridge, 1937), Seton-Watson's analysis of the Schleswig-Holstein question represents the median, in time as well as character, between Ward's approach and Mosse's. His account is based on a vast body of literature and his grasp of European politics is more secure than that of most British diplomatic historians. He looks briefly but squarely at the policies of Bismarck and Napoleon III. He also carefully evaluates the British response to what was definitely a very delicate situation in 1863-4. Seton-Watson is critical of the British government and rightly sees that the Danish crisis tended to diminish

British influence and prestige on the continent. He shows clearly how inconsistent was Russell's Schleswig-Holstein program and deftly relates Britain's failure here to her errors in Poland. He indicates that the court exerted considerable influence to prevent a divided cabinet from involving Britain in a war with Germany, and he also examines the major parliamentary debates on the Dano-German question. Most of his notions have been confirmed by Mosse's more specialized studies. On the debit side, Seton-Watson does not attempt to explain or to estimate the role of the British press during the crisis, and his account of the London conference of 1864 is sketchy. In analysing parliamentary opinion, he might also have examined profitably the serious divisions over the matter within both liberal and conservative ranks. But given the scope of his work and the nature of the sources available to him, Seton-Watson deserves praise for the overall competence with which he has dealt with British policy in the Danish duchies.

While other British survey-historians have tended to sidestep the Schleswig-Holstein crisis, Sir E.L. Woodward, in *The Age of Reform, 1815-70* (Oxford, 1962), analyses it quite soundly. Here (pp. 317-24) he is too brief on the Danish problem to throw much new light on it, but he demonstrates a satisfactory understanding of the question in its European context. He is perhaps a trifle too partial to Palmerston, and he passes little judgment on Russell's work. There is no mention of Clarendon or Granville in his summary, and he deals with the queen only in a footnote. But, on the whole, Woodward's treatment of the British role is very good. His view of British public opinion with respect to foreign affairs in general, and the Schleswig-Holstein question in particular, is eminently reasonable.

The most recent British survey of the Schleswig-Holstein crisis appears in Bourne's *Foreign Policy of Victorian England, 1830-1902* (Oxford, 1970). This work provides a good general summary of Victorian foreign policy, but on the question of Schleswig-Holstein (pp. 107-10), Bourne accepts too readily the orthodox view of Palmerston's later diplomacy. He glosses too rapidly over the earlier history of the Dano-German quarrel and therefore fails to take properly into account the difficulties facing the British Foreign Office in 1864. Even so, Bourne makes a number of perceptive observations, and his selection of documents is carefully considered. His conclusion (p. 110) that ministerial disagreements prevented Britain from pursuing a Palmerstonian line in the Schleswig-Holstein crisis is certainly valid.

Of all the British biographers, the most scholarly in their treatment of the Danish crisis are W.B. Pemberton, D. Southgate, A.W. Tilby, and Sir Spencer Walpole. Not surprisingly, they are all biographers of either Palmerston or Russell. And since no discussion of Palmerstonian biography can be complete without some mention of his most famous biographer, the name of H.C.F. Bell, a naturalized American, must be included in this group.[1]

In Bell's *Palmerston* (London, 1936), there is good coverage of the Dano-German quarrel during the two periods of crisis, but there is nothing on this subject between 1852 and 1862. As a result, Bell speaks glibly (ii, 361–400) of Palmerston's failing memory in 1863, although indeed Russell and Palmerston had conducted a vigorous correspondence with European courts on the question of the duchies ever since 1859. At any rate, Bell analyses Palmerston's difficulties in 1864 with skill as well as sympathy. He attributes the British failure to Palmerston's declining mental and physical powers, the pacific and mercenary attitude of the public, divisions within the cabinet, the constant meddling of the queen, and the British fear of France. Rather than blame Palmerston for the rebuffs suffered by Britain in the Danish crisis, Bell accepts them philosophically as the signal that the age of Palmerstonianism had passed. The European forces at work here are not always soundly grasped by Bell who fails also to deal thoroughly with either the London conference or the Schleswig-Holstein debates in Parliament. On the whole, however, his assessment of the British role in the conflict is quite satisfactory, even though space did not permit him to deal as fully with the matter as he would have wished.

Pemberton's *Lord Palmerston* (London, 1954) is not as carefully researched as Bell's and was not intended to be as ambitious a project. Still, Schleswig-Holstein is dealt with here (pp. 329–47) in greater detail than in other biographies written on a similar scale. Although Pemberton minimizes Russell's role, his analysis of Britain's policy is sound enough. By assuming, however, that there were certain straightforward options available to Palmerston in the attempt to solve this puzzle, Pemberton seems unduly critical of his hero. He is the only one of Palmerston's biographers who admits the validity of the queen's stand on the Schleswig-Holstein dispute.

Southgate contrived, in *The Most English Minister: Policies and Politics of Palmerston* (London, 1966), to produce a fine synthesis of all the known printed materials on this outstanding Victorian. Here, he follows the orthodox interpretations of Britain's involvement in the Schleswig-Holstein drama, and agrees (p. 518) with Mosse and A.J.P. Taylor that the cabinet meeting of 25 June 1864 marked a turning-point in British diplomacy.[2] But, by accepting too readily the normal criticisms of the British program, Southgate has failed to answer the following questions: How obvious was it in 1863 that Prussia was leading Germany? Why was it really necessary to meet the queen's objections on the question of a plebiscite in the duchies? Why should Denmark expect British help after she had so consistently disobeyed British advice? If the London Treaty of 1852 was an error, when and how should Russell have abandoned it? Had Southgate tried to answer these questions, his otherwise scholarly summary would have been more favourable to Palmerston and Russell who were trying to follow a confused public opinion, to lead a divided and reluctant cabinet, to forestall the Russians and the French while restraining the Germans, and to cope with an unduly Germanophile court. In fairness to the 'two dreadful old men,' criticism of their Schleswig-Holstein policy must be tempered by the realization that they were also hamstrung in the 1860s by Gladstonian finance and Cobdenite economics.

Tilby's *Lord John Russell* (London, 1930) is very much a product of its immediate circumstance. In an age when warlike programs were being disavowed by Englishmen, Tilby describes Russell's policy in the Danish crisis as 'folly' (p. 245). He recommends a program of indifference since the Baltic was not in any case a direct British interest. He is critical of Russell for failing to understand the motives of Bismarck and to appreciate the measure of Prussian strength. Moreover, he feels that this fundamental lack of understanding was due simply to Russell's ignorance of the issues involved. In this analysis, Tilby does an injustice to Russell. It was not merely a question in 1864 of remaining indifferent, for clearly there was too much British sympathy for Denmark; Parliament itself recommended diplomatic intervention early in that year. It was all right for Palmerston and Russell, like Tilby in 1930, to resign themselves in the end to the consolation that the Baltic was not a direct British interest – but this view would not have been acceptable to the vast majority of Englishmen as late as 1863. There is, nevertheless, some validity in Tilby's claims (pp. 235-45): the Schleswig-Holstein crisis of 1864 was to some extent created by British bungling in the immediate past, and the policy of 'meddle and muddle' certainly reduced British prestige abroad. Tilby, however, is exaggerating when he declares that Britain ceased to count in European affairs for half a century after Denmark's defeat.

In *The Life of Lord John Russell* (London, 1891) by Walpole, the foreign secretary received his most lenient treatment. This is done (ii, 380-410) at the expense of Denmark. Walpole blames the Danish downfall in 1864 on the obstinacy of the Danes themselves. Perhaps because the queen was still alive, his treatment of her influence is imperfect, and he fails likewise to deal adequately with the question of ministerial discord. But Walpole is useful for his long extracts from Russell's correspondence, and while he does not try to estimate the French contribution to the Danish tragedy, his remarks on Napoleon III's motives and policies are sometimes perceptive.

Many British biographers have accomplished a strange feat in that they have dealt at some length with Schleswig-Holstein without attempting to provide any analysis or to reach any conclusions. They have merely reproduced the ideas of the statesmen of whom they have written. By tending to accept the opinions of their subjects they have contrived to perpetuate the Dano-German controversy by transforming it from an actual into a historiographical one. Thus the ministerial struggle, which severely hampered British policy in 1863-4, has not yet ended. In fact, most British historians who have addressed themselves to the Danish problem have curiously assumed the same moral positions as those held by the politicians in the 1860s. Consequently no fewer than six distinct schools seem to be participating in this eternal debate: Palmerstonians (the advocates of a vigorous British policy); Mancunians (the peace-at-any-price party); Royalists (the admirers of Queen Victoria who give her credit for maintaining peace despite the stupidity of her advisers); Danophiles who feel that Britain should have defended Denmark in her hour of need; Germanophiles who complain of Danish misrule in the duchies; and Disraelians who totally condemn the policies of the liberals as a matter of course.[3]

The existence of so many separate schools in the British historiography on Schleswig-Holstein bears ample testimony to the complex nature of the Elbe puzzle and also to the enormous difficulty facing Palmerston and Russell in their search for a solution. The contrariety of advice still being offered by British historians must serve as proof that Palmerston and Russell had no clear-cut options in 1864. Even British material interests, which by virtue of their very nature are normally measurable, have been a source of controversy. Whereas, for example, Molesworth, Pemberton, and Tilby deny that Britain had genuine interests in the Baltic, Lord Strang speaks of Denmark as a 'prime British interest.'[4] Some of the queen's supporters do not believe that British honour was compromised in 1864, but many other British writers do. Some historians, like Hassall, recommend war;[5] several others suggest that non-intervention was best.[6] Many of them, however, make no positive recommendation although they see fit to criticize the British program. And even so knowledgeable a historian as A.J.P. Taylor has admitted, in *The Struggle for Mastery in Europe, 1848-1918* (Oxford, 1954), that it is still difficult to determine exactly what else the British government could have done in 1864 (pp. 153-4).

Taylor's caution in this matter is based on his vast knowledge of nineteenth-century European diplomacy. But apart from Mosse and possibly Seton-Watson, the other British historians who have dealt with the Schleswig-Holstein question are not so familiar with the continental background. In fact, only a small number of British writers have attempted to place the Dano-German struggle properly within its historical and European context. Moreover, even those who have examined the problem simply as an issue in British politics and diplomacy have circumscribed their own vision by the flimsiness of their research. As a result, the majority of British historians make the elementary mistake of assuming that the crisis of 1864 sprang suddenly upon Palmerston and Russell and found them ridiculously unprepared. They invariably ignore the voluminous correspondence on Schleswig-Holstein conducted by the British Foreign Office during the period 1848-63. This is an error committed even by Bourne and Southgate whose analysis of the British role in the Danish crisis is sounder than most. Jasper Ridley, for example, in *Lord Palmerston* (London, 1970), speaks of the revival of the old legal arguments in 1863 (p. 569) as though the whole matter had lain dormant since 1852; and John Prest, in his recent biography of Russell, actually refers to Palmerston's speech in the House of Commons on 23 July 1863 as 'the original and greatest mistake' in Britain's handling of the whole affair (p. 396).

Few British historians stress the fact that Britain's anterior negotiations helped to place her in her dilemma during the actual crisis. To say that Britain was confused in 1863-4 is clearly not sufficient: Britain, after all, had followed the Schleswig-Holstein question perhaps even too closely during the preceding fifteen years. Britain committed the blunder of adhering too tenaciously to the London Treaty of 1852, which both the Danes and the Germans were determined to circumvent. But, given the chaotic circumstances of 1848-52, the London Treaty appeared the least of evils, and it might have succeeded had the Danes been more co-operative. The British government recognized this, and therefore constantly urged Denmark to be more conciliatory. There was really no other course, for the foreign secretary could scarcely have offended parliamentary and public opinion by appearing to take up cudgels for Germany. Indeed, when Russell came forward with his notorious 'Gotha Despatch' in 1862, he was promptly denounced by the British Parliament, the press, and even the cabinet.[7] Had not the Crimean War embittered the Russians, and the Polish question frustrated the French, Britain might well have managed to prolong the settlement of 1852 for many more years. The circumstances prevailing in 1864, however, could not easily have been foreseen by Palmerston and Russell in the 1850s.

British historians do not generally consider any of these matters. Instead they do Palmerston a grave injustice by quoting out of context the oft-repeated remarks made by the prime minister in July 1863. The reply that Palmerston gave to an innocent question about the threatened federal execution in Holstein was the only possible one that he could then have given. For no one, in the summer of 1863, could rationally have predicted that Denmark would ultimately be left alone to face a German invasion. Palmerston's response to Seymour Fitzgerald in the House of Commons was based on Britain's entire policy in Schleswig-Holstein since 1848. He was warning the Germans to be wary of starting a disturbance on the banks of the Elbe that was likely to expand in ways for which they had not bargained. He was also advising the Danes to fulfil the engagements they had contracted in 1851-2. British historians (like Bourne, Prest, Ridley, and Southgate), who criticize Palmerston for raising Danish hopes by threatening Germany with war in July 1863, do not realize that Palmerston was talking about a general European reaction against German aggression and not about British acts of hostility. Indeed, as Steefel has suggested (p. 61), it seems clear that Palmerston confidently expected France to resist the Germans should they encroach upon Danish soil. Furthermore, most British historians seem unfamiliar with the remainder of the same speech in which Palmerston refers to the Germans in Schleswig in a manner that could hardly have satisfied the Danes. To quote this speech and then dismiss Britain's Schleswig-Holstein policy as one purely of bluff, as so many historians have done, is simply to misinterpret what Palmerston, and certainly Russell, thought they were doing. In any case, even if it can be proved that Palmerston was indeed bluffing in July 1863, diplomatic historians must surely realize (as Palmerston himself did) that the European situation had changed drastically by January 1864.

The fact is that the majority of British historians have no enthusiasm for investigating the British role in the Danish crisis. Most of their remarks on Schleswig-Holstein are superficial – sometimes even inaccurate. But now that most of the relevant correspondence, both private and public, is available, there is no longer a good excuse for inaccuracy in the British treatment of Schleswig-Holstein. There are volumes of records in the Royal Archives which throw light on the attitude of the court and the motives of individual cabinet members. The latter have also left volumes of private correspondence, of which the Palmerston, Russell, Clarendon, Gladstone, Granville, Halifax, Somerset, and Ripon Papers are most important. Also very useful are the Cowley, Hammond, and Layard collections. The parliamentary Blue Books have been used by many British historians, but often without the necessary double-check on the Foreign Office documents. Among these, indeed, there is a vital collection (FO 97) devoted entirely to the British correspondence on Schleswig-Holstein during the period 1851-9. Few historians, either British or European, have utilized this source. The British Parliament also displayed an unusually keen interest in Danish vicissitudes in 1863 and 1864. More use needs to be made of these parliamentary debates. British historians, as a rule, are familiar only with Palmerston's famous reply to Fitzgerald on 23 July 1863 and with the long motion of censure in July 1864. The Victorian press, too, followed the Dano-German controversy with remarkable zeal. Countless editorials, letters, and miscellaneous items on Schleswig-Holstein appeared in most London and provincial journals. Dailies, weeklies, monthlies, and quarterlies all devoted an astonishing amount of space to the Elbe riddle, as it was then called. Only *The Times,* the *Morning Post* and the *Quarterly Review* have so far been examined by a few of the British historians writing on the Danish crisis. In addition to all this, the Dano-German controversy was the kernel of much pamphleteering activity in Britain after 1846.

This largely untapped body of resources could effectively be used to bridge the current gaps in our knowledge of Britain's reaction to the Schleswig-Holstein crisis. Her official policy has been analysed often enough by British and European diplomatic historians working in archives all across the continent, but it will never be properly understood until the domestic background is further illuminated. Mosse has examined masterfully and in detail the important role of the queen. The part played by the cabinet, however, has only very recently been investigated with equal care.[8] The ambivalent attitude of Palmerston towards this whole Danish business in 1864 has not yet been thoroughly considered by any of his biographers. The influence of Parliament has also been neglected thus far, and only vague hints have been made about the increasing passivity of the Palmerstonians within the cabinet after the House of Commons refused to encourage warlike designs in February 1864. Obviously, then, there are huge gaps in the common knowledge of Britain's response to the Danish crisis, and it is the purpose of this book to fill them.

The most glaring vacuum in this area has been created by the lack of published work on mid-Victorian public opinion. British scholars have often emphasized the significance of public opinion as a factor in Victorian politics and diplomacy, but nobody has yet examined its influence over British policy in the Danish duchies. Without pursuing the theme in depth or detail, most writers have simply indicated that British public opinion was very important since, by refusing to sanction Palmerstonian tactics in 1864, it ultimately forced the government to adopt the discreet rather than the heroic approach. This has, for instance, been part of A.J.P. Taylor's conviction that, by eventually accepting Cobden's gospel, the British public persuaded its leaders to conduct a passive foreign policy for almost sixty years after the Crimean War.[9] No one has yet successfully challenged this interpretation.

British historians have invariably discerned a striking correlation between public opinion and foreign policy from Canning's day to our own, and they have rightly emphasized the significance of public opinion as a force in British politics, particularly after 1832. Certainly Victorian statesmen themselves considered it of paramount importance, and it is well known that they tried, with varying degrees of skill and success, simultaneously to mould, lead, interpret, and follow this considerable, albeit vague and elusive, force. Yet studies of Victorian public opinion are rare.* Historians have seldom attempted to demon-

---

* This, of course, is not meant to belittle the work of scholars like Christine Bolt, Mary Ellison, Kingsley Martin, Dora Raymond, Bernard Semmel, and R.T. Shannon.

strate how public opinion was manipulated in the nineteeth century, who influenced it, and with what effect. They have generally assumed that the Victorian press spoke for the public and, in doing so, have tended to overstress the role of such outstanding papers as *The Times* and the *Morning Post*.

On matters diplomatic, however, Victorian opinion was influenced to a remarkable extent by governmental propaganda and European counter-propaganda. The British Foreign Office periodically set forth its own defence in sessional papers to which most Victorians could find easy access. Successive governments traditionally influenced editorial opinion on foreign policy by publishing their celebrated Blue Books. These edited versions of diplomatic correspondence often formed the basis of newspaper commentary. This indeed was the most overt fashion in which Victorian political leaders attempted to manipulate press opinion on foreign affairs. But foreign governments were aware of this practice and tried to combat it by supplying information of their own. This was done mainly through their ambassadors in London, many of whom (under strange pseudonyms) wrote long letters to various newspaper editors. Some European ministers accredited to London, like Count Karl Frederick von Vitzthum of Saxony, used subtler forms of persuasion. Vitzthum seems to have kept in close touch with the British political leaders, especially Derby and Disraeli, and to have wielded much influence upon their approach to the Schleswig-Holstein crisis.[10] His behaviour was by no means unusual, for during the peak of the Dano-German quarrel in the winter of 1863–4 many European documents and reports appeared in the leading British newspapers.

The Victorian Blue Books formed only one segment of an overall pamphleteering campaign, as all interested parties tried to rig the market of opinion in their favour. Several tracts, pamphlets, and books appeared on the Schleswig-Holstein question during the period 1846–64. This war of words was actively waged by foreign diplomats who wished to publicize their government's policies, opposition members who were attacking Britain's official program, and British as well as European merchants who feared that an Anglo-German war might injure their trade and shipping. The most prolific among such writers were Baron Christian von Bunsen (the Prussian minister in London, 1842–54), Lord Robert Cecil (the future marquis of Salisbury), Carl August Gosch (a Danish agent in Britain), Sir Robert Morier (a British diplomat attached to the legation in Berlin), and Dr Travers Twiss (a Fellow of University College, Oxford). It is impossible to measure exactly the effect of these publications, but one must conclude that they all contributed to that remarkable confusion of ideas that prevailed in Britain throughout the century on the subject of the Danish duchies.

Mid-Victorian public opinion was also aroused by politicians who arranged huge public meetings to discuss matters of national importance. Members of Parliament often used these opportunities to meet the leaders of opinion within their constituencies. This was then the best method of gauging the temper of the voting public. As it was vital, on these occasions, for the speakers to strike exactly the right chord, political scouts in local districts tried hard to keep MPs in touch with the general feelings of their constituents. For these reasons, public meetings in the 1860s constitute an important index of contemporary public opinion. Several such public meetings were held in the winter of 1863-4 when most of the younger liberals, following the example of the radicals Bright and Cobden, made a strong plea for a British policy of non-intervention in the Dano-German conflict on the dual ground that British interests were not directly involved and that Britain in any case should attend to her own domestic problems. The warm and enthusiastic reception which these speakers invariably received seems to indicate that they were saying precisely what their listeners wanted to hear.

It is partly for this reason that more attention ought to be focused on parliamentary speeches, many of which were aimed directly at the electorate – particularly when the parliamentary session was so far advanced that a general election seemed imminent. This, in fact, was the case in 1864 during the great debate on Schleswig-Holstein. As Henry Brand, the liberal chief whip, had warned Palmerston, many of the MPs who took part in this motion of censure did so with an eye on the hustings.[11]

Certain organizations in Britain also tried to influence official policy by manipulating and shaping public opinion. Perhaps the most important of these, in the area of foreign affairs, was the Peace Society, led by Samuel Gurney, Joseph Pease, and Henry Richard. Itself an off-shoot of the famous Anti-Corn-Law League, this group tried to persuade the British cabinet to stay clear of foreign entanglements that might lead to war. Its importance cannot be measured with any certainty but it obviously wielded considerable influence, especially in the north of England, and it also controlled the *Morning Star* – one of the most powerful organs of the Manchester School.

Victorian public opinion was thus shaped and moulded by public organizations, politicians, intellectuals, and diplomats, as well as by journalists. Pamphlets, tracts, books, and sessional papers were used freely to influence British policy. Lectures and public speeches were also employed by such leaders of British opinion as Lord Brougham, John Stuart Mill, John Ruskin, and others. But it was the Victorian press which still played the leading role in creating public opinion. This was inevitable in an age before the advent of radio and television, when the newspaper was still the chief source of information on current affairs, and when even educated Victorians did not always have the means of checking the accuracy of press reports. The British press in the nineteenth century has also remained the most accurate indicator of contemporary opinion because most publishers felt that they had to speak for their respective constituencies in order to maintain or to increase the circulation of their journals. Equally important perhaps is the fact that, even when editors were expressing purely personal opinions, their contemporaries generally felt that they were appealing to a certain kind of audience. And it must surely be significant that, throughout the nineteenth century, British politicians seemed to believe that the newspapers wielded some kind of magical power.[12]

There are, however, two very serious considerations to which few historians have addressed themselves in analysing nineteenth-century British opinion. In the first place, taking into account the relatively high levels of Victorian poverty and illiteracy, one must conclude that only a very small minority of Victorians in the mid-century could possibly have bought, read, or understood the journals of that period. To give point to this observation, it is necessary only to add that *The Times*, that 'great potentate,' sold for three pence a day in the 1860s when the average daily wage was less than four shillings; and that, in fact, its average daily circulation of 60,000 copies amounted to approximately one for every five hundred persons in Britain at that time. Secondly, and perhaps even more importantly, a great deal of what appeared in the mid-Victorian editorial columns was actually inspired, if not put there directly, by political leaders seeking support for their own personal views. This suggests the paradoxical conclusion that Victorian politicians did as much to influence newspapers as the latter did to affect politics.

It takes only a brief examination of the political affiliations of the leading British newspapers in the 1860s to demonstrate this second point. Notwithstanding its much vaunted independence, *The Times* was then closely attached to Palmerston, the liberal prime minister, Austin Henry Layard, and Lord Clarendon (although this last link was almost broken in April 1864 when Clarendon joined the cabinet as chancellor of the duchy of Lancaster).[13] John Thadeus Delane, the famous editor of *The Times*, remained a staunch Palmerstonian throughout the last ten years of that great man's life. The avowed Palmerstonian mouthpiece, however, was the *Morning Post*, controlled by the Borthwicks who were Palmerston's close friends. They remained faithful to the prime minister to the very end, and Lord Glenesk indeed claimed that Palmerston had been the inspiration of his paper during the period 1850–65.[14] It has often been alleged with some justice that Palmerston dictated many of the editorials which the *Morning Post* devoted to foreign affairs. This immensely energetic politician wrote leaders also for the *Globe* and remained in close contact with the editors of that paper until his death.[15] As he also gave financial assistance to the *Observer*, Palmerston could rely upon the support of this weekly as well.[16] Since another of his friends,

Thornton Hunt, helped to establish the *Daily Telegraph* in 1855, the prime minister found consistent support from this quarter too.[17] In fact, Palmerston wielded an enormous influence over the London press during the last ten years of his career by deliberately cultivating the friendship of the leading journalists of that period.

The *Daily Telegraph* (with an average daily circulation of almost 150,000 in the early 1860s) soon became one of the most successful of the new penny papers. While trying to defend Palmerston's foreign policy, on the domestic front it idolized Gladstone, the chancellor of the exchequer, and continued to do so until the Eastern crisis of 1876, largely because of his intimate friendship with its editor, Edward Lawson, the first Lord Burnham.[18] The *Daily News*, another successful cheap daily, gave wholehearted support to Earl Russell mainly because its editor, Thomas Walker, was a close friend of Russell's 'kinsman,' the dean of Bristol.[19] The radical *Morning Star* was under the direction of Bright and Cobden.[20] Disraeli, the opposition leader in the House of Commons, is thought to have wielded some influence over the *Standard*.[21] Lord Derby, the leader of the conservatives, secured the support of the *Herald* by lending it money,[22] while another conservative, Lord Robert Cecil, wrote several leaders for the *Saturday Review* as well as for the *Quarterly Review*.[23]

It is insufficient, therefore, for a study of this kind, to examine only a handful of newspapers without taking note of their political and social connections. The sample must also be wide enough to include the better-known provincial publications. The investigation of journalistic thought should then be supplemented with careful analysis of other contemporary observations; for public opinion must be seen as the sum of informed and articulate expressions together with the miscellaneous and often inarticulate reactions to them. As it is difficult to measure the feelings of the silent majority, the historian dealing with the mid-Victorians has no choice but to depend on the private and public correspondence of the *élite*, their assessment of popular opinion, editorials and news items, reports of public meetings, memorials, petitions, memoirs, and biographies. The historian must also understand that, although it is impossible to examine *all* informed opinion, the more extensive his sample the greater are his chances of emerging with reliable indices of the public temper.

This book is based on a thorough investigation of eleven important dailies, seven weeklies, two monthly magazines, and five quarterlies. Several memoirs and biographies, and the private correspondence of the leading cabinet ministers have also been utilized. This sample has been selected so that liberal, conservative, radical, and independent views have all been considered. The choice of newspapers is based, to a large extent, on circulation statistics and general reputation. Among the most influential London dailies, only the *Morning Advertiser*, the

Morning Star, and the *Sun* have been omitted, and their omission is largely due to the feeling that their inclusion would have resulted in a too emphatic imbalance in favour of liberal, radical, and free-trading views already represented here by the *Daily News* and the *Daily Telegraph*. The *Morning Post* and *The Times* are automatic selections since they are universally regarded as the two most powerful British newspapers of the mid-Victorian period. The *Morning Herald* and the *Standard* are chosen mainly because they were then the most important of the conservative journals. The *Globe* is used partly because it can be taken to represent whigs slightly to the right of centre, and partly because of its reputation at that time for lively writing on political subjects. Chosen from among the provincial press are the conservative *Dublin Daily Express*, the moderate and independent *Glasgow Herald*, the *Manchester Guardian* with liberal prejudices slightly to the left of centre, and the liberal *Liverpool Mercury*. These ought to provide a fair cross-section of provincial journalism – although it is arguable that the *Leeds Mercury* (also liberal) might have been a choice superior to its counterpart from Liverpool. With the exception of the liberal *London Review*, the popular *News of the World*, and the conservative *Press*, the most reputable weeklies and quarterlies have been pressed into service here.

2
Great Britain and
the Dano-German conflict, 1848-52

The Schleswig-Holstein question was one of the most perplexing of all the issues that confronted European statesmen in the nineteenth century. It was an aggravating affair, as much because it persistently defied amicable settlement as because it often tended to exert an unwarranted influence over other European questions, although it was not in itself an issue of major importance. Thus European statesmen were forced to devote more attention to the Elbe riddle than was its intrinsic due. The seriousness of the problem lay in the perpetual threat which it posed to European peace and stability, for it was basically a conflict between Danish and German nationalism in which both sides consistently proved reluctant to make moderate concessions or to accept reasonable compromise. The major European powers were anxious to prevent the dispute from resulting in open warfare. They feared that such hostilities would not only alter the status quo in the Baltic but might produce unsavoury repercussions elsewhere. Indeed, the Schleswig-Holstein question led directly to two Dano-German wars between 1848 and 1864. It was essentially to avert this clash of nationalities that European statesmen strove so hard to find a peaceful solution to the problem.

For Great Britain the Schleswig-Holstein question was of considerable importance. Britain was herself a great maritime power, and her position demanded the strictest vigilance over strategic naval zones like the Baltic. The Baltic Sea was also a useful trade-route for British commerce and shipping. Although her advances in naval technology had already freed her from her old dependence on Baltic ports for timber and naval supplies,[1] Britain was still trading in that region to the extent of more than £30 million sterling each year. As late as April 1864, indeed, the conservative Charles Newdegate was able to remind the House of

Commons that approximately one quarter of the total of British tonnage passed through the Sound between 1860 and 1862.[2] British interests therefore seemed to require the maintenance of the status quo in the Baltic. Britain simply could not allow any powerful European state to extend its influence in northern Europe. She wanted to preserve the integrity and independence of Denmark mainly because she feared that a united Germany which included Schleswig and Holstein could become a most dangerous rival. She could not therefore view the Schleswig-Holstein problem with indifference. She earnestly desired to settle the Dano-German dispute in a manner favourable to Denmark in order to frustrate any ambitious plans cherished by the tsar of Russia or the liberal-nationalists in Germany. Britain failed miserably to accomplish this kind of Baltic settlement, mainly because the majority of her people never understood the problem. Even her leading statesmen in the nineteenth century did not attempt a detailed examination of the Elbe puzzle before it was too late.

The Schleswig-Holstein question was indeed a very complex one. In the first place, Denmark, Schleswig, and Holstein were related to each other in different ways. Holstein's attachment to the other duchy and to the kingdom was chiefly 'personal' in so far as her duke was also the duke of Schleswig and king of Denmark; but the bond between Denmark and Schleswig was much closer: it was at once religious, linguistic, and ethnological.[3] The southern boundary of Denmark, in fact, had been set at the river Eider ever since the ninth century. Schleswig was a fief of the Danish kingdom and quite distinct from Holstein which the king held as a fief of the Holy Roman Empire. By the Capitulations of 1460, however, the king of Denmark promised never to separate Schleswig from Holstein, and this was one of the conditions on which the two duchies resigned themselves to Danish rule. This intricate arrangement was rendered even more confusing by the Schleswig-Holstein Estates who, in the sixteenth century, consented to a series of partitions which left the two duchies, despite a common administration, divided between the ducal-royal and ducal-Gottorp families.

Ultimately, however, the right of succession to both duchies belonged to the male heirs of the elder royal line, the descendants of Christian III, with reversion to the Augustenburgs and Beck-Glücksburgs who were the heirs of the younger royal line. Next in line to the royal descendants stood the Russian, Swedish, and Oldenburg branches of the old ducal-Gottorp family.[4] But Frederick III of Denmark added to the confusion in 1665 by altering the law of succession with his famous *Lex Regia*, which permitted the succession of female descendants to the throne of Denmark. This was the historical basis for the quarrel over the succession which became so integral a part of the Schleswig-Holstein question in the nineteenth century. For the Germans eventually argued that the *Lex Regia* did not alter the law of succession in Schleswig, and that in fact it was not competent to modify the law of succession in one duchy so independently of the other.[5]

Further complications developed early in the eighteenth century as a result of the Scandinavian wars, during which Frederick IV of Denmark twice drove the Swedes from his southern territory and was, in 1720, acknowledged by Sweden as the ruler of the ducal-Gottorp portion of Schleswig which had hitherto been administered jointly by the dukes of Schleswig-Holstein-Gottorp. A guarantee of this transfer was given by Britain, France, and Russia, and Frederick proclaimed the acquisition of the two duchies in 1721.[6] Whereas the Danes were to argue, in later years, that these transactions represented the conquest of Schleswig and Holstein, the Germans claimed that the Peace of Fredericksborg of 1720 merely settled the question of the ownership of the Gottorp estates in Schleswig.[7]

It would now seem that the Danish kings missed several opportunities during the eighteenth century to incorporate Schleswig into the monarchy, and it is clear that both duchies could have been annexed outright in 1721 with little difficulty. But Denmark continued to adhere to the outmoded principle of Schleswig-Holstein indivisibility even after the dissolution of the Holy Roman Empire in 1806. When the Germanic Confederation was established by the Congress of Vienna in 1815, Frederick VI failed to detach Holstein from its old connection with Germany or to liberate Denmark from the restrictions of 1460. He simply entered the new German Diet as duke of Holstein, swearing to preserve the *nexus socialis* between the two duchies.[8]

Not only had the Danish crown throughout the ages persisted in adhering to the anomalous Capitulations of 1460, but in later years it encouraged the infiltration of German ideas into the southern parts of its domains. As no corresponding Danisation was employed to combat these influences, Holstein had become solidly German and South Schleswig predominantly so by the beginning of the nineteenth century.[9] The middle regions of Schleswig had become almost evenly divided between Danish and German elements, and by the middle of the nineteenth century German influences had penetrated into North Schleswig as well. This gradual Germanisation of the duchies encouraged the interference of the Bund after 1815, and it became increasingly difficult for the Danish king to rule over Schleswig and Holstein since his subjects there tended more and more to regard themselves as belonging to the Germanic Confederation.

This strong sense of German feeling in the south of the kingdom gradually stirred the corresponding Danish nationalism in the north. The Danish national-liberal movement in fact made vast strides within the second generation after Waterloo, and Denmark began to democratize her institutions. This program offended the conservative governments in Europe, but failed to reconcile the

Kongeaa River

Christiansfeld

Haderslev

Løgumkloster

Åbenraa

Norborg

Augustenborg

Tønder   Kliplef

Sonderborg

Flensburg

Schlei

Schleswig

Husum

Eider

River

Kiel

H O L S T E I N

Adapted from Biernatzki

	Danish spoken		German and Danish spoken in equal parts.
	German spoken		More German than Danish spoken
	Frisian spoken		More Danish than German spoken

Areas in which German and Danish are used alternately in church.

0   10   20   30   40   50 MILES

0   10   20   30   40   50 KILOMETRES

Map II Language map of Schleswig, 1849. Reprinted from W. Carr:
Schleswig-Holstein 1815-48, by permission of Manchester University Press.

Schleswig-Holstein liberals. In keeping with the general tendencies of the age, agitation against the Danish system of government in the duchies steadily developed into a conflict between German and Danish nationalities.[10]

It was a complex struggle for it involved four distinct movements each in its own way a manifestation of the liberal and nationalist attitudes then commonly struck: Scandinavism, Eiderdanism, Schleswig-Holsteinism, and Germanism. Scandinavism flourished particularly in Sweden where liberals dreamed of a union of Swedes, Danes, Norwegians, and Finns under Swedish leadership. The Eiderdanes clamoured for the incorporation of Schleswig into the monarchy, the complete separation of Schleswig from Holstein, and the establishment of Denmark's southern boundary at the Eider river. Schleswig-Holsteinism embodied the principle of setting up the two duchies as an independent state, free from Danish control and attached to the Bund. The German nationalists, meanwhile, desired to unite all the German communities in one vast, federal state. These were the main conflicting tensions which endangered the status quo in the Baltic and made Danish rule over Schleswig-Holstein a very precarious business.

The explosion occurred in 1848 when the Danish king Frederick VII, under pressure from the Eiderdanes, promised to bring Schleswig directly under Danish control and to grant Holstein a separate constitution. This immediately led to a revolt in the duchies which was openly supported by the Augustenburgs – the inveterate enemies of the Danish ruling house. The Schleswig-Holsteiners also successfully appealed to the Diet and to Prussia for military aid. In April 1848 an army of 30,000 Prussian and federal troops, led by Friedrich von Wrangel, overran Schleswig and drove the Danes as far north as Düppel. In these circumstances, Denmark appealed directly to Britain, France, and Russia who had guaranteed the union of Schleswig and Denmark in 1720. These three powers all wished, for various selfish reasons, to preserve the status quo in the Baltic. They feared that a disruption of the balance of power in that region might lead to consequences over which they would ultimately have little control. They therefore co-operated to bring about a peaceful settlement of the Dano-German quarrel.

Tsar Nicholas I of Russia was especially anxious to thwart the advance of the Prussian troops: he not only feared the repercussions of the revolutionary movement within his own dominions but he was also highly suspicious of German ambitions in the Baltic. He also feared that if the duchies were captured from Denmark she might be inevitably driven into the fold of a Scandinavian union which could effectively frustrate Russia's hopes of expanding in the Baltic. Sweden in fact was already assuming a menacing attitude. Posing as the champion of Scandinavia, she mobilized her forces and threatened to give active support to Denmark should the German troops advance into northern Jutland.[11] These factors prompted the tsar to despatch a squadron into Danish waters and threaten to declare war on Prussia unless she withdrew her army.[12] Nicholas felt that any victory for nationalism in this area would make the Baltic unsafe for Russian commerce, while a stalemate might redound only to the advantage of his major rivals, Britain and France. He was therefore determined that the struggle should end and the status quo be restored at once.

France was experiencing domestic convulsions of her own and had no desire to encourage a disturbance on the Elbe that might possibly result in Russian expansion. Nor did she relish the prospect of a united Germany that could become 'a power very much more redoubtable to its neighbours' than a divided Germany then was.[13] A strong Germany in central Europe would obviously present an effective obstacle to future French expansion beyond the Rhine. As her republican leaders were also anxious to secure the goodwill of the other great powers, France could give no moral support to the national liberals in the duchies. She wanted Denmark and Prussia to compose their differences and restore the status quo in northern Europe as soon as possible.

The British foreign secretary, Palmerston, viewed the Danish crisis of 1848 in the same light as did the French and Russian governments. It is true that he had consistently preached a gospel of constitutionalism since 1830, but he was alarmed by the violence of the revolutionary movements of 1848 which he feared might throw the whole of Europe into a state of chaos. He came out strongly on the side of law and order in central and northern Europe. He was first and foremost an anglo-centric British representative, and it was his aim to defend the public law of Europe whenever it seemed to promote British interests. The Treaty of Vienna had established a certain delicate European equilibrium which seemed best suited to the perpetuation of British maritime supremacy. Palmerston believed that any major shift in this continental balance might endanger Britain's position. Except in the case of Italy (which he considered unique), he did his utmost therefore to prevent the triumph of the national liberals. He considered the Schleswig-Holstein rebellion a dangerous affair that could expand into a general European war. He was convinced that the integrity of the Danish monarchy was essential to the European system, and he was resolved to impede the progress of German nationalism – especially since he also felt that a united Germany (with an extended Zollverein) could become a serious rival to British commerce and shipping.[14]

Given the nature of British interests, the general British reluctance to take an active part in this Dano-German war, and the disturbing restlessness of the Chartists in 1848, there was not much that Palmerston could do beyond persuading both sides to lay down their arms – even had he wished to do otherwise. But his role was by no means a straightforward one, for although he deprecated the conduct of Prussia and the Diet, he could not but admit that some of the Schleswig-Holstein grievances were valid.[15] Moreover, the pro-German court was much offended by Palmerston's attitude, as the queen and the prince consort felt that he was too sympathetic to Denmark.

The awareness that both sides were wrong, and the fact that the British court and public were at variance over the matter made the Schleswig-Holstein question a very awkward one for Palmerston during the period 1848-52. The British press and people were vehemently pro-Danish, largely because they sympathized with the underdog. They simply felt that big Germany was attempting to bully little Denmark on the flimsiest of excuses, and even in Parliament strong language was being used against the Germans. Disraeli, indeed, on 19 April 1848, delivered a powerful speech in the House of Commons, in which he argued that Britain was morally bound by the terms of the Treaty of 1720 to give active assistance to Denmark. He thought that Britain should either help the Danes to drive the Prussian troops from Schleswig 'or we must practically announce ... that England no longer respects guarantees.'[16]

Palmerston was under pressure from the court and a handful of radicals to give moral support to the Schleswig-Holsteiners,[17] and he was also being urged by Danophiles like Disraeli to take direct steps to persuade the Prussians to retreat. In these circumstances, active interference on Britain's part was hardly possible. The foreign secretary did not wish, in any case, to take part in the war. His objective was to accomplish a Prussian withdrawal by means of diplomacy. Thus when Denmark appealed to Britain for help on the basis of the 1720 guarantee, Palmerston forthwith offered to mediate. He did so, in his usual style, without royal approval and thus added to the discord between the Foreign Office and the court.[18]

Notwithstanding the court's suspicions and complaints, Palmerston's approach to the Schleswig-Holstein question during at least the first year of the crisis was not obviously or particularly pro-Danish. He used similar language to both sides in his efforts to bring the war to an end. His response to the Danish appeal, as he explained to Disraeli in April,[19] and to David Urquhart in May, was that the guarantee of 1720 did not apply; Denmark's right to rule over Schleswig was not in dispute; the Germans were attempting to defend the rights of Holstein which was an undisputed part of the Germanic Confederation; and in this sense the issue was an internal one. Moreover, as Britain had already agreed to mediate, there could be no question of invoking the guarantee of 1720.[20]

As mediator, Palmerston geared his efforts towards arranging an armistice, but both sides were so obstinate that nothing resulted from his exertions until the aggressiveness of Russia and Sweden forced the Prussians to relent.[21] It is difficult therefore to measure the value or impact of Britain's mediation during 1848-50. Certainly she tried hard for several months to play the part of a neutral, but it was this very role which seemed to aggravate rather than solve the problem. Palmerston used strong language to both parties alternately and thus succeeded mainly in frustrating them both. It was only after the tsar had made it plain that Russia was not prepared to tolerate the Prussian activity in Schleswig that Palmerston adopted a decisive anti-Prussian stance. Now that he had secured the vigorous co-operation of Russia, he consistently urged Prussia to seek a truce and abandon the duchies.

It was in fact the powerful Anglo-Russian alliance that eventually compelled Prussia to withdraw in 1849 and to accept the London Protocol of 1850. As Austria, France, and Sweden also wished to suppress the Schleswig-Holstein rebellion, Prussia (herself in the throes of domestic squabbles) had no choice but to retreat. Her withdrawal from the duchies in the mid-century was a diplomatic victory for Palmerston and Brunnow, the Russian ambassador in London. By working very closely together, these two statesmen thus ensured the localization of the war, the eventual suppression of the Schleswig-Holstein revolt, and the immediate frustration of the ambitions of the German liberals in the duchies.

The British court continued to object violently to Palmerston's curious brand of mediation; but while the queen was looking at the dispute in its German context and thinking only of preserving the peace for the moment by thwarting the Danish scheme to annex Schleswig,[22] the foreign secretary was viewing the problem in its broader, European, setting. He realized that the Schleswig-Holstein question involved more than the simple incorporation of Schleswig, and he fully appreciated that as soon as the present ruling line became extinct the issue would be further complicated by the thorny question of the succession – for Frederick VII had no male heir and was unlikely now to produce one. To Palmerston's mind, the integrity of the Danish monarchy was vital to the European balance; he hoped therefore to arrange a European concert to settle the question of the Danish succession in a peaceful manner while preserving the Danish state intact even after the death of Frederick VII. It was for this reason that he advised the rest of Europe to decide on a successor to the Danish king. He requested the major European powers to draw up protocols on this subject with a view to reaching an amicable solution which might later be ratified in a more formal conference. At the same time, Palmerston instructed Sir Henry Williams Wynn, the British minister at Copenhagen, to impress upon the Danish government the vital necessity of settling the succession question once and for all. He argued that Frederick VII could effectively thwart both the ambitions of the German liberals and the schemes of the Eiderdanes by helping to arrange the Danish succession in such a way as to keep the entire monarchy under one ruler 'in personal union.' Palmerston also suggested that perhaps the king of Denmark might consider the son of the duke of Oldenburg as a likely successor.[23]

For many months this project languished, for a variety of reasons. Not only was the king of Denmark initially reluctant to accept Palmerston's advice,[24] but the duke of Oldenburg appeared indifferent, and the Austrian government expressed a preference for a Glücksburg successor to the Danish king.[25] The duke of Augustenburg also raised objections on the simple ground that his claim to the Danish succession was stronger than any other.[26] In addition to this, Queen Victoria, fearing that its direct object was to do violence to German interests, totally rejected the project. She denounced the principle of settling a German issue without considering the wishes of the Diet.[27] Bunsen, the Prussian minister in London, also bluntly refused to co-operate.[28]

Despite these obstacles, Palmerston, supported by Brunnow, pressed on with the scheme for a London protocol to solve the difficulty of the Danish succession. Eventually, on 4 July 1850, he succeeded in persuading representatives from Austria, Britain, Denmark, France, Russia, and Sweden to discuss the matter at a conference in London. They unanimously agreed to preserve the integrity of the Danish monarchy; to help solve the Dano-German problem with Britain as mediator; and to support the final settlement of the Berlin Treaty (which Prussia had been forced to sign only two days before). These powers thus pledged themselves to seek an immediate suspension of arms for the present and to arrange a Schleswig-Holstein settlement for the future.[29] A more formal London Protocol was then drawn up along these lines and signed by the same ministers on 23 August.

But the situation remained bleak for many months. The duchies were still in a state of chaos and it was not actually before 1851 that the evacuation of Schleswig was completed and the Danish king's authority re-established in Holstein.[30] Dano-German relations remained strained and the negotiations that followed the Berlin Treaty were desultory and tedious. Austria then made unexpected difficulties for Palmerston's project by requiring that assurances be given to the Diet that German rights would be respected.[31] The Russian government, moreover, declared itself unwilling to accept a Glücksburg prince as Frederick VII's successor.[32]

Palmerston's reaction to this difficult situation was to keep up a regular correspondence with all the governments involved, urging Denmark to respect the rights and privileges of the Germans in the duchies, and persuading the Germans to adopt a more conciliatory approach. Above all, he kept the matter of the succession constantly in the foreground. His persistence finally began to produce results in the summer of 1851, when Prussia declared herself ready to participate in negotiations on the topic of the Danish succession,[33] and Cowley, the British minister at Frankfurt, was able to report that Germany as a whole was willing to concede the claims of Augustenburg so long as the duke was handsomely indemnified.[34]

Palmerston now began to promote the idea that a reasonable cash settlement would avoid much unnecessary strife,[35] even though he himself did not think that Augustenburg's pretensions were valid. This proposal, which was supported even by the Prussian government,[36] was eventually accepted by the Danish king. But the negotiations between Augustenburg and Denmark progressed very slowly since the king refused to treat the duke as an equal, and since the duke showed himself increasingly reluctant to accept an annual income in return for the surrender of his estates.[37] Augustenburg's intransigence eventually exhausted the patience of the European great powers, and, late in 1851, Prussia finally withdrew her support from the duke. She now assented formally to the principle of the integrity of the Danish dominions and to the choice of the Glücksburg prince as Frederick VII's successor.[38]

When Palmerston was removed from the Foreign Office at the end of 1851, his Schleswig-Holstein policy was too far advanced for his immediate successors to alter it. As it was, Lord Malmesbury, who became foreign secretary in a conservative ministry in February 1852, was an avowed protégé of Palmerston and had no desire to undo his mentor's work. He continued Palmerston's policy in the duchies by trying to expedite any official settlement that would restore the 1848 status quo in the Baltic. Malmesbury at once urged Prussia to force Augustenburg to accept Denmark's offer, and recommended haste now that the circumstances seemed favourable.[39]

By the spring of 1852, Britain, Denmark, France, and Russia were all tired of the Schleswig-Holstein question and were anxious to settle it without further ado. The king of Denmark issued an ultimatum to the effect that the terms he had offered Augustenburg in February would have no binding force after 30 April. This gave the duke four weeks to make up his mind, and he reluctantly accepted the Danish conditions just before the deadline.[40]

The settlement of the dispute between Denmark and Augustenburg followed the lines laid down by Palmerston in 1851. He had recommended a satisfactory compromise which did not leave the duke with any sense of injury. His suggestion was that the king of Denmark should offer the duke 'somewhat more than the real value of his Estates.' Palmerston's object was to ensure that Augustenburg's eventual claims were 'quashed' by his own consent.[41] His advice was ultimately accepted by Frederick VII who expressed himself prepared, early in 1852, to offer generous terms to his turbulent vassal.

The king of Denmark agreed to pay three million rix dollars (the equivalent of £330,000) as compensation for Augustenburg's estates. He was also willing to remove the entail to allow the duke to make any redistribution he wished. In return, Frederick VII required the duke to surrender his rights to the Danish succession and to leave Denmark altogether. Augustenburg was prohibited from purchasing property within the Danish dominions or from undertaking 'anything whereby peace may be disturbed or endangered within the Royal Estates.' These were the terms offered by the Danish king in February.[42] Meanwhile, he had satisfied the requests of Austria and Prussia by issuing the proclamation of 28 January 1852, which promised to preserve intact the constitution of the kingdom of Denmark while granting separate constitutions to the three duchies.[43] The king pledged himself to respect the liberties of Germans within his realm, and to grant the Estates in the duchies enough power to prevent tyrannical acts on the part of the central authority. This ordinance was well received by the rest of Europe, and was later even ratified by the Diet at Frankfurt.[44] Augustenburg thus found himself suddenly isolated and he had no choice but to accept the Danish terms.

The royal proclamation of 28 January was the immediate result of the famous Dano-German negotiations of 1851-2. These were discussions held by Austria, Prussia, and Denmark in an attempt to restore peace to the Baltic. Austria and Prussia, bent on preserving German (and consequently their own) influence in Danish affairs, refused to allow Denmark to detach Holstein from the old connection with Schleswig. They insisted that Denmark should rule the duchies in accordance with the rules and traditions of the Bund. They deplored any attempt at Danish incorporation of Schleswig and they demanded that the Estates in the duchies should be consulted before any changes be foisted upon them by the Danish government. These were the conditions upon which Austria and Prussia were ready to guarantee the integrity of Denmark. If Denmark could adhere to these principles, Austria and Prussia would, for themselves as well as the Diet, consent to the Danish arrangement of the succession whereby it was hoped to maintain the kingdom and the duchies under a single jurisdiction.[45]

As Denmark accepted this bargain, Malmesbury now aimed at a speedy settlement of the question, and did all he could to prevent the Diet (notorious for its delaying tactics) from discussing the matter. He suggested that Austria and Prussia could answer for the whole of Germany.[46] Despite Prussia's objection to this proposal, the London conference met on 28 April and swiftly ratified all the stipulations that had been agreed upon since 1850.[47]

The London Treaty of 8 May 1852 was the logical conclusion to Palmerston's whole Schleswig-Holstein policy since 1848. It recognized the integrity of the Danish monarchy as a vital part of the European system and acknowledged the arrangements that had been made for the Glücksburg succession. It provided for a European revision of the question of the Danish succession upon the extinction of the Glücksburg line. It agreed to perpetuate the existing relationship of Holstein and Lauenburg to the Bund. But it avoided any mention of 'guarantee' since Britain expressly refrained from undertaking such an obligation. The Russian government also insisted that the agreement should be one between the six powers on the one hand, and Denmark alone on the other. Thus it was that the ratification by each of the six powers were exchanged with Denmark alone.[48]

The London Treaty therefore affirmed no new principles. It merely ratified those conditions which had earlier been agreed upon with respect to the reorganization of the Danish administration in the duchies and the means of achieving Danish unity for the future. But it satisfied neither the Germans nor the Danes, and since it contained too many technical loopholes both sides were encouraged to violate it whenever they safely could. Even the agreement between Denmark and Augustenburg was unsatisfactory, for although the duke had unquestionably signed away his rights not only for himself but for his entire house, he was not legally competent to do so. His son was already of age and the duke therefore could not, in accordance with German law, speak for his immediate heir in 1852. The Augustenburgs were thus left with an obvious avenue of escape, which they put to effective use in 1863. Furthermore, as the Dano-German engagements of 1851–2 and the London Treaty itself were decided upon without the direct participation of the Diet, the smaller German states were later able, on very strong moral grounds, to question the validity of the London settlement. In fact, the various engagements left the Germans with an abiding sense of grievance. On the very day the London Treaty was signed, Bunsen (who almost resigned rather than be a party to it)[49] remarked that it represented little more than a 'declaration of bankruptcy.' He saw it simply as a triumph of the major powers at Germany's expense, and his only consolation was the possibility that Germany might derive some future advantage from the fact that the Diet had not been consulted.[50]

If Bunsen was dissatisfied with the results of Prussian diplomacy in Schleswig-Holstein, the Danes were no more content with the consequences of their own. The London Treaty not only disappointed the German liberals but it produced a bitter pill for the Eiderdanes to swallow. All their ideals were undermined by the European great powers despite Danish military triumphs at Idstedt and Fredericia. The London Treaty not only restored the status quo (which they had long considered offensive), but it even provided for the succession of a Glücksburg prince who was notorious for his German sympathies. Denmark had fought to free herself from German interference in her domestic affairs and at least to make herself supreme in Schleswig. Her efforts resulted merely in the artificial resurrection of the odious and outmoded Capitulations of 1460. In the interests of European peace, the great powers sacrificed at once the principles of Eiderdanism and Schleswig-Holsteinism – the conflict between which had led to the Dano-German war in the first place. But the simultaneous suppression of these divergent ideals failed utterly to guarantee Schleswig-Holstein tranquillity. Predictably, neither the Danes nor the Germans proved willing to fulfil the engagements of 1851-2. The London Treaty, as a result, led directly to the Schleswig-Holstein crisis of 1863-4.

It is difficult to exaggerate Britain's role in the temporary settling of the Dano-German dispute after the crisis of 1848. In an age when her foreign secretary was still allowed sufficient freedom of manoeuvre to handle his department as he saw fit, Palmerston proved to be the dominant personality throughout the negotiations. It was his persistence more than any other single factor which kept the question of the Danish succession in the foreground after 1850, and it was he who did most to induce the king of Denmark to buy off the duke of Augustenburg. All the weaknesses of the London Treaty were the direct offspring of Palmerston's diplomacy. He objected to the Augustenburg claims on the selfish British ground that, under the Augustenburgs, the Danish dominions were likely to fall too readily within the commercial orbit of the Prussian Zollverein. Yet, had the Augustenburgs been appeased, most of the Schleswig-Holstein difficulties of the next fifteen years might have been avoided. At one point Palmerston agreed with the principle of nationality and supported the idea of dividing Schleswig into two parts, attaching the southern section more securely to Holstein and the Diet, and incorporating the Danish and the so-called 'mixed' portions of Schleswig in the Danish kingdom.[51] This principle of demarcation in accordance with nationality became a recurrent theme in the Schleswig-Holstein discussions during the ensuing sixteen years. Palmerston, however, abandoned this potential solution in 1849 when both Denmark and Russia rejected it. It is possible that the timely partition of Schleswig in the late 1840s might have prevented Denmark from losing all of the disputed duchies in 1864. Palmerston failed to recognize that the German portions of the Danish monarchy had become a liability rather than an asset to the Danish king. By insisting so vehemently on the integrity of the Danish dominions, he really helped to prolong the quarrel between the Schleswig-Holsteiners and the Eiderdanes.

These criticisms of Palmerston's Schleswig-Holstein policy, however, are based too securely on hindsight. In 1852 Palmerston had every reason to feel satisfied with his adept handling of a very delicate problem. He had, without recourse to war, achieved some solid (albeit transitory) British successes. He had persuaded Prussia to retreat from the duchies; he had prevented either France or Russia from making capital out of the Baltic upheaval; he had frustrated the Scandinavian union which, for commercial reasons, he had feared; he had preserved the integrity of the kingdom of Denmark – a friendly power occupying a strategic zone; and he had, in short, done much to restore the pre-war status quo without

losing either Danish or German friendship. Britain, essentially a maritime commu-
nity, could resume trading with the Baltic ports on pre-war terms. The dreaded
expansion of the Zollverein in the Baltic had been thwarted.

Palmerston maintained a lively interest in the Danish duchies because he felt
that Denmark stood in the same relation to Britain and the North Sea as Turkey
and the Mediterranean in the south-east of Europe. He firmly believed that British security depended to some extent upon the perpetuation of Danish control
over the 'Dardanelles of the North.'[52] The same selfish logic that inspired so
many generations of British statesmen to support the tottering Ottoman Empire
governed Palmerston's approach to Denmark throughout his long career. In his
view, the Napoleonic Wars had amply demonstrated how dangerous it was for
the Danish navy to fall into the wrong hands. He was also convinced that the
interests of peaceful trade required the preservation of the old order in the north
of Europe. The real triumph of his Schleswig-Holstein diplomacy during the
crisis of 1848–52 lay in the fact that he not only succeeded in re-establishing the
Baltic system of 1848 without going to war with Prussia but actually compelled
her to participate in this arrangement. Here he clearly made ample use of the co-
operation of Austria and Russia which, for obvious political reasons, disapproved
of Prussia's involvement in the Schleswig-Holstein rebellion.

This diplomatic 'coup' was achieved in the face of the most vigorous and
unrelenting resistance from the British court. Queen Victoria and Prince Albert
were too pro-German to accept the Palmerstonian view that Britain stood to lose
from an expansion of the Prussian Zollverein to the borders of Jutland. They
saw Britain's role in Schleswig-Holstein as that of an arbiter rather than a partisan; yet they themselves were anxious to give moral support to the national
liberals in the duchies. They considered that the paramount motive of a mediating power was not its own material interests but the moral rights of the disputants involved.[53] Inspired by this idea, Prince Albert could not but be distressed
to feel that the 'rights of the poor people of Schleswig and Holstein were to be
the price for which Lord Palmerston would repurchase the goodwill of France
and particularly Russia.'[54] It was the constant bickering between the court and
the Foreign Office over the Danish question that contributed as much as anything else to Palmerston's dismissal late in 1851. The court won that particular
round but lost most of the others, essentially because the majority of British
people within and outside Parliament agreed with Palmerston's foreign policy.
It is an interesting index of his political as well as diplomatic skill that, during
the Dano-German conflict, he succeeded in mollifying a rabidly pro-Danish Parliament without ever supporting the Danish cause by force of arms and without
making any promises of a material sort to the Danish government. He kept the
House of Commons in check simply by denying the applicability of the 1720

guarantee and by claiming, after the manner of Prince Albert, that it would not be proper for a mediating power to join the fray.

Yet, for all his diplomatic and political skill, history was to prove that Palmerston was wrong and the British court right. Even after the spectacular expansion of Prussia and a united Germany under Bismarck later in the century, British trade in the Baltic continued to flourish. That the volume of British trade in the North and Baltic seas was not ultimately dependent upon Danish ownership of Schleswig and Holstein was a fact of commercial and economic life that Palmerston was not capable of grasping. He could not possibly have foreseen in 1848 that the volume of Britain's Baltic trade would actually increase after the boundaries of Denmark were seriously circumscribed in the 1860s. The statistics presented to Parliament by the Board of Trade, however, disclose that the real value of the merchandise imported from, and exported to, the Baltic region by Britain in 1862 totalled approximately £40 million when Denmark was still in possession of Schleswig, Holstein, and Lauenburg. In 1865, after Denmark had lost these duchies, the real value of this trade had risen to more than £47 million.[55]

Nor could Palmerston easily have prophesied the diplomatic upheavals of the 1850s that were destined to undermine the foundations of the London Treaty. It was his misfortune that the settlement of the Baltic question which he did most to accomplish in 1852 should have to rest inevitably upon such uncertain props: the mutual jealousy of Austria and Prussia; Anglo-Russian co-operation in the north of Europe; and the goodwill of France. When these underpinnings were eroded by the Crimean War, the Italian question, and the Polish revolt, the London settlement gradually collapsed notwithstanding Palmerston's own strenuous efforts to defend it.

3
Great Britain and the
Danish duchies, 1852-9

Few historians have given much thought to the development of the Schleswig-Holstein dispute in the interval between the two periods of crisis. Indeed, many British writers have tended to assume that this quarrel had been settled by the London Treaty and was suddenly revived in 1863. In fact, however, the provisions of 8 May 1852 served generally to aggravate rather than solve the problem, and the dispute continued with much bitterness and violence throughout the 1850s. Britain consistently took an active interest in this controversy and tried desperately to bring it to an end. This is made crystal clear by an examination of the thirty-four volumes of public correspondence (FO 97/120-53) which deal exclusively with the Schleswig-Holstein question during 1851-9. It is on this material, largely neglected by both British and European scholars, that this chapter is based. The investigation shows that, for seven years after signing the London Treaty, Britain pursued a wonderfully constant policy in the Danish duchies. Her Schleswig-Holstein program was founded almost inflexibly upon a keen determination to preserve the arrangements of 1851-2. But this proved increasingly difficult since both Denmark and Germany were unwilling to fulfil their treaty obligations.

Denmark was obviously the more guilty party in this regard during the years immediately following the Treaty of London. Frederick vii himself was so hostile to the Glücksburg prince and so sympathetic to the Eiderdanes that, for several months, he encouraged their stout resistance to the treaty by doing as little as possible to implement its main provisions or to settle the question of the succession.[1] Malmesbury became so impatient with Denmark's delays that he warned her, in December 1852, not to endanger her own independence and integrity by violating the terms of the London Treaty. Great Britain, he declared, could accept no excuses from Denmark for failing to fulfil her obligations. The British government had no intention of releasing Denmark from her recent engagements, and it was even determined to prevent the re-opening of the Schleswig-Holstein discussions at the international level.[2] This admonition elicited a promise from Frederick VII that he would do all in his power to keep the Eiderdanes firmly under control and to preserve the settlement of 1852.[3]

The king of Denmark not only gave assurances that he meant to abide by his engagements but he even expressed himself anxious, in conjunction with the major powers, to make the London Treaty binding upon the whole of Europe by inducing the states which had not participated in the London conference to give the settlement their formal approval.[4] Britain warmly supported this plan, and it was eventually decided that all the signatories to the agreement should invite the rest of Europe to adhere to it. Malmesbury himself had suggested that the Diet should merely be notified of Article IV (whereby the Danish succession had been regulated), after Denmark had requested the other European powers to accede to the treaty.[5] As this now met with general agreement, the Diet was once again treated with contempt by the major powers although the individual German states were asked to give their formal assent to the treaty.

All the non-German powers signified their agreement, and the majority of the German states, despite the treatment meted out to the Diet, immediately gave their unqualified assent. In fact, only Bavaria questioned the propriety of neglecting the Diet, and her chief minister, Pfordten, refused to accede to the treaty before the Frankfurt assembly had pronounced a verdict on the case.[6] This example was ultimately followed by Baden, Hesse-Darmstadt, and the two Mecklenburgs.[7] The minor German states were by no means unanimous on this question of the Danish succession. Nor were they prepared, in 1853, to make any sacrifices for the Schleswig-Holstein liberals. Moreover, they could not afford to alienate themselves from Austria and Prussia who had both signed the London Treaty. The majority of the German states accordingly assented to the treaty, although it was generally believed that the rights of Germany had been violated and should be restored at a more favourable opportunity.

Lord John Russell, who went to the Foreign Office when a coalition government replaced the conservative administration late in 1852, continued Malmesbury's policy in Schleswig-Holstein. He not only repeated the British intention of upholding the London Treaty but he censured the Bavarian government for its refusal to accept it. He declared that the question of the Danish succession could not have been left to the whims of the Diet for it was more than a purely German issue. It was a serious international affair which endangered European peace. He warned Bavaria that she was inviting an unnecessary isolation upon herself as there was nothing she could then do to alter the treaty. Britain, he added, was determined not to re-open any discussion of the question.[8] This was the identical stand taken also by the earl of Clarendon who replaced Russell at the Foreign Office in February 1853. He refused to tolerate any European attempt to undo the London Treaty. Hence he dealt cursorily with the Augustenburgs when they tried to re-open the discussions by denouncing the settlement and appealing to Britain.[9]

Now that the rest of Europe had acceded to the London Treaty, Denmark wanted to prevent future European intervention in the duchies by trying to persuade the governments which had signed the treaty to declare that its intention was to supersede the antiquated *Lex Regia* of 1665,[10] which she herself now revoked in 1853. Clarendon readily agreed with the Danish decision to rescind the *Lex Regia*, for this was precisely what Palmerston had been recommending since 1850.[11] Sweden also publicly approved of the abolition of the old Danish law of succession,[12] but the Germans answered evasively and this all-important matter was consequently allowed to slide despite the efforts of the Danish crown to solve the problem once and for all.

After passing the new law of succession, however, the Danish government hesitated to promulgate it or to make any real effort to execute the provisions of the London Treaty. Sir Andrew Buchanan, who was now the British minister at Copenhagen, regretted this unnecessary delay and attributed it to the blatant intrigues of certain members of the Danish royal family who still hoped to exclude the Glücksburg house altogether. Buchanan deplored this state of affairs and formally protested to the Danish government,[13] but in spite of his remonstrance the new law of succession was not eventually proclaimed until 31 July 1853.[14] The truth is that it was almost impossible for Denmark to fulfil her engagements. It was only with the greatest difficulty that her own Rigsdag[15] had been induced to accept the London Treaty.[16] The war itself had increased Dano-German animosity and the king was now finding it very hard to restrain the immoderate Eiderdanes in Copenhagen or to control the rebellious Schleswig-Holsteiners in the duchies.

The king of Denmark began by submitting the draft of a new constitution to the Estates of the duchies and instructing them to overlook the sections dealing with the relations between the separate parts of the monarchy. He ordered them to consider only those clauses which referred specifically to the proposed plan for the Estates and their competence to regulate the affairs of the duchy they represented. Largely because of these restrictions, the Holstein Estates rejected the Danish scheme while the Schleswig Estates proposed a number of major amendments. The Eiderdanish party advised the king to circumvent this opposition by imposing these separate constitutions on his own authority. Frederick VII accordingly did so in 1854 when he established a constitution for the affairs of the monarchy as a whole without the sanction of the Rigsdag or the Estates.[17] This arrangement failed to satisfy the majority of his subjects and Frederick VII replaced it with another Common Constitution in 1855, without the consent of the Estates and with only the informal approval of the Rigsdag.[18] The new plan soon proved to be as unworkable as its predecessor as it was too unsympathetic to the German claims. It increased the opposition to Danish rule in the duchies and drove Schleswig-Holstein further into the arms of the Diet.

Fortunately for Denmark, the German states were too preoccupied with the Crimean War to interfere actively in Schleswig-Holstein at this stage. Both Austria and Prussia, in fact, were profoundly disturbed by the Near Eastern crisis and pursued a tortuous diplomacy in the Crimea that kept them always on the threshold of active participation in the war. Determined to thwart Russian expansion in the Balkans, Austria mobilized her forces and gave strong moral support to the western allies, but Prussia, more concerned about French aggression on the Rhine, resolved to remain neutral. Their common feeling of insecurity, however, led them on 20 April 1854 to conclude a defensive alliance whereby Prussia promised, in case of need, to help Austria defend her possessions in Italy in return for Austrian assistance in defence of Germany on the Rhine.[19]

Great Britain was also devoting her major energies to the Crimean crisis and played no effective part in the Danish trials of the period. She tried to stay clear of the dispute and confine herself to counsels of moderation on all sides. Indeed it was difficult for her to do otherwise for there was too much disagreement on the question even among her own ministers abroad. Buchanan, who considered the Estates far too hostile towards the king, tended to take a pro-Danish stand.[20] On the other hand, the German point of view was strongly defended by Colonel Hodges, the British representative at Hamburg, and Sir John Ward, the British consul at Leipzig.

Hodges held Denmark entirely responsible for the prevailing tension. He argued that her arbitrary acts alienated her not only from the German element in Holstein but from her otherwise loyal subjects in Schleswig. He was particularly critical of the way in which the Danish government had suddenly introduced into the two duchies the unpopular system of Danish currency.[21] In the same vein, Ward suggested that Britain should advise Denmark to repudiate the obnoxious constitution of October 1855, as it was at once a violation of Schleswig-Holstein rights and a breach of the London Treaty. He warned Clarendon that serious complications must ensue so long as Denmark persisted in her acts of doubtful legality.[22]

Few people, in fact, considered the constitution of 1855 in any other light, although Buchanan (without defending its legality) reported that Holstein was really so truculent that no Danish measure could succeed so long as it threatened to strengthen the ties between Denmark and Holstein.[23] This opinion was also voiced by Sir Alexander Malet, the British minister at Frankfurt, who felt that agitation in Holstein was encouraged more by German propaganda than by Danish misrule. Malet observed that, while Holstein continued to denounce Danish tyranny, the duchy was yet loath to accept the reforms which Denmark was so willing to concede in 1854.[24]

In the face of this ambassadorial discord, Clarendon chose the path of moderation and advised both sides to avoid extreme measures. He urged Denmark to redress the real grievances of which the duchies complained and to remove those inequalities between Denmark and the duchies which were given so much prominence in the German press.[25] Austria and Prussia, who had not yet decided on a common policy and were naturally reluctant to act positively in the duchies until they had done so,[26] seemed willing enough to follow Clarendon's advice. In the wake of the Crimean War, they were anxious to avoid a Baltic crisis and they were therefore treating the Schleswig-Holstein question in a most conciliatory manner. They protested only mildly against the Danish constitution of 1855.[27] Denmark, however, missed this opportunity of allying with the two major German powers to keep the minor German states in check. In spite of Clarendon's advice, she even refused to send a satisfactory answer to the Austro-Prussian remonstrance and thus left Austria and Prussia with little alternative but to refer the Schleswig-Holstein question to the Diet.

Britain and France wished to prevent the Diet from complicating the matter even further. Britain was especially anxious that Denmark should solve the problem herself by a policy of moderation. Clarendon warned her that, if she could not settle her differences with Austria and Prussia, then no one could prevent the Diet from settling the dispute in an anti-Danish fashion. He observed that Germany was becoming dangerously excited, and that this could easily lead to a revolt in the duchies which the Diet might feel disposed to support.[28] But Clarendon's warning failed to produce the desired effect, and in November 1856 Austria and Prussia jointly demanded the revocation of the Constitution of October.[29]

Denmark's refusal to comply with the Austro-Prussian demand alarmed the British government whose conviction was that any appeal to the Diet would serve only to arouse the violent political feelings of the minor German states. Britain believed that in such a case the Schleswig-Holstein problem would become immeasurably more difficult to solve. Clarendon therefore promptly accepted the French proposal for a conference in March 1857 and tried to persuade the Russian government to follow his example. Without debating the competency of the Diet to settle this matter, Clarendon argued that it would be easier to persuade Denmark to listen to the advice of the great powers than to submit to the dictation of the Bund 'should any pressure become necessary in order to secure for the Duchies the reforms of which they clearly stand in need.'[30]

The Russian government, however, made an evasive reply. On the morrow of the Crimean War, Russia was still mindful of Anglo-French hostility in the Turkish affair. Licking her wounds, she was trying to buy enough time for them to heal and had thus embarked on a deliberate program of withdrawal and retrenchment.[31] Russia was not prepared therefore to play a prominent part in settling the Dano-German quarrel at this time. Gorchakov, the Russian foreign minister, merely observed that the Schleswig-Holstein question was a purely German one – that is, within the sole competency of the Diet – and could not be regarded as an international complication until the Diet should threaten to disturb the London Treaty. Gorchakov thought that Denmark could prevent German interference in the duchies by redressing all the wrongs of which Schleswig and Holstein complained. He concluded that if Denmark's allies all gave her this discreet counsel she could hardly fail to obey.[32]

Britain and France therefore had to abandon the idea of a conference. They now sought to end the Dano-German stalemate by bringing their combined pressure to bear directly upon Austria, Prussia and Denmark. As a result Austria and Prussia declared themselves willing to keep the Schleswig-Holstein discussions out of the Diet if Denmark would promise to convene the Holstein Estates and listen to their complaints.[33] In recommending this course to Denmark, Clarendon suggested that she should put her own house in order rather than be forced to do so by European command, or worse still, give the impression of doing so only in deference to the Bund.[34] Although she condemned as 'uncourteous in style, and peremptory in tone' the Austro-Prussian request to convoke the Holstein Estates, Denmark announced that she would follow the advice of France and Britain; and it was eventually decided that no appeal should be made to Frankfurt until after the meeting of the Holstein Estates.[35]

Unlike Palmerston and Russell, Clarendon was not really in the habit of interfering in the domestic concerns of European states, but now that the Schleswig-Holstein question was becoming dangerous he was anxious to familiarize himself with all the relevant details. This is why, in the face of conflicting reports from abroad, he decided to send Sir John Ward to Holstein to ascertain the real condition of affairs in that duchy. Going there with an avowed German bias, the British consul could not but discover ample material to strengthen his prejudices. He spent three weeks in Holstein before submitting a comprehensive report to the Foreign Office on 28 May 1857.

Not surprisingly, Ward's report turned out to be a bitter assault on the Danish system of administration in the duchies. Ward regarded the whole problem as deriving fundamentally from conflicting nationalisms. Its solution therefore rested upon an admitted principle of Dano-German equality in the duchies. The main cause of the strife was Denmark's failure to concede to Holstein the rights and privileges she had so often promised. The constitution of 1855 was such an obvious encroachment upon these rights that an uprising in Holstein was practically inevitable. Ward suggested the repeal of this constitution. Holstein was too solidly German to be oppressed by Danish rule which made no allowance for popular feeling. As Holstein was still part of Germany, Ward felt that Denmark should alter her policy in that duchy and thus avert a clash with the Diet. He enumerated all the harsh measures recently imposed on Holstein and contended that they served only to drive her more securely into the arms of the Bund. In fairness to Denmark, Ward admitted that these crude attempts at Danisation were probably the result of the Vienna Treaty, which had reduced too severely the size of the old Danish kingdom. This constriction had forced Denmark to resort to a program of centralization as a means of holding more securely what was left to her. Holstein, however, had not been accustomed to this idea of a corporate state, having been traditionally attached to Denmark only by the 'personal tie.' This was perhaps the main reason why the Holsteiners resented the Danish attempts at incorporation.

Ward's report was a masterful study of the question despite the bias of its author. The British consul not only paid careful attention to the relevant statistics but he emerged with a number of interesting conclusions. As a solution to the Schleswig-Holstein problem he proposed the restoration of the pre-war status quo in its entirety; or, failing this, the division of Schleswig according to nationalities, attaching the northern portion of the duchy to Denmark proper and the southern section of Holstein. Above all, he felt that a thorough liberal system of government throughout the Danish monarchy was the best guarantee against revolt.[36]

Acting promptly on Ward's suggestions, Clarendon now addressed a strong letter to Copenhagen, instructing the British minister there to warn Denmark against the adoption of any half-measures in Holstein, to urge her to fulfil all the promises made in the royal proclamation of 28 January 1852, and to remove every reasonable grievance which Holstein had just cause to lament.[37] At the same time, to placate the minor German states that were eager to have the dispute settled by the Frankfurt assembly, Clarendon announced that while Britain could not allow the Diet to settle a matter of international importance, she still admitted the competency of the Diet to treat the Holstein question. Great Britain, he added, had never questioned that federal right.[38]

It is true that Britain had never really denied the Diet's right to discuss the question of Holstein, but Bavaria and Württemberg had an unanswerable case. Until the London Treaty was threatened, Europe was not justified in interfering in a German dispute. On this point even the great powers were divided, for Russia regarded the question as a purely German issue. It was this division among the great powers and the excitement among the members of the Bund that forced Denmark to relent. For many months she had been most reluctant to follow Britain's advice, and her steps towards the pacification of Holstein were painfully and deliberately slow. But she now suddenly announced that she would convoke the Holstein Estates at once and give them ample opportunity to enumerate their needs.[39]

Denmark, however, was still not sincere in her treatment of Holstein. No sooner had she made the pledge to Austria and Prussia than she neutralized it. She convoked the Holstein assembly but did not allow it to put forward its case. Instead she prepared a draft constitution and required the Estates to vote on it. Despite the firm opposition of Britain and France she even limited the freedom and scope of the Itzehoe debates.[40]

Buchanan did his utmost to persuade Denmark to leave the Estates free to discuss their own affairs. This advice was not based on any respect for Schleswig-Holstein liberties but on a genuine concern for Denmark's future. Buchanan's whole argument was that Denmark should give the Holstein assembly enough liberty to embarrass itself.[41] This was sound advice indeed for the Estates would most likely have forfeited their German protection by demanding liberal institutions alien to the very character of Austria and Prussia. Moreover, such an attitude on Denmark's part would have deprived the Bund of its pretext for interfering in the internal affairs of Denmark. The Danish government, however, refused to heed this judicious counsel, and the Itzehoe debates came rapidly to nought.[42] Still trying to save the day, the British and French ministers at Copenhagen urged Denmark to ask the deputies to state clearly their demands so that Denmark could at least meet them half-way.[43] But the Danish government rejected these proposals also.

British ministers abroad were disappointed by this Danish obstinacy. They felt that Denmark's strategy had been faulty. Had she chosen to meet Holstein on liberal rather than national grounds, she might have succeeded in overthrowing the whole Schleswig-Holstein movement, for Austria and Prussia were more anxious to lead the nationalist movement in Germany than to champion the cause of liberalism. This feeling that a liberal approach on Denmark's part would have split the German movement asunder was shared by Bloomfield, Buchanan, Clarendon, Orme, and Ward. Bloomfield, in fact, tried hard to urge the Prussian government to induce Holstein to draw up a catalogue of concrete proposals which Denmark might fairly be required to accept.[44] He was convinced that this approach would not only encourage the Holstein liberals to overreach themselves, but would prevent the duchies from hiding behind the support of the Bund in future and making vague complaints as to invaded rights as they had done in the past. Had Denmark adopted this policy, it is doubtful whether the Itzehoe deputies would have reached an agreement among themselves as to what, in concrete terms, they really desired. But she began at once by restricting their freedom of debate and thus gave them a focal point around which they could unite.

Throughout the deadlock Britain and France suggested that Denmark should take the matter in her own hands and offer distinct concessions both to Holstein and Schleswig; but Denmark argued that such a policy would merely lead to further demands.[45] By the end of the year she had convinced herself that it would be better, after all, to bring the matter before the Diet. This misguided view led her to permit the Schleswig-Holstein question to come before the assembly at Frankfurt. This was the very course that Britain had consistently deprecated and had tried so hard to avoid since 1848.

Austria and Prussia referred the question to the Diet in November 1857. This step could no longer be avoided. Even the French government seemed willing at last to admit what had been only too true from the start: the Schleswig-Holstein problem was a German one with which the European powers should only interfere when it extended beyond German bounds.[46] This was so reasonable a view that it is difficult to understand why Britain refused to accept it. By consistently endeavouring to prevent the Diet from discussing the question of Holstein, she actually helped to strengthen the German sense of suffering. It is not surprising therefore that, when the German states were at last allowed to pronounce a verdict on the case, they did so in an intemperate manner. Had the Diet been invited to deal with the legitimate grievances of Holstein as early as 1853, it might have dealt more leniently with Denmark.

At all events it was precisely this German belligerence, as exhibited by the Diet after 1857, that Britain had wished to avoid. Even after the fiasco at Itzehoe, Clarendon deplored the Austro-Prussian decision. He was prepared to admit that a question was purely German when it related to two members of the Bund, but the quarrel between Germany and Denmark was an entirely different matter.[47] Clarendon declared that Britain would regard any strong federal measures as a European complication, and he reproached Buol, the Austrian foreign minister, for his casual references to physical action on the part of the Diet.[48] He also protested, in February 1858, against the truculent behaviour of the Hanoverian government.[49]

Whatever may be said of the wisdom of Clarendon's policy, it was at least consistent. Throughout the period he was determined to prevent the Dano-German quarrel from resulting in open warfare. He consistently warned Denmark against her impolitic approach and he consistently urged the Germans to moderate their tone. He was always ready to use Britain's 'good offices' to bring about an amicable solution. The overall impression left by his diplomacy in this affair is that he was too pro-Danish. Hence his annoyance at the shortsightedness of Danish policy and the readiness of Denmark to engage in war with Germany in spite of the overwhelming odds. It was this Danish indifference to the horrors of war that disturbed him most. Clarendon managed to preserve peace between Denmark and Germany but he failed to force Denmark to execute the London Treaty or to prevent the Diet from taking the Schleswig-Holstein question into its own hands. But these failures were not really Clarendon's fault. They were the result of Danish stubbornness and German excitement.

Unfortunately for Clarendon and the other neutrals, the real trouble was that the rising tide of nationalism both in Denmark and Germany could no longer be contained. Denmark, by 1857, had become bent on the Eiderdanish program in spite of the London Treaty.[50] The Diet had also become too impatient by the end of 1857. It at once appointed a committee to investigate the nature of Holstein's grievances, and proclaimed (on 11 February 1858) that the Common Constitution of 1855 could not be recognized as legally in effect for Holstein and Lauenburg as it directly violated those German rights which Denmark had promised to defend in 1852. The Diet called formally upon Denmark to fulfil her engagements, and to state exactly how she intended to honour her obligations.[51]

Denmark was inclined to deal firmly with the Diet, but France and Britain strongly recommended a policy of conciliation.[52] Frederick VII was caught between the desire to placate the powerful Eiderdanes at home and the necessity of preserving the goodwill of the major powers. In these circumstances vacillation and delay were inevitable. The German states meanwhile grew more impatient and, at the end of May, the Diet peremptorily ordered Denmark to declare her intentions within six weeks.[53] Denmark resented this order so bitterly that she even seemed ready to sever diplomatic relations with Frankfurt and refuse altogether to revoke the Constitution of 1855. But Elliot, the new British minister at Copenhagen, demonstrated how dangerous such an approach could be both to Denmark and to Europe; he advised Hall, the Danish chief minister, to state clearly the nature and form of such concessions as Denmark was prepared to make.[54]

Elliot's prudent language was approved by Malmesbury who had replaced Clarendon as foreign secretary in February 1858. Malmesbury was sympathetic to the Danish cause but he could not permit Denmark to injure her own position by pursuing the wrong course. He was convinced that her defiant attitude was based on the fact that she took French and British aid too much for granted. He accordingly tried to dispel this fallacy by warning Denmark that she was mistaken in assuming that Britain would assist her under every contingency. He suggested that Denmark should take all necessary steps to meet the requirements which the Diet might lawfully demand. If she failed to do this, then she could expect neither the sympathy nor the assistance of the British government.[55]

Malmesbury's warning produced an immediate effect. The Danish government suddenly expressed a willingness to negotiate with the Diet on the basis that the Constitution of 1855 was not valid for Holstein and Lauenburg.[56] Denmark replied to the Diet on 15 July, acknowledging that its authority in Holstein was beyond question. At the same time, however, she stoutly asserted that

the General Constitution of the Danish monarchy, and consequently also the position of Holstein in that monarchy, belongs to the internal affairs of Denmark: any criticism of the same that the Confederation may permit itself is an unjustifiable attack upon the independence of the Danish State as a whole, which has been recognised by Europe. Moved by her love of peace, however, Denmark is willing for the time to regard the General Constitution as suspended, and declares herself ready to enter into negotiations concerning arrangements of a different nature.[57]

This was the first intelligible reply that Denmark had made to the many German despatches of 1858, and still it was little calculated to allay the Diet's wrath. The Diet had repeatedly proclaimed the illegality of the Common Constitution; yet Denmark now merely offered to 'suspend' its operation in Holstein and Lauenburg, leaving it in force over the rest of the kingdom. She had also failed to state specifically how she intended to fulfil the promises made in the proclamation of 28 January 1852.

Britain and France regretted the arrogant tone of the Danish reply. The British and French ministers at Copenhagen had desperately tried to have the original draft altered to make it more conciliatory.[58] Elliot was most dissatisfied with its wording. He ruefully observed that Denmark, by merely offering to suspend the Constitution, had imprudently 'left an arm in the hands of the Diet.'[59] Malmesbury likewise regretted the Danish decision but hastened to persuade Austria and Prussia to accept Denmark's reply in a spirit of conciliation in order to bring about an amicable solution. Meanwhile he advised Denmark to revoke the Constitution altogether as it related to the German duchies.[60] These recommendations ultimately prevailed: the Diet made a more conciliatory reply to Denmark than had at first been expected and feared;[61] and, after much delay, Denmark decided to abolish the Constitution of 1855 in so far as it concerned Holstein and Lauenburg, and to summon the Holstein Estates to consider new measures.[62]

On the surface, this was a large concession for Denmark to make. The British ministers abroad, with few exceptions, certainly felt so. Elliot expressed the view that Hall had thus satisfied the demands of the Diet.[63] Malet rejoiced to see that Denmark had thus removed all grounds for German interference.[64] Malmesbury himself was pleased to learn that Denmark had at last followed Britain's advice.[65] Forbes, the British minister at Dresden, optimistically declared that Denmark's prudent acts had 'set this affair at rest.'[66]

The Diet, however, took a different view of the edict promulgated by Frederick VII on 6 November 1858. The German states declared that the ulterior object of the decree was the incorporation of Schleswig. Ward reported that the Germans were becoming even more excited now that Denmark seemed bent on flagrantly violating the engagements of 1851-2. He himself agreed with the German interpretation of the edict and warned Malmesbury that the recent proclamation was merely a preliminary to the annexation of Schleswig.[67] When Malmesbury relayed Ward's letter to Elliot, the latter replied that its arguments only served to demonstrate how impossible it was for Denmark to give satisfaction in this dispute. He did not deny that the measure tended towards the incorporation of Schleswig; he was simply annoyed that Germany should react in this manner when Denmark was merely complying with the recent demands of the Diet.[68]

The royal proclamation of November, by tending undeniably towards the illegal annexation of Schleswig, naturally drew to that duchy some of the German attention that had hitherto been focused primarily on the affairs of Holstein. As it was accompanied by indiscreet acts of Danish severity in Schleswig, Dano-German relations deteriorated even further. Denmark was now bent on the consummation of the Eiderdanish principle and was becoming more and more jealous of any European or German attempt to interfere with the administration of Schleswig. In fact, late in 1858, the king of Denmark issued a number of unpopular decrees which were specifically designed to hasten the process of Danisation in Schleswig by suppressing all forms of Schleswig-Holsteinism in that duchy.[69]

Britain had never questioned the right of the Diet to settle disputes in Holstein, but she had also defended the principle of Danish supremacy in Schleswig. She feared that any attempt on the Diet's part to meddle with the affairs of Schleswig would immediately transform the quarrel into a European crisis, and she had therefore always urged Denmark to avoid such a complication by giving that duchy no grounds for complaint.[70] Denmark, however, had pointedly neglected this advice, and even the Danophile Elliot was forced to admit, early in 1859, that Frederick's latest measures in Schleswig were crude and inopportune.[71]

Although Malmesbury deplored the Danish tactics in Schleswig, he urged Prussia to use her influence in the Bund to prevent its more warlike members from advocating extreme measures.[72] The keynote of his policy was moderation, and while it produced no effect upon Denmark, it induced the Diet to await the outcome of the next session of the Holstein Estates. Malmesbury demanded a faithful adherence to the London Treaty and urged both Denmark and Germany to fulfil their respective engagements. He advised the Germans to stay clear of Schleswig, a duchy in which they could claim no jurisdiction,[73] and he exhorted the Danes to abandon such policies as might endanger European peace.[74]

When the Holstein Estates met in March 1859, they rejected the king's propositions and put forward counter-resolutions diametrically opposed to the Danish point of view. Elliot could not but remark that the session was pervaded by an overt sense of hostility to Denmark.[75] The deputies demanded that no constitutional alterations concerning the whole monarchy should ever be attempted without the prior acquiescence of the separate legislatures. They also denounced the royal proclamation of 31 July 1853 by which the new law of succession had been decreed.[76] Denmark could not accept these resolutions, and a deadlock resulted.

Malmesbury's policy in Schleswig-Holstein had thus, like Clarendon's, come to nothing. Throughout 1858 he succeeded admirably in restraining the Diet (which Clarendon had failed to do), but he could make little impact on the stubborn Danes. Denmark's determination to secure her supremacy in Schleswig drove a solid wedge between her and the Holstein Estates, and as neither side was disposed to yield there was little that the French and British governments could do. It was unthinkable for them to threaten Denmark with war because there was simply too much pro-Danish sympathy in Britain and France; nor could they threaten the Germans who, after all, were basing their objections to Danish policy precisely on the same London Treaty that Britain and France wanted so desperately to maintain. It was also impossible for them to secure the much needed support of Russia (either during or after the Crimean War) for the sake of convening a European conference to revise the settlement of 1852.

In these circumstances the British Schleswig-Holstein policy of moderation in the 1850s was basically sound. It is perhaps true that Britain's anti-Germanism inspired the Danes to be more aggressive than they might otherwise have been, but at no stage did the British government give even moral support to the Eiderdanish principle. Throughout this period her policy in the duchies was founded upon a simple and explicit faith in the validity of the Dano-German engagements of 1851-2. Her unequivocal advice to Danes and Germans alike was to adhere faithfully to the Treaty of London.

This remarkable consistency of British policy in the Danish duchies after 1846 was in some ways due, ironically enough, to the frequency of British political changes in the 1850s. The fact that the foreign secretaryship changed hands no fewer than six times in the nine years after 1850 tended inevitably to make the expanding Foreign Office staff more important than it had been previously.[77] In fact, Edmund Hammond, the permanent under-secretary (1854-73), gradually became a major cog in the administrative wheel. By 1865 he had virtually ousted the parliamentary under-secretary from the diplomatic business of the Foreign Office. He not only wrote first drafts of despatches and abstracts of incoming letters, but he offered advice freely on all diplomatic matters and prepared several memoranda which eventually formed the basis of important despatches. Hammond, who played a prominent role in the selection of diplomats and consuls, kept in close touch with political leaders at home as well as the major British ministers abroad. He thus became a key figure in the formulation of British policy. Indeed Clarendon and Granville, two of his closest friends, often sought his opinion and followed his advice.

The spectacular increase in the volume of diplomatic correspondence during the Crimean War also made it humanly impossible for the foreign secretary to attend to all the minute details of his office, as Palmerston had been known to do in his younger days. Clarendon complained bitterly in 1856 that he had actually been required to handle 56,000 despatches in the previous year.[78] In this period of political instability, therefore, Britain's diplomacy came to depend more and more on her civil servants at home and her ministers abroad. As most of these men had been trained in the Palmerstonian school, this tended to provide a certain semblance of continuity. It also partly explains why, at least until his death in 1865, some version of Palmerston's views seems to have prevailed at every level of the Foreign Office.

This character of the Foreign Office was not popular with the court which had fallen, after 1840, completely under the influence of Prince Albert. The two institutions came increasingly into conflict after 1846, and eventually (during Palmerston's second ministry) the cabinet became the arbiter between them. The court held, among other things, that Palmerston was too unsympathetic to Germany. Even so, it had little cause to object to British policy in the Danish duchies after 1852 although Clarendon, Malmesbury, and Russell all found it necessary to refer to Palmerston's memoranda of 1848-51 when dealing with the problem.

4

Lord John Russell and
the Schleswig-Holstein question, 1859-63

The failure of the Itzehoe session to solve the Dano-Holstein problem restored the Elbe riddle to the status it had occupied in November 1857. The question was once more referred to the assembly at Frankfurt, where the Hanoverian representative tried hard to persuade his colleagues to resort to vigorous federal action in Holstein.[1] But German attention gradually shifted at this stage to the Italian War, and Denmark was momentarily left with a free hand in the duchies. She proposed an interim constitution for Holstein until a permanent solution could be found. This *provisorium* prevented the Diet from taking further action and the threatened federal execution was thus postponed.[2]

This was the state of affairs in Schleswig-Holstein when Russell replaced Malmesbury in June 1859. To break the deadlock, he told Sir Augustus Paget (who had succeeded Elliot in Copenhagen) that Britain would willingly use her 'good offices' to facilitate a settlement of the dispute. At the same time he remarked that the constitution recommended by the Holstein Estates needed considerable revision 'before it can be made practically useful.'[3] Paget thereupon promised Hall that, if Denmark were to make a reasonable concession to Holstein, Britain would use her influence to persuade the Germans to accept it. He was careful to add, however, that his country could commit herself to no concrete pledge of material support to Denmark.[4]

Russell tried at first simply to continue Malmesbury's policy by insisting upon an attitude of Danish as well as German moderation. He repeatedly asked Denmark to liberalize her administration of Schleswig and he constantly warned the Diet of the dangers inherent in a federal occupation of Holstein. This program failed mainly because Denmark refused to pacify Schleswig, preferring instead to continue the strict policy of Danisation initiated by Frederick Tillisch, who had served in 1850-1 as the royal commissioner in Schleswig.[5] The resultant growth of agitation in that duchy induced the Diet, in March 1860, to demand a complete fulfilment of the Danish pledges of 1852.[6]

The Diet did not claim any jurisdiction over Schleswig but it insisted that Denmark should keep all the promises she had made to Germany. It threatened to proceed with a federal occupation of Holstein if Denmark were to pass any law or budget affecting the kingdom as a whole without the approval of the Holstein Estates. Denmark now complained to Britain, arguing that the federal decree was a clear-cut encroachment upon her independence in Schleswig.[7] The British government could not deny the impropriety of that edict, but it merely besought Denmark to alter her policy in Schleswig. Paget denounced her treatment of that duchy and reported that

until the Duchy of Schleswig is placed on a more equal footing with the rest of the Monarchy in regard to the freedom of the press, the right of petition and public meeting, and a greater amount of liberty is allowed to individuals as to the education of their families, there is little hope of the agitation which exists there ceasing, or of more loyal feelings towards the Danish Government being exhibited by a certain portion of the population.[8]

Russell himself advocated a 'Liberal and separate Constitution for Schleswig' as a means of conciliating the German powers.[9] Paget embodied this suggestion in a rough constitutional plan and discussed the matter with Hall, but the Danish government remained unmoved.[10]

The refusal of the Danes to modify their tone, and the growing restlessness of the Germans impressed Russell with the gravity of the situation. He instructed Paget to study the history and cause of the current impasse and to report as fully as possible to the Foreign Office.[11] The upshot was an able summary of the entire Schleswig-Holstein dispute in which Paget contended that the Danish engagements of 1851-2 had been consistently violated. He concluded that 'the great point to be obtained from the Danish Government is, a frank and loyal recognition of the freedom and equality of the nationalities of the Duchy [of Schleswig]; the removal of every unnecessary and vexatious restriction; and that as much independence should be granted to the Provincial Assemblies of both Holstein and Schleswig as is compatible with the integrity and preservation of the Monarchy.'[12]

On the very day that this memorandum was written, the Danish government published the new budget for the monarchy without consulting the Holstein Estates.[13] This was a clear violation of German rights as well as the federal decree of 8 March. Oldenburg proposed a resolution for the federal occupation of Holstein,[14] and although the Diet was as yet unwilling to adopt such an extreme measure, it had no alternative but to demand satisfaction from Denmark. Emboldened by the knowledge that Britain and France were opposed to the federal execution, Denmark announced that the alleged budget was no more than a statistical summary. It was neither a budget nor a law, and it had, in any case, been drawn up prior to the edict of March.[15] The Diet rejected this explanation, but decided to follow the advice of the great powers and await the meeting of the Holstein Estates.

Denmark agreed to convene the Holstein Estates to discuss the new constitutional arrangements. Russell was pleased with this decision as well as with the temporary constitution which Denmark had announced for Holstein. But he also felt that if the Danish government 'would, in addition, grant Schleswig a Constitution, guaranteeing to the Duchy legislative and administrative independence, and would leave the question of the language to be used in the churches and schools to be determined by the wishes of the population in the so-called Mixed Districts, it appears ... that they could not fairly be liable to the charge of not having fulfilled their engagements, or of seeking to incorporate the Duchy.'[16] However, Russell was soon to be disappointed. On 25 September 1860, Frederick VII issued a proclamation that directly affected the administration of Holstein although that duchy had not been previously consulted on the matter.[17] This was so obvious a violation of federal law that many British ministers expressed dismay. Indeed Sir Henry Howard, the British ambassador in Hanover, denounced the Danish program in the duchies as 'extremely impolitic' and 'at variance with the spirit of the age.'[18]

When, in the face of these Danish indiscretions, Prussia now appealed to the British sense of justice,[19] Russell expressed his dissatisfaction with both parties in a pontifical despatch to Berlin and Copenhagen. 'These promises,' he argued,

constitute an engagement which His Danish Majesty is bound in honour to fulfil. He is bound not to incorporate Schleswig with Denmark; to maintain in Schleswig representative States; and to protect the Danish and German nationalities in the Duchy of Schleswig.

But neither in form nor in substance ... do these promises give a right to Austria and Prussia, or to the German Confederation collectively, to interfere in all the details of administration in the Danish Duchy of Schleswig.[20]

Federal execution could now hardly be avoided. On 7 February 1861 the Diet decreed that the Danish budget of July 1860 and the royal fiat of 25 September were both invalid. It commanded Denmark to lay the budget for the fiscal year, beginning 1 April 1860, before the Estates of Holstein and Lauenburg. It threatened to occupy these duchies if Denmark failed to obey this injunction within six weeks. This attitude was given added weight by the menacing temper of the Prussian king, who had publicly declared on 14 January that it was Prussia's duty to pacify the duchies.[21]

Thus had Denmark, in defiance of Britain's friendly advice, brought upon herself the prospect of federal punishment which had threatened ever since 1858. The Swedish government, alarmed by Denmark's defiant attitude, sought to settle the question by means of a conference. Sweden now proposed the complete separation of Holstein from the Danish kingdom and a European guarantee of the integrity of the rest of the monarchy. She was ready, that is, to accept the Eiderdanish program in its entirety. She also recommended the absolute neutrality of Holstein. The great powers, however, disliked the principle of the neutrality of Holstein, and the Swedish scheme consequently failed.[22] Even Russell dismissed it summarily on the ground that Germany would hardly consent to such an arrangement.[23]

The idea of a conference was perhaps the best, but Sweden destroyed her own plan by proposing to alter the status quo in the Baltic. This is precisely what the major powers were trying to avoid. It was indeed to preserve the status quo in the Baltic that they were then resisting the idea of federal execution. They suspected the Germans of ulterior motives and were resolved to prevent the occupation of Holstein by prevailing upon Denmark to submit to federal law. In this they succeeded,[24] although they failed to persuade the Danish government to submit 'for the approbation of the Holstein Estates the quota to be contributed towards the general expenses of the Monarchy.'[25]

Denmark avoided the federal execution by summoning the Holstein Estates but, as she refused to let them discuss the common budget, their meeting was as addled as those that had preceded it.[26] The Diet, therefore, on 27 April 1861, referred the whole case to a Schleswig-Holstein committee. The latter worked at a leisurely pace, while Russell continued to warn the German states not to embark upon a reckless course. He suggested that the federal occupation of Holstein, which might be just as dangerous for the Bund as for Denmark, ought to be adopted only after all other resources had been exhausted.[27] Russell did not deny the Diet's right to perform a federal execution in Holstein; he merely questioned the expediency and the prudence of such a tactic. His main contention was that Germany ought to avoid unnecessary complications.

In the hope of settling the dispute amicably, Russell came forward, towards the end of April, with an elaborate scheme. He now proposed

1 That the quota of the common budget of the Monarchy which affects the Duchies of Holstein and Lauenburg should be submitted to the States of Holstein and Lauenburg respectively for their assent, amendment or rejection.

2 That the laws which are to affect the Duchies of Holstein and Lauenburg shall be submitted to the Diets of Holstein and Lauenburg for their assent, amendment or rejection.

3 That the Duchy of Schleswig shall send Representatives to the Parliament of Denmark, to vote in that Parliament the common expenses of the Monarchy, and to vote on all laws affecting the Monarchy.

4 That the separate Diet of Schleswig shall continue to be elected and meet according to the present law. The functions of that Diet to consist in voting such sums as may be necessary for the maintenance of churches and schools and other local expenses, and in providing by equal laws for the welfare of the Danish, German and other inhabitants of Schleswig.

5 When those terms are assented to, and solemnly proclaimed by the King of Denmark, the four Powers, viz., France, Great Britain, Russia and Sweden, to guarantee to the Crown of Denmark the possession of the Duchy of Schleswig.

6 That Commissioners should be appointed, one on the part of Denmark, one on the part of Germany, and one on the part of the four Powers, to define the boundary of the Duchy of Schleswig. The guarantee mentioned in a former Article to comprise the Duchy thus defined and bounded.

7 That the Treaty and Engagements of 1852, so far as they are not altered by these Articles should be inviolably maintained.

Russell trusted that all Europe would see in these propositions an evidence of Britain's desire to do justice to the contending parties and to save 'Denmark and Holstein from the chances and calamities of war.'[28] These proposals, however, were promptly rejected by France, Russia, and Sweden, and Russell's plan had to be abandoned.[29]

Delighted to find that the Swedish and British solutions tended to favour the Eiderdanish line, Denmark now proposed to grant Holstein complete independence without infringing the rights of the other parts of the kingdom. But France and Russia objected to this plan as they feared that it might lead to the development of German sea-power in the Baltic with a convenient base at Kiel. And Prussia's suggestion that Schleswig be partitioned was at once vetoed by Denmark.[30]

Russell, who was anxious to avoid a greater European complication, was disappointed by the failure of these various proposals. His primary aim was to maintain peace. It was for this reason that he induced Denmark, in August 1861, to make guarded concessions to the Diet in order to postpone federal action in Holstein.[31] He also used his influence to persuade Austria, Prussia, and Denmark to agree to solve the dispute by means of direct diplomatic understanding between themselves, independently of the Diet.[32] Russell hoped to prevent the Diet from discussing the matter further since the smaller German states were making Denmark more intractable by their tendency to interfere in the affairs of Schleswig. But, in spite of Russell's efforts, the Dano-German negotiations of 1861-2 foundered on the rock of Schleswig.[33]

After the breakdown of the negotiations between Austria, Prussia, and Denmark, Paget, fearing open warfare, advised a European conference in which Denmark and Germany would be obliged to come forward and state their intentions more clearly.[34] And Russell, who seems to have blamed Austria and Prussia for the new impasse, proposed that a joint remonstrance should be made to Germany in the name of the integrity of Denmark. He felt that in the interest of peace the Germans should be compelled to declare their hand in a conference rather than hide behind vague phrases about obscure rights.[35] France, Russia, and Sweden, however, displayed no enthusiasm for a joint remonstrance, and the project had to be abandoned.[36]

In the face of this European refusal to accept Britain's lead in Schleswig-Holstein mediation, Russell now emerged with his famous 'Gotha Despatch,' which was designed to settle the question in both its local and its international contexts. This proposal was destined to become one of the most controversial of all the diplomatic notes written by Russell, but although its immediate impact was astonishing its ultimate effect was strangely negligible. Hitherto his concrete proposals for the administration of the two duchies had tended to favour the Eiderdanish principle. The Danish government as a result had looked upon him as one of its staunchest friends, and he had given signal proof of this bias in the spring of 1862 when he had vainly tried to organize a European concert to resist the German claims in Schleswig. His whole Schleswig-Holstein policy since 1859 had been based mainly on the suspicion that Germany harboured evil designs on the duchies. Yet his despatch of 24 September 1862 supported the chief contentions of the Austro-Prussian note of the previous month. Denmark could not but be distressed by his *volte face*.

The despatch began by regretting the state into which the Dano-German negotiations had fallen and summarizing the main points of the controversy, which seemed to Russell to focus on the administration of Schleswig and the establishment of a common constitution. Russell denied the right of Denmark to impose taxes or laws upon the duchies without the consent of their Estates. He denied the validity of the constitution of 1855 as it related to Holstein, Lauenburg, or Schleswig, since it had not been formally accepted by these duchies. He admitted that Denmark could competently legislate for herself and impose taxes on the kingdom proper without reference to the three duchies. These were his major premises.

With respect to the administration of Schleswig, Russell proposed to grant complete autonomy to that duchy; to let the Schleswig Estates deal independently with questions relating to religion, education, and language in the duchy. As for the common constitution, he felt it was absurd to expect the concurrence of the four Estates of the monarchy before any law or budget could be passed. He suggested instead that the normal budget for the whole kingdom should be drawn up and placed before the separate Estates in the following manner:

Obtain that sum from the four Representative Bodies. Confide its distribution to a Council of State, formed, two-thirds of Danes, and one-third Germans. Let the votes of this Council be taken in public, and accounts of the expenditure be published yearly.

The normal budget to be voted in gross for ten years. The distribution or expenditure to be voted yearly.

In conclusion, Russell summed up his proposal under four main heads:

1 Holstein and Lauenburg to have all that the German Confederation ask for them.
2 Schleswig to have the power of self-government, and not to be represented in the Rigsraad.
3 A normal Budget to be agreed upon by Denmark, Holstein, Lauenburg, and Schleswig.
4 Any extraordinary expenses to be submitted to the Rigsraad, and to the separate Diets of Holstein, Lauenburg, and Schleswig.[37]

This proposal was markedly different from the one which Russell had made in April 1861. He had then defended the idea of a separate constitutional position for Holstein in what was little more than personal union with Denmark. Now he was, in essence, repeating the demand for a quadripartite organization of the Danish monarchy which the Holstein Estates had made. Even as late as July 1862, Bismarck had found him rather disposed to the Eiderdanish principle and arguing that the limit of Danish concession ought to be the autonomy of Holstein on the analogy of Luxembourg.[38]

Many explanations have been offered for this remarkable change of front. The most obvious one is that Russell was won over to the German side by the anti-Danish environment of Coburg, whither he had journeyed in the summer of

1862 in the company of the queen. Certainly he could have been influenced by Queen Victoria who had become even more German in her outlook after the death of the prince consort in December 1861. He could also have been moved by the arguments of Robert Morier, the able secretary to the British legation at Berlin, who served as his private secretary during his tour of Saxe-Coburg-Gotha. Morier, indeed, claimed to have written the Gotha despatch himself, and declared that its object was to provide Britain with the means of an honourable escape from the obligations imposed by the Treaty of London.[39] It is possible that Russell saw the wisdom of Morier's scheme, for he gave every indication of withdrawing from the Schleswig-Holstein dispute after Denmark rejected his Gotha proposals. It is also possible that Russell was influenced by the anti-Danish report of the vice-consul, Reinals, whom he had sent to investigate the nature of popular unrest in Schleswig.[40] Yet another possibility is that Russell was deliberately trying to improve Anglo-Prussian relations. Ever since the French seizure of Nice and Savoy in 1860, Britain had been faced with the prospect of isolation on the continent. She had become distrustful of Napoleon III, and had not yet composed her differences with Russia, against whom she had fought in the Crimean War. It was now also impossible to count on the support of Austria, whose diplomacy in the Balkan crisis had been blatantly suspect, and which had since been considerably weakened by the Italian War as well as by domestic difficulties.[41] These explanations, however, are largely conjectural, and it is perhaps best to consider Russell's Coburg message of 1862 as the result of a combination of factors rather than any single cause.

The Gotha despatch took Europe by surprise. The surprise was, on the whole, of a pleasant kind, for only the Scandinavian governments objected to it. France, Russia, and the majority of the German states (including Austria and Prussia) expressed their approval, but Russell's plan came to nothing as it was summarily rejected by Denmark and Sweden.[42]

The Coburg missive was also rejected, interestingly enough, by Russell's own countrymen. *The Times*, for instance, which was then working in close association with such important political leaders as Clarendon, Layard, Lowe, and Palmerston, denounced it in a scathing editorial on 18 November. Convinced that Prussia wanted to seize the port of Kiel, the liberal *Examiner* thought it necessary to urge the British government to defend the integrity of Denmark.[43] Even the conservative *Saturday Review*, which was considered pro-German, criticized the despatch.[44] On this question the British press reflected the mood of Parliament. Lord Derby, the conservative leader, rejected Russell's proposals, which Malmesbury was certain had actually been made without Palmerston's sanction.[45] The cabinet, in fact, was divided over the issue, and Morier was left to regret that his recommendations were only 'pooh-poohed' by the British ministers.[46] Knowing little of the history of the quarrel, Englishmen tended instinctively to favour the Danish cause. This pro-Danish sentiment was further enhanced by the tremendous enthusiasm over the impending marriage between the Prince of Wales and the daughter of Prince Christian of Glücksburg. The announcement of this marriage-alliance was made on 9 September and was warmly applauded in Britain.[47]

Encouraged perhaps by these manifestations of British sympathy, the Danes remained adamant and the Holstein case was thus once more left in the hands of the Diet. Russell now announced that since Denmark had rejected his advice, she was now free to solve her own problems in any manner she chose. He warned her, however, that as there was no escape from her treaty obligations, she could best ensure her independence and integrity by adhering to the engagements of 1851–2.[48] He also circulated a memorandum to British ministers abroad, defending British policy in Schleswig-Holstein and regretting that his attitude of moderation had failed. Great Britain, Russell concluded, now had no other course than to withdraw from these unsatisfactory proceedings and to hope for a satisfactory outcome.[49]

Denmark's persistent refusal to fulfil her promises of 1851–2 and to treat her German subjects liberally provided the duchies with a just cause for making repeated appeals to the Bund. Had she redressed the wrongs of Schleswig, as Britain had so often advised, Denmark would at least have removed the German pretext for interfering in that duchy. As it was, most of the German proposals after 1859 related specifically to the administration of Schleswig, and it was largely to maintain her supremacy in this duchy that Denmark finally determined, early in 1863, to detach Holstein altogether from the monarchy. The king of Denmark accordingly issued the patent of 30 March, promulgating a new and separate constitution for Holstein without the consent of her Estates. Although this proclamation declared the necessity of settling the constitution of the monarchy 'so far as possible in accordance with the demands of Germany,' its object was to exclude Holstein from the Rigsraad,[50] while bringing Schleswig directly under its control. The patent also announced new financial arrangements which were calculated to increase the burden of the duchies by two million dollars.[51] This March Constitution, as it came to be called, was an unequivocal violation of the pledges made by Denmark during 1850–2. It was an affront to Europe, for it was at variance with the Treaty of London, and it was a direct challenge to Germany.

Denmark chose exactly the right moment for throwing down the gauntlet. The diplomatic circumstances of March 1863 offered Danish defiance the best chance of success. The Poles had just risen in revolt against Russia, and this meant that Austria and Prussia had to take steps to safeguard their own government in Galicia and Posen. They were unable, therefore, to concentrate all their energies against Denmark. In Prussia, serious disagreements between the king and the liberals in the legislature seemed likely to prevent that country from pursuing an effective policy. Austria, still trying to recover from the scars of the Italian War, was experiencing diplomatic isolation and economic difficulty. The Diet, too, had been practically paralysed since 1860 as a result of the bitter quarrel between Austria and Prussia over the question of federal reform within the Bund.[52] Moreover, the two great German powers took divergent stands on the Polish rebellion. Prussia came to an understanding with Russia and offered military assistance to quell the insurrection,[53] while Austria joined the western powers in a denunciation of the Russian system in Poland. The policy of Britain, France, and Austria in this crisis almost led to a full-fledged war. In these circumstances Denmark was justified in thinking that she could afford to flout the warnings of the Diet.

Austria and Prussia were so preoccupied with the Polish affair that they had to content themselves with brief identical notes of remonstrance, reserving their right to intervene in the Schleswig-Holstein question at a later stage.[54] The Diet was left free to act in its slow and cumbersome fashion. It was July before it condemned the patent of March and demanded its repeal. Denmark rejected the Diet's propositions in August and thus exposed herself to a federal execution in Holstein within six months of the Diet's ultimatum.[55]

Many of the British ministers abroad regretted Denmark's determination to push matters to a head in Schleswig-Holstein, and even the Danophile Paget had to admit that, in the final analysis, the patent of March was contrary to the Danish engagements of 1851–2.[56] But opinion within Britain seemed very much in favour of the Danish cause. *The Times*, for example, felt that the whole Schleswig-Holstein question was being kept alive by the Germans purely for the sake of German ambition. 'If they are encouraged by the language of Lord Russell to use violence to Denmark,' it warned on 16 May 1863, 'they may find that he has led them to misunderstand the feeling of England and of Europe.' Similar sentiments had been expressed on the previous night in the House of Lords, where Derby, Ellenborough, and Wodehouse advised Britain to co-operate with France and Russia to thwart German designs in the duchies and to protect the integrity of Denmark.[57]

Russell was perturbed by this debate. The House of Lords was too pro-Danish at the very time when he was doing his utmost to discourage the Eiderdanes. He tried hard to convince the House that it was not simply a question of German greed. The whole problem, he pleaded, was complicated by the fact that wrongs had been committed by both sides. In these circumstances, he could only conclude that 'the best position for the English Government to hold is to maintain and adhere to treaties that have been made, and not to advance on this dangerous and questionable path of denying to Germany those rights which fairly belong to her. Our best position is, with any difficulty that may arise, to look rather to peace and conciliation than to the extreme issue of war.'[58] As Russell later explained to the queen, Great Britain, in the midst of Polish and American problems, surely needed to do no more than 'express to Austria and Prussia our intention to respect, and if necessary, maintain, the independence and integrity of Denmark.'[59]

The Danish question was, in fact, becoming increasingly complicated. Hitherto the neutral powers had achieved a fair degree of co-operation in this affair. They had often combined, albeit in vain, to press moderate counsels upon Denmark. The fact is that Britain, France, and Russia had striven to preserve the status quo in the Baltic ever since 1848, because none of them could expect to derive any advantage from the destruction of the London Treaty. Only very recently had they objected to the patent of March and tried to persuade Denmark to pursue a conciliatory course.[60] Now the French government, apparently in the process of clearing the ground for a vigorous policy in Poland (or so Paget suspected), was beginning to intrigue at Copenhagen for a rupture between the Germans and the Danes.[61]

Austria meanwhile was hoping to curry favour with the German liberals, not only by supporting the Polish rebels but by agitating for aggressive federal measures in Holstein. Bismarck, who had isolated Prussia in Germany by opposing federal reform, was driven to seek closer ties with Russia. The resultant Alvensleben Convention made the Polish affair, from the British point of view, far more serious. Prussia withdrew from the more violent proceedings of the Diet, but could no longer prevent that assembly from assuming an attitude of menace. In spite of this German excitement, Denmark made a defiant answer to the Austro-Prussian note, and Russell's policy of moderation thus failed once again.[62]

Since he could not force Denmark to change her policy in the duchies, Russell now attempted to apply pressure on Austria, whose truculence he feared might embolden the Diet to order an immediate federal execution. To prevent this, Russell instructed Bloomfield to remind Rechberg that the Austrian and Prussian governments had 'declined in 1861 to negotiate on the affairs of Holstein without arranging those of Schleswig. But the affairs of Schleswig are matters of international concern, and should be discussed with the utmost calmness and deliberation by the Powers of Europe, and cannot be decided by the Diet of Frankfort.'[63] Russell's main concern was to keep Schleswig out of the discussion so that Denmark might be persuaded to fulfil her undoubted obligations with regard to Holstein. He therefore wanted Austria and Prussia to use their influence over the minor German states to prevent them from precipitating a war by interfering in Schleswig. But neither Austria nor Prussia, each vying for the same position within the Bund, cared to offend the Diet at this point. The Diet consequently could not be dissuaded from issuing its ultimatum to Denmark. On 9 July it demanded the immediate repeal of the patent of March,[64] in spite of Russell's protests.[65]

The Diet's resolution accentuated the anti-German prejudices in Britain and led to Seymour Fitzgerald's anxious enquiry in the House of Commons as to the meaning of this recent aggressiveness on the part of the Bund. Palmerston made a short and sober reply which has curiously received almost as much attention from diplomatic historians as the great speech he delivered in the Don Pacifico debate of 1850. Palmerston's reply to Fitzgerald, coming as it did at the end of the parliamentary session, attracted little notice in Britain at the time – even though Morier complained afterwards that it had 'produced all the effect which the most determined well-wisher to European disquiet could desire.'[66] Palmerston merely permitted himself to say, on 23 July 1863, that Britain had always been interested in the integrity and independence of Denmark; that any violent attempt to destroy these things would lead to serious complications; that Holstein was part of the Bund and the Diet therefore had every right to interfere in the affairs of that duchy; that although Schleswig did not belong to the Germanic Confederation there were enough Germans there to make it 'perfectly justifiable' for the Diet to 'make representations to the King of Denmark requesting that the German population should be put on a fair and equal footing with regard to the Danish population of Schleswig'; that the Germans were too sensible to act rashly in this matter; that Britain would do all in her power 'to induce the disputing parties to confine the question within the limits of diplomatic intercourse'; and that he himself did not anticipate 'any immediate danger, or indeed any of that remote danger which the hon. Gentleman seems to think imperils the peace of Europe arising out of the Danish and Holstein question.'[67] The only hint of menace was buried in the middle of his speech when he suggested that, given 'the great interest which the Powers of Europe feel in the independence of the Danish monarchy,' anyone trying to disturb the status quo in the Baltic 'would find, in the result, that it would not be Denmark alone with which they would have to contend.' This last sentence, often taken out of its proper context, has repeatedly been used by British historians to discredit Palmerston and Russell. They see it as a deliberate threat to Germany which served to encourage the Danes to defy the Diet in 1863. As has been clearly shown here, however, the Danes had been defiant long before 1863, and they were now resisting the Diet in spite of Britain's consistent plea for moderation.

Russell's Schleswig-Holstein policy in the summer of 1863 consisted mainly in urging Austria to restrain the Diet. He warned Rechberg that if the Diet persisted 'in confounding Schleswig with Holstein other Powers of Europe may confound Holstein with Schleswig, and deny the right of Germany to interfere with the one any more than she has with the other, except as a European Power.'[68] He observed also that any invasion of Schleswig would be detrimental to the independence and integrity of Germany, for it would provoke the intervention of Napoleon III. Russell advised Austria, in the face of these hazards, to confer first with the great powers before impelling the Diet to a definitive resolution. This warning yielded no result. Rechberg merely told Bloomfield that it would be better for Britain to use her influence at Copenhagen to bring about the immediate and total repeal of the illegal patent of March.[69]

Rather than follow Russell's advice, Denmark was actually trying to establish a European concert for the purpose of resisting the Diet, even though the western powers were trying to discourage the project.[70] These Dano-Swedish proposals, in fact, tended to complicate the plans of France and Britain who were then acting in concert with Austria on the question of Poland and were therefore anxious to preserve peace in the duchies. Russell agreed that the Danes should withdraw from Holstein and take their stand on the banks of the Eider, as the king of Sweden had advised, but he did not think that Britain could make the same material pledges to Denmark as the Swedish government had apparently done. As both sides were 'so much in the wrong,' Russell did not see how Britain could interfere – 'at all events till the peace of Europe is actually in danger on the subject of Schleswig.'[71]

Palmerston, in the meantime, was becoming increasingly irritated by the German determination to proceed with a federal execution, and he even seemed willing to support the aggressive Scandinavian project. He complained to the queen in mid-August that the Diet had 'not as yet intelligibly shown that the Danish patent of March last for Holstein is contrary to any law or rule of the Confederation.'[72]

When, on 27 August, Denmark rejected the Diet's ultimatum, Russell now tried to persuade the Germans to limit their activities to Holstein in the hope of forcing Sweden to abstain from interfering in a purely German matter. As Swedish intervention could widen the scope of the war, he was anxious to avoid it. He accordingly warned Austria, Prussia, and the Diet to beware the results of their indiscretion. He was now prepared to hold Austria and Prussia responsible for any untoward consequences since they were acting contrary to Britain's advice by promoting the idea of federal execution in Holstein. Russell again insisted that the Diet was by no means competent to judge matters relating to Schleswig, and he reminded the Germans that the Danish dominions had been recognized by all the great powers.[73] This latest warning served only to elicit a curt rejoinder from Bismarck who bluntly declared that federal execution was a legal proceeding and not a declaration of war: since Denmark was being legally penalized for her transgressions, it was difficult for her to escape full responsibility for any war that could possibly result.[74]

It was now obvious therefore that Britain needed French co-operation if she hoped to make any impression on the Germans, whom she had hitherto refused to take steps to coerce. The coercion of Germany had certainly not been feasible during the period of the Polish crisis when she needed to retain the co-operation of Austria. But Russell's whole Polish diplomacy had just been blown to bits by Russian defiance and Austrian vacillation. He could not but harbour a certain sense of resentment towards Austria and Russia. Besides, the moment seemed ripe for a strong anti-German stand. Prussia's refusal to attend the congress of German princes, convened by Austria for the purpose of revising the federal constitution, had left the Bund in a state of confusion.[75] Even though he still felt that Germany and Denmark were both too much in the wrong for Britain to play the role of a partisan, Russell now agreed with Palmerston that the western powers should employ the strongest measures if Germany refused their mediation.[76] He therefore proposed to France that the two powers should offer their mediation while reminding Austria and Prussia to obey their engagements of 1851-2.[77]

The French foreign minister, Edouard Drouyn de Lhuys, was in ill-humour over the British 'desertion' on the question of Poland. Britain, France, and Austria had vigorously protested against Russian tyranny in that country but when they were openly snubbed by the tsar, Austria and Britain immediately retreated. Drouyn was eager to proceed further, as much to defend the liberty of the Poles as to preserve the dignity of France; but with France left shamelessly in the lurch, he was compelled to share in the Austrian and British humiliation.[78] It was an episode which the French government could not easily forget. Drouyn declared that France was reluctant to repeat the Polish fiasco. He could not see what purpose mediation would serve unless the British government determined to do more. To draw German attention to the stipulations of the London Treaty seemed to him too similar to the manner in which Russia had been uselessly reminded of the Treaty of Vienna. France, in a word, was much less anxious to present an identical note to Germany than to preserve her freedom of action in the Schleswig-Holstein dispute.[79] Conscious of the growing isolation of France after the Italian War, Napoleon III was already contemplating an alliance with Prussia – especially since the behaviour of Austria and Britain during the Polish crisis had demonstrated their unreliability as allies.[80]

Britain was thus beginning to pay for her mistakes on the Polish question. Now that Anglo-French co-operation was needed to prevent a Dano-German war, her policy in Poland was making France reluctant to act in concert with her on the Danish affair. With the French government in this mood, Russell had to make a non-committal reply to the proposal made on 11 September by Ludvig Manderström, the Swedish foreign minister, who was seeking French and British support for the consummation of the Eiderdanish principle. Great Britain, Russell declared, was willing to mediate alone or with France; should this policy fail, she would have to reconsider her course in the light of future developments. She preferred to see the matter settled by negotiation rather than by war.[81]

When it became clear that neither France nor Britain would commit herself to help Sweden defend the integrity of Denmark, the Swedish government began to withdraw gradually from the policy it had pursued in the summer of 1863. By October, Sweden was following a course almost as prudent as that of the western powers. But by this time the Eiderdanish program was too far advanced to be abandoned. Frederick VII, indeed, opened the session of the Rigsraad on 28 September with a bellicose speech in which he promised to enforce the edict of March.[82]

The Diet finally voted on 1 October that its decrees so often disobeyed by Denmark were to be enforced by federal execution. It called upon Hanover and Saxony to provide the commissioners and troops for the military occupation of Holstein and Lauenburg. Austria and Prussia were required to prepare a force in reserve – in case Denmark resisted.[83]

In spite of Denmark's wayward policies, Russell continued to denounce the very principle of federal execution. He regarded it as a most dangerous measure. If Denmark resisted the German occupation, as she seemed determined to do, federal execution would at once be transformed into a Dano-German war. No one could tell where such a war, beginning on the Elbe, would end. Even if Britain managed somehow to localize the conflict, it would still result in the hampering of British trade as had been the case in the Dano-German war of 1848–50. Russell's main aim, therefore, was to dissuade the Germans, by threat if necessary, from invading Holstein; and he hoped, if federal execution could not be avoided, at least to limit the Diet's interference to the purely German territories of the Danish king. Hence he reminded Austria and Prussia of their obligations under the treaty of 1852, and trusted that the Diet would claim no objectives beyond the boundaries of Lauenburg and Holstein. At the same time he announced that

It appears to Her Majesty's Government that instead of resorting at once to a Federal Execution, the Diet ought to demand from Denmark a clear and explicit declaration of the meaning of the words 'explanations' and 'negotiations,' which she has used in relation to the Royal Letters Patent of March 30.

If these explanations open the way to a satisfactory arrangement, all grounds for a Federal Execution will be taken away; and if they do not, the Diet can still resort to a Federal Execution.

Her Majesty's Government are willing to offer their good offices to bring about a conciliatory termination of these difficult affairs.[84]

Russell's offer of mediation met with little success, and his continuing efforts to persuade the Diet to reconsider its order of 1 October were equally futile. The Diet would admit of no mediation on the question of Holstein even though it acknowledged that the question of Schleswig might be solved by a European conference.[85] By the end of October Germany could no longer be satisfied with anything less than the unconditional surrender of the patent of March and a strict adherence to the federal edict of 1860. Russell was thus left with nothing but the hope that Denmark would acquiesce in the impending execution. Supported by France and Sweden, he urged her to avert a war by allowing the Diet to occupy Holstein as it had recently done in the case of Hesse.[86] If Denmark could be induced to accept the occupation of Holstein as a legal device, then it might still be possible to arrange an amicable settlement after all.

Thus had the patent of March made Russell's Schleswig-Holstein policy, such as it was, immeasurably more difficult to execute. Striving always to maintain peace, he discovered by the end of October 1863 that war was practically inevitable. The more determined the Germans became to occupy Holstein the more convinced Russell felt that they should be thwarted. He grew increasingly hostile to the Diet, and his policy after July 1863 was markedly different from the one he had pursued in the previous eleven months. This change is hard to justify, for it was the Danes who had grown more and more intractable since 1852. They had persistently refused to follow Britain's advice and had indeed often acted in a spirit diametrically opposed to it. Yet, paradoxically, Russell became more and more unsympathetic to the German cause. This obvious lack of a consistent and definitive program did much to undermine British policy in the Danish duchies after 1859.

Some of Russell's inconsistency was doubtless due to public pressure. By the autumn of 1862 he had come round to a partial acceptance of the German claims. But he was forced to reconsider his Coburg views when they were so emphatically rejected by British public opinion. He began to feel that the Germans were using Holstein as a pretext for threatening Denmark's position in Schleswig. Thus he became increasingly reluctant to resist the current of British opinion on the question. The conduct of the Diet after July 1863 focused the attention of British newspapers on what they considered to be flagrant acts of German aggression. The British press was solidly pro-Danish, and Russell eventually swam with

the tide. Had the journalists paid more attention to the Schleswig-Holstein question during the 1850s when Denmark was committing a series of provocative
acts, it is possible that they might have taken a more objective view of the quarrel. As it was, the British journals became interested in the controversy only in
the summer of 1863 when the Diet appeared to be the aggressor. Until this time,
Russell was left fairly free to vacillate in Schleswig-Holstein as he chose, so long
as he did not offend the Danophiles by appearing to take up cudgels for Germany (as they were led to believe in September 1862).

Throughout September and October 1863, *The Times*, the most influential
London daily, conducted a vigorous campaign against German pretensions in the
duchies. It ridiculed the Bund and was outraged when such a nondescript collection of pompous princelings ventured to reject Russell's mediatory proposal. It
had no doubt that the western powers would easily foil the German plans, for
it seemed to take French co-operation very much for granted, even though it was
still suspicious of Napoleon's designs upon the Rhenish provinces. *The Times* did
not see how a federal execution could be effectively performed, and it was convinced that, even if the occupation of Holstein did take place, the Great Powers
could not abandon Denmark. Quite clearly, the editors of this paper had not
carefully studied the history of the dispute. They took for granted the validity
of the Danish claims and did not even consider the prudence or legality of the
patent of March which had precipitated the crisis of July.

Equally negligent in their research were the leader-writers for the *Morning
Post*, the liberal daily which was still very closely linked with Palmerston. This
paper considered federal execution harsh and groundless. On 9 October it declared that 'the Danes, in truth, have done all that they could in reason be
expected to do, in the way of compliance with German demands. The Danish
Court is therefore entitled to the countenance of this country and of France, as
the party that is aggrieved in the dispute which it has had to maintain with Germany, and if any event of an international character should arise.' Without discussing the recent impolicy of the Danish government, the *Morning Post* simply
hoped that the Diet would accept the British mediatory proposal and thus prevent German embarrassment. It confidently predicted that under the influence
of Britain and France the Schleswig-Holstein question would 'sink again into its
chronic obscurity.' On 24 October the *Morning Post* vehemently denied that the
patent of March was a violation of Denmark's pledges. It considered that proclamation indeed as evidence of Danish conciliation since it 'more than satisfies
the wants of the Holsteiners.' The *Morning Post* warned the Germans not to push
the issue to the point of war as this would merely bring upon themselves an unnecessary chastisement.

The *Daily News*, a liberal newspaper enjoying close links with the foreign
secretary, was just as pro-Danish. 'The proposed federal execution,' it remarked

on 14 October, 'is no longer a domestic question, but one involving the peace of Europe.' While warning the Diet not to flout the counsels of the major powers, it also complained of the lukewarm attitude of Napoleon III who was thus encouraging the foolish Germans to implement their ulterior schemes.

The *Observer* (another Palmerstonian mouthpiece) was at first inclined, on 20 September, to feel that Denmark was in no real danger since the Diet was not united. Believing that the whole crisis sprang from German designs on the port of Kiel, it did not see how Europe could possibly permit such a German violation of Danish soil. When the execution was finally ordered, the *Observer* warned the Diet on 25 October to beware the intervention of the great powers which could not but oppose this blatant German aggression as the Danish king had 'already done much to satisfy all reasonable men.'

The liberal *Globe*, which had long been sympathetic to Palmerston, also regarded the Schleswig-Holstein crisis as the product of German greed. It was therefore much distressed by that curious 'monomania' which 'afflicts the German people.' It did not question the legality of the patent of March but cursorily dismissed the German demands as inadmissible. Anticipating European resistance to the federal execution, it expressed the view, on 24 October, that 'no sensible man who reflects on the complexity of the relations subsisting between the powers of Europe, and on the peculiar position of Austria and Prussia, can avoid the conclusion that it would be an act of wisdom on the part of the German Courts to back out of the dispute in that way which they may deem most suitable to their dignity.' The *Globe* and the *Observer* were thus re-echoing opinions that had been vigorously stated by the liberal *Examiner* almost a year before. This weekly had declared on 1 November 1862 that 'what Prussia wants to get from Denmark – by hook or crook, both shores of the harbour of Kiel, with all the surrounding naval stations ... is inconveniently obvious to men who are awake, and to the Germans themselves, nakedly put, inconveniently immoral.' The *Examiner* remained convinced that Denmark's dignity, let alone her integrity, required the stoutest resistance to the German demands.

The *Manchester Guardian*, another liberal newspaper, was perhaps the most reasonable among the Danophile journals. It admitted that Denmark was much too reluctant to fulfil her obligations and suggested that Britain should persuade her to adopt a more conciliatory course. Although the *Manchester Guardian* suspected that Prussia was seeking to escape from her domestic problems by means of military adventure abroad, it did not foresee, on 10 October, that the Schleswig-Holstein crisis would result in open warfare. It thought that the European powers would have ample time to solve the problem by diplomacy since the Diet was usually so slow and hesitant in matters of this kind.

Apart from the court, Germany found few reliable champions in Britain during the summer and autumn of 1863 to counter the Danish arguments that were being propagated freely. The conservative journals were no more sympathetic to the Diet, and even the normally pro-German *Saturday Review* was reluctant to support German policy. It is true that on 17 October it warned Britain against letting Denmark 'use us to get her own way in everything,' and advised Russell to avoid helping Denmark to commit acts of injustice; but two weeks earlier it had itself acknowledged that the German behaviour was suspect. The *Saturday Review*, on 3 October, marvelled at the spectacle of a Prussian despotism posing as the champion of Schleswig-Holstein liberalism.

British opinion rejected the Diet's policy chiefly because of the growing fear that the crisis could not but redound to the advantage of France. The British press and a number of British politicians perceived in this tedious Danish business a golden opportunity for Napoleon III. This fear of France, this curious opposition to German aspirations, and the instinctive British sympathy for Denmark were all clearly expressed by the *Spectator* when on 10 October it declared that

No treaty has ever given Germany the right to terminate Danish independence, and in defending her freedom Denmark will have the aid of the sympathy, if not of the arms, of Great Britain. Both will be more readily and more heartily conceded if the King will only remove those grievances which are the avowed, if not the real cause of the movement which, to the irritation of all sane men, now threatens Europe with conflagration, and Germany with the loss of the Rhine.[87]

Faced with this kind of public opinion at home, Russell would have found it impossible, even had he been so disposed, to continue the Coburg policy he had briefly pursued towards the end of 1862. The fact is that while the foreign secretary recognized that both sides were responsible for the crisis in the duchies, the pressure from the Danophiles within Britain was simply too powerful. The majority of Russell's colleagues in the cabinet, the vast bulk of the parliamentary members in both houses, and the newspaper editors almost to a man, were all passionately committed to preserving the integrity and independence of Denmark.

As most of Britain's diplomats on the continent, with the notable exception of Hodges, Howard, Morier, and Ward, were also deeply opposed to the German claims in Schleswig-Holstein, the Danes could not but have been aware of the immense moral support they were then receiving from the British public. Russell was consequently unable to discourage the Danish government from proceeding to extreme measures in 1863. It can thus be argued that the strong expression of pro-Danish feeling within Britain after the publication of the Gotha despatch in September 1862 increased Russell's difficulties in Schleswig-Holstein, at the very time when the need to keep a closer watch than usual over American developments and to find an honourable escape from involvement in the Russo-Polish quarrel dictated a British policy of caution in the duchies.

5

Great Britain and the federal execution

The patent of 30 March 1863, against which most of Europe had agitated, remained in force until November, only to be replaced by the definitive constitution for which it had itself provided. This Constitution of November was in many respects a revival of the Constitution of 1855, but it went further than all the Danish policies since 1852. It provided for the complete detachment of Holstein from the monarchy and the unequivocal annexation of Schleswig by Denmark.[1] It was, in short, a flagrant violation of the engagements of 1851-2 as well as a direct challenge to the Bund.

Although this Eiderdanish constitution was based mainly on his own proclamation of March, Frederick VII refused, on his death-bed, to sanction it. In accordance with the London Treaty he was succeeded by Prince Christian of Glücksburg who was known to be sympathetic to the German cause.[2] For this reason, the majority of the Danes feared that the new king would refuse to grant the constitution for which they were clamouring. These suspicions made the Eiderdanes all the more determined, and Denmark found herself on the brink of revolution. In spite of the excitement prevailing in Copenhagen, however, the European courts, with the exception of Sweden, insisted upon the royal veto.[3] On 17 November Russell telegraphed to Paget advocating delay. He seriously felt that the king should not consent to the constitution until the international question had been solved.[4] But, as Paget explained, the situation in Copenhagen was so desperate that the king could not comply with the wishes of the European powers.[5] On 18 November Christian IX signed the bill and announced that it would take effect from 1 January 1864.

Russell, who had so repeatedly demanded the recall of the edict of March, could not but be distressed by the Constitution of November. It was a severe blow to his hopes, especially since it came just when Denmark seemed on the point of yielding. When the Diet vetoed the Danish offer to modify the patent of March, Hall had expressed himself, at the end of October, quite willing to accept British mediation.[6] Bismarck also appeared interested in British mediation, and he suggested that Britain should again use her good offices at Frankfurt.[7] But Austria and the Diet had become so belligerent that Russell wisely refrained from exposing the British government to another rebuff. 'It is clear,' he wrote to Buchanan,

that Her Majesty's Government cannot expose themselves to another refusal of their suggested mediation at Frankfort. It would not be enough that Prussia should support the proposal of Great Britain, or that the Diet should put forth conditions for their assent which Denmark would refuse.

Her Majesty's Government have no immediate interest in this question. Their interest is bound up with the general interest of Europe.

The line which Her Majesty's Government have taken upon this question is clear and distinct. They think that the Federal question in Holstein should be settled according to Federal Laws, and in conformity with the views of the Federal Diet.

But the German Diet have unfortunately mixed this purely Federal question with those of the general Constitution of the Danish Monarchy and the position of Schleswig.

It is obvious that these are international questions, and as they are also questions of great difficulty upon which passion has been listened to, and reason has been disregarded, it is very desirable that Powers neither German nor Danish should be permitted to mediate upon them.

The German Diet have refused the mediation suggested by Great Britain. They had a right to do so.

But Great Britain also has a right to reserve any further interference till a prospect shall arise of such interference being salutary and effectual.[8]

By mid-November therefore Russell was preparing to withdraw from the Schleswig-Holstein quarrel. All his arguments against federal execution had produced no result; he could not again take the lead in mediation; and he could not commit Britain to active military intervention. His diplomacy had exhausted itself. Britain could now do no more than preserve her liberty of action and let the Diet fulfil its order. The attitude of Russia was far from friendly, and that of France was ambivalent. Russell had the satisfaction of inducing Hall to admit the right of the Diet to perform its execution in Holstein, and Britain now had no motive for immediate action unless the federal occupation of the German duchies should be improperly conducted.

It was possible for Russell to produce such a clear outline of British policy in Schleswig-Holstein in mid-November mainly because the whole question had been reduced to a simple matter of federal chastisement which Denmark had promised not to resist. But the death of Frederick VII, the passage of the Eider-danish constitution, and the collapse of the Anglo-French concert all conspired to complicate the issue at this very point. The western alliance, already shaken by the Polish crisis, was further undermined by the British reaction to Napoleon III's proposal that the European powers should meet in a congress to revise the settlement of 1815. Napoleon's aim was to restore his damaged prestige and to avenge himself on Austria, whom he blamed most for the failure of French diplomacy in Poland.[9] His project, however, was ridiculed by the British press, and Queen Victoria herself described it as 'an impertinence.'[10] Still hoping for French support on the Danish affair, Russell was really inclined to accept Napoleon's suggestion and leave the other powers with the responsibility of rejecting it;[11] but his arguments could not prevail against those of Cowley (the British minister in Paris), Hammond, Palmerston, and the queen.[12] After vacillating for a fortnight, during which he asked Drouyn to specify the concrete arrangements the emperor had in mind, Russell eventually declined Napoleon's invitation altogether on 25 November.[13] Britain had thus rejected the French proposal before the other powers had committed themselves, and thus left the latter with an avenue of escape without having to share Napoleon's displeasure. This supreme impolicy cost the British government the goodwill of France during the climax of the Danish crisis.

Frederick VII's death, which inevitably revived the dispute over the Danish succession, produced considerable excitement and speculation in Britain, where the press emerged with a variety of analyses. Some newspapers, like the liberal *Daily News*, *Morning Post*, and *Daily Telegraph*, and the conservative *Morning Herald* described as hopeful the circumstances under which Christian IX was ascending the throne. They suggested that the German character of the new king was bound to lead to a satisfactory compromise between the crown and those subjects whom Frederick had offended. They even felt that the succession of the Glücks-burg prince would avert the threatened Dano-German conflict. The liberal *Globe* was hesitant. Their editors expressed great concern for the new dynasty on 17 November, although they had thought only the day before that it was at last reasonable to look forward to a satisfactory settlement of the Dano-German dispute.

Many British journalists, however, immediately predicted that the new succession would aggravate the dispute between the Diet and Denmark. This was the view expressed by the conservative *Standard*, for instance, when it declared, on 16 November, that Christian IX had inherited a legacy of woe as a direct result of Russell's diplomatic blunders. On 21 November the *Economist*, the *Saturday Review*, and the *Spectator*, following the example set by *The Times* on the 17th, all observed that Frederick VII's death had elevated the Schleswig-Holstein question to an international one of grave anxiety. They gloomily warned the British government of new and sudden complications.

Frederick's death, in fact, inspired a good deal of pessimism in Britain. The queen herself was

much alarmed at the danger which this entails of immediate war, the arrangement of 1852 *never* having been accepted by the Diet, and being, as Lord Russell *well knows, contrary* to the rights of succession existing in Holstein and Schleswig.

She urges the Government *most* strongly to do *nothing* without *consultation* with the other *Powers*, but *especially* with Germany.[14]

The queen eventually resigned herself to the Glücksburg succession but hoped that Christian would deal fairly with his German subjects. She felt that he should be induced to veto the constitution. Her main concern was that Britain should give Germany no further ground for complaint at this critical juncture.[15] She was therefore very disappointed when she heard that Christian had signed the very constitution which the Diet had outlawed. Her opinion was that if only Denmark could be persuaded to fulfil her part of the bargain, then the London Treaty might work, bad as it undoubtedly was. She thought that arbitration or mediation would be most useful if it could somehow be arranged. Apart from her obvious concern for German rights, the queen was particularly fearful of what Napoleon III might do in the midst of the confusion.[16] Palmerston and Russell were also alarmed, as much by the worsening of the situation abroad as by the queen's reaction itself. Palmerston regretted her persistent derogation of the London Treaty and thought that she ought to be reminded 'that she is the Queen of England, and not a German sovereign.'[17]

Russell was perturbed by the prospect of having to retrace his steps only a few days after announcing the British determination to withdraw from the Schleswig-Holstein quarrel. He now instructed Paget, on 18 November, to inform the Danish government that Britain was ready to offer her sole mediation and that she was doing so at Prussia's instigation.[18] But while Denmark was willing to accept Russell's mediation,[19] she showed no desire to appease the Germans by revoking the constitution as he had also advised. The Germans therefore could not be restrained.

The November Constitution was such a glaring breach of federal law that a violent German response was more or less predictable. Its immediate effect indeed was to throw the whole of Germany into a state of frenzy, especially since the son of the duke of Augustenburg now put himself forward as the rightful duke of Schleswig-Holstein. The Augustenburgs were clearly acting contrary to the spirit of the London Treaty and ought to have found little support from those parties who had acceded to it. The minor German states, however, gave zealous support to the pretender, and even the Prussian court was sympathetic to his cause.[20]

Palmerston and Russell were outraged by the revival of the Augustenburg claims, the original validity of which they had never admitted. On this question they were wholeheartedly supported by their colleagues in the cabinet who also refused to countenance the behaviour of the Augustenburgs. The British ministers advised the Foreign Office to acknowledge the succession of Prince Christian in accordance with the London Treaty. The cabinet based its stand on the settlement of 1852 and tried to persuade the court to do likewise.[21]

The queen agreed that the London Treaty should be observed but she did not think that the Danes could expect Germany to adhere to that settlement if they themselves persisted in violating it. She was not surprised to see so many German states supporting the Augustenburg claims, for Christian IX had succeeded to the Danish throne only by virtue of the very treaty he had infringed by signing the Constitution of November. The queen denounced Danish malpractices in the duchies and continued to regret that the London Treaty (concluded by the major powers without consultation with the Diet) had foisted an unpopular sovereign upon Schleswig and Holstein.[22]

Although the queen and her ministers admitted the necessity of adhering to the settlement of 1852, it was clear that they were viewing it from diametrically opposite points of vantage. The queen wanted to maintain the treaty only for the sake of protecting German rights whereas her ministers wished to preserve it for the purpose of combating the pretensions of the Diet. At all events the court and the cabinet were for the moment united on two basic ideas: the preservation of peace and the validity of the Treaty of London.

It was in this sense that Russell now addressed the disputants on 23 November. In a circular despatch of that date he reminded the rest of Europe that Britain still adhered to the London Treaty and could not therefore give any support to the claims of Augustenburg.[23] At the same time he urged Austria and Prussia to make an honest effort to temper the belligerence of the Diet. He also issued an unmistakable threat to the Germans: Britain maintained the right to interfere in this controversy should the Diet attempt in any way to meddle with the affairs of Schleswig.[24]

Despite Russell's warnings, the Diet not only questioned the validity of the London Treaty but was ready by the end of November to contest the Glücksburg title both to Holstein and to Schleswig. It was thus preparing openly to exceed the limits of federal jurisdiction. Annoyed by the truculence of Bavaria, Saxony, and Württemberg, Palmerston urged Russell to remind them in the strongest language that the Treaty of London still prevailed, to warn them of their folly in upholding the dubious Augustenburg claims, and to impress upon them that this course could lead to serious war.[25] Russell obeyed,[26] but succeeded only in evoking the curt reply from Bavaria that she regarded the question of the succession in the duchies as a case for the Diet to judge.[27]

This German policy was bitterly criticized in Britain. Clarendon regretted that circumstances should have resulted in Napoleon's indifference, as this was only serving to embolden the Germans, who were being carried away by 'that blatant blockhead, the Duke of Coburg.'[28] Hammond was also irritated by what he considered the manifest dishonesty of the Diet whose actions seemed to prove that it was just as eager to interfere in Schleswig as to defend German rights in Holstein.[29] Both Clarendon and Hammond were all the more displeased because they imagined that the German manoeuvres were creating excellent opportunities for the French emperor. Clarendon, however, appreciated Russell's dilemma when he remarked that while Britain needed to work in concert with France, she could not really permit, or participate in, any French coercion of Prussia.[30]

The views of Clarendon and Hammond typified British opinion of that day. Britain condemned the German policy not only because it seemed morally wrong but because it appeared inadvisable at a time when France was so restless. The queen, pro-German as she was, regretted occurrences which could only place temptations before Napoleon III. The cabinet held this view, and the British public concurred. The press, anti-German as always, denounced the revival of the Augustenburg claims, ridiculed the Diet, and blamed the Bund for provoking a general war.

The Times strongly opposed the Augustenburg pretensions and expressed the hope on 20 November that the young duke would find no support for his cause as his family had been 'set aside both by solemn treaty and by law.' The Times exhorted the British government to uphold the London Treaty in spite of the irresponsible antics of the Diet. On 27 November it advised the king of Denmark to 'fulfil the Federal duties incumbent upon him,' so as to prevent the Germans from encroaching upon his rights or repudiating the settlement of 1852.

The Palmerstonian Morning Post was more outspoken in its assault on the house of Augustenburg and in its defence of the London Treaty. It rebuked those who held that the treaty was invalid because the people of Schleswig-Holstein had not been consulted as to its terms, and indignantly asked its readers on 19 November whether Europe should be 'plunged into a general war, of we know not what duration, merely because Germany wants some ports and coastlines belonging to one of her neighbours?' The *Morning Post* also observed that there was no mention in the treaty of a 'provisional execution of it by any one of the contracting parties.'

The *Daily News* declared on 23 November that the great powers could 'hardly permit the petty Princes of Germany to destroy, under an impulse of selfish zeal, what they consider so important to the interests of Europe and have taken such pains to secure.' Two days later, it described the Augustenburg title as 'so full of flaws, and crossed by so many other claims, that even if it were barred by no treaty and no act of renunciation, few responsible statesmen would be disposed to recognize it.' The *Daily News* felt that Britain was morally bound to prevent a foreign movement from setting up a pretender who openly flouted an international agreement.

The *Morning Herald*, whose owners and editors were in close contact with Lord Derby, was inclined to dismiss the Diet's violence as a tempest in an Augustenburg teapot, for it did not believe that even the Germans could be so stupid as to draw upon themselves the wrath of all Europe. It declared, on 19 November, that the Diet's policy was likely to be more detrimental to Germany than to any other state.

The Disraelian *Standard* refuted the claims of Augustenburg on the double ground that they had been solemnly renounced and were in any case inferior to those of the house of Hesse. It was therefore appalled by the measure of support which the pretender was finding in Germany.[31] The *Standard* remarked on 20 November that the whole dispute rested upon the will of Austria and Prussia, without whose assistance the prince of Augustenburg must perforce 'return to his castle at Dolzig to meditate upon the vanity of human wishes, and to count the costs to which his little spurt of sovereignty has put him.'

The *Observer* likewise held on 29 November that Augustenburg was an insupportable pretender. It considered foolish the Diet's apparent intention to flout the law of Europe, since the great powers simply could not allow Denmark to suffer a German invasion. The *Observer* added that if Austria and Prussia chose to promote another order of succession in the duchies, they would 'place themselves in the position of never being treated with again.'

The *Spectator* warned Prussia that the western powers would not permit her to expand at Denmark's expense, but it was mainly concerned with thwarting the ambitions of Napoleon III. It differed from most British newspapers by suggesting that the London Treaty should be abandoned. On 21 November it recommended an Eiderdanish solution which it considered best attainable through a plebiscite.

The *Saturday Review* also thought that the London Treaty should be given up since it had failed for eleven years to provide any stability at all. It suggested that the dispute could be settled most fairly by partitioning Schleswig, and urged the British government on 28 November not to give Denmark free rein to oppress her German subjects in the duchies. The *Saturday Review*, however, could not resist the temptation to contrast the German attitude towards Schleswig-Holstein with the conduct of Austria and Prussia in Galicia and Posen.

Although the *Globe* had also admitted on 17 November that a revision of the London Treaty might be appropriate, it deplored the manner in which that settlement was being repudiated by the Diet. Like the majority of British newspapers, it suspected that Germany aimed at objectives in Schleswig as well as Holstein. It was outraged by the brazen dishonesty of the Augustenburgs and by the attitude of those German states which had acceded so readily to the treaty of 1852. On 27 November the *Globe* made a strong plea for moderation when it advised the new king of Denmark to put himself in the right by revoking the patent of March – notwithstanding the fact that this edict had already been superseded by the November Constitution.

Conspicuously isolated on the subject of Augustenburg was the *Daily Telegraph* which argued on 19 November that it was 'unfair to the Germans to represent their advocacy of Prince Frederick's pretensions as a crusade in favour of abstract legitimacy.' On the following day, it admitted that the pretender's claims were dangerous in the circumstances of 1863, but it still maintained that the whole controversy was so complicated that each party could construct a plausible defence for itself. The *Daily Telegraph* expressed annoyance on 23 November at the British tendency to treat the question too much from the Danish stand-point, and it regretted that Europe was more concerned about German and Danish rights than the welfare of the inhabitants of the duchies. It advised Denmark to give up the idea of annexing Schleswig if the Schleswigers did not wish for it, as the duchy would become a mere liability if annexed against its will. The *Daily Telegraph* on 26 November seemed disturbed by the prospect of Prussian protection of Schleswig-Holstein liberties when the Prussian government notoriously held Posen under a galling yoke. But, on the whole, this paper considered the entire question a trivial one and it urged the British government on 25 November not to become involved in any controversy, much less a war, on account of Schleswig-Holstein.

Even though the *Daily Telegraph* and the *Saturday Review* focused attention on Denmark's failure to fulfil her obligations, they were equally ready to assert that Germany was less interested in defending German rights then in seeking northward expansion. This was the view of all the pro-Danish newspapers which were eager to show that Germany had precipitated the crisis. Without examining the basic causes of the conflict they were willing to accept that the current deadlock was the result of the Diet's pugnacity. Even the November Constitution, which played such an important part in aggravating the dispute, was imperfectly understood by the British press. Some editors actually assumed that it had been intended as a concession to Holstein. This failure to understand the nature of Danish policy made the British public starkly hostile to the apparent aggressors. Despite this strong anti-German feeling, however, the British people recognized the need for moderation and peace.

It is not at all clear whether Russell consciously or deliberately followed this kind of public opinion; but it is significant that his policy at this stage was in keeping with the attitudes of the nation as a whole. He disapproved of both the high-handed measures of the Diet and the imprudent tactics of Denmark. He wanted to settle the dispute without resorting to war. This is why he had so often fallen back on mediation. The Diet's refusal to accept British mediation, and Denmark's failure to rescind the constitution, compelled him to try different methods of diplomacy at the end of November.

Russell now accepted the Russian proposal that the five powers which had signed the London Treaty with Denmark should act in concert to compel Denmark to fulfil her engagements and thus to preserve peace. The idea was that they should send envoys to Copenhagen ostensibly to congratulate Christian IX on his accession and to attend the funeral of Frederick VII, but in fact to bring all the diplomatic pressure of a combined Europe to bear upon the Danish government. Acting in concert in Denmark, the envoys were to assure the king that Europe still defended the principle of the independence and integrity of the Danish monarchy, but to explain that this was, as in 1852, conditional upon the fulfilment of Denmark's obligations. Above all, they were to insist on the repeal of the November Constitution.[32] This project collapsed when Austria and Prussia refused to co-operate.[33]

Austro-Prussian co-operation was now, in fact, impossible to purchase. The two great German powers had suddenly decided, in November 1863, to reconstruct their foreign policy. Deeply disturbed by Napoleon's congress proposal and painfully conscious of their diplomatic isolation, they were impelled, by a strong and common feeling of insecurity, to put a temporary halt to their disagreements, which indeed had brought them precariously close to open warfare in August and September.[34] Austria's situation had become particularly delicate. During the Crimean War, she had alienated herself from Russia without earning the gratitude of the western powers; and she had just repeated the same error in the Polish revolt. The hesitancy of the Mittelstaaten during the Fürstentag crisis in the recent summer had also demonstrated that she could not count upon the assistance of the other German states. In her desperation, Austria, without a friend in Europe, sought moral support from her German rival. Prussia, meanwhile, had estranged herself from the bulk of Germany by her stand on the question of federal reform of the Bund. She had also incurred the enmity of Britain and France by her policy in Poland without, as yet, ensuring the goodwill of Russia. She was consequently eager to work in concert with Austria to keep Napoleon III in check, while at the same time holding out to France the prospect of a Franco-Prussian understanding.[35]

Bismarck and Rechberg resolved therefore to work closely together on the Schleswig-Holstein question – especially since they were anxious to avoid a federal attack upon the London Treaty. The Diet was already considering the idea of changing the plan of federal execution to one of simple occupation since the former scheme would implicitly recognize the validity of Christian's title to the duchies. To forestall this dangerous tactic, Bismarck and Rechberg found it necessary to expedite the original order for federal execution. On 7 December they compelled the Diet to proceed immediately with the occupation of Holstein and Lauenburg, and thus acknowledge tacitly the title of Christian IX. On 12 December the usual week's notice was served on the Danish government to withdraw its troops from those duchies. Preparations had been so carefully made for this federal action that by 24 December the Diet's forces had entered Holstein and Lauenburg, and the two duchies lay under effective occupation by the end of the year.[36]

In accordance with the advice of the non-German powers, Denmark offered no resistance to the federal execution. This prudent decision deprived the Diet of any further *casus belli*. The dreaded federal execution had thus occurred despite the frantic opposition of the British government. The Frankfurt assembly had treated the British notes, both threatening and mediatory, with singular disrespect. Russell had also failed to influence the Diet indirectly, by working through Austria and Prussia.

Russell objected strenuously to the Diet's policy, but his attitude served only to annoy the queen who had always held that the Danes were the guilty party. In the summer of 1863 she protested vehemently against his attempts to threaten the Diet, and at least on three occasions compelled the foreign secretary to modify his approach.[37] On this question, however, Palmerston was in agreement with Russell, and so too, on the whole, was the cabinet. Despite occasional differences of opinion, as in the case of the Gotha despatch of 1862, there was, as yet, no deep ministerial rift over the Danish affair. Indeed, as late as 30 November, when the queen objected to Russell's proposed draft of a despatch to Buchanan, the cabinet overruled her objections.[38] She had argued vainly that the note tended too strongly to suggest that the fault lay more with Prussia than with Denmark, and that Prussia was more likely to heed British advice 'if the reciprocity of the obligations of the two parties were explicitly admitted.' On 2 December she reluctantly sanctioned the despatch – notwithstanding her own fears that it was 'little calculated to effect the object her Government professes to have in view.'[39]

Now that the Dano-German war was imminent, the queen was doing her utmost to prevent the British Foreign Office from pursuing an anti-German policy. She began to seek the support of her other ministers to curb the pro-Danish sympathies of Palmerston and Russell. As the two cabinet leaders also began to see the need for ministerial support to counter the German bias of the court, their colleagues gradually became the intermediary between themselves and the queen during the Schleswig-Holstein crisis. This, of course, by the end of 1863, was neither a novel nor an unusual role for Russell's colleagues. Although he had insisted on obtaining the foreign secretaryship in 1859, he was universally regarded as unfit for the post. The other ministers therefore had thought it necessary from the very beginning to keep a careful watch over his diplomatic activity. As a result, on all the major issues of the period – the Italian War, the American Civil War, the Mexican adventure, the Syrian upheaval, the Polish insurrection – there had been considerable ministerial involvement in the formulation of British foreign policy. The cabinet, however, had seldom been united on any subject, be it domestic or foreign, as it was sadly lacking in fundamental cohesion. This difficulty arose from the simple fact that Palmerston's second ministry was really a coalition between the leading forces in mid-Victorian politics: Palmerstonians, Peelites, Mancunians, and Whigs. In December 1863 the only reliable Palmerstonians in the cabinet, apart from the prime minister, were Argyll (himself an ex-Peelite), Lord Stanley of Alderley, and Lord Westbury. Cardwell, Gladstone, and the duke of Newcastle carried the Peelite banner; while Milner-Gibson and Villiers represented the Manchester School. The cabinet also included a handful of 'courtiers,' like Granville, Grey, and Wood, who generally kept the queen informed of ministerial developments and often tried to mediate between the court and its official advisers in times of critical stress.[40]

Despite the effort of her minions, the queen failed to prevent the despatch of 2 December to Berlin. But it was this skirmish that proved to be the turning-point in the struggle between the court and the Foreign Office for control of British policy in the Danish crisis. While Palmerston ably refuted the queen's propositions by insisting on the obvious distinction between the London Treaty itself and the anterior Dano-German negotiations of 1851-2, and by boldly asserting that the German powers were morally bound to acknowledge Christian's title,[41] Sir Charles Wood, the secretary for India, warmly supported the queen. He expressed the view that Britain should compel Denmark to fulfil her pledges instead of offending Austria and Prussia.[42] This was – on the question of Schleswig-Holstein – the start of the ministerial rebellion against Palmerston and Russell. Henceforth an increasing number of their colleagues would join the ranks of the 'peace-party' within the cabinet.

It was in this unsettled atmosphere that Russell had to contend with the aggressiveness of the Diet. Austria and Prussia, unwilling to irritate the great powers, pledged themselves to uphold the Treaty of London, but this was the limit of their concession to British feeling. Indeed, they were tending more and more to make their adherence to that treaty contingent upon Danish behaviour, and it became clear that unless Denmark obeyed the stipulations of 1851-2, Britain could not persuade the German states to do so. This is why Russell agreed eventually, despite the indifference of Austria and Prussia, to join France and Russia in sending special envoys to Copenhagen with the object of compelling the Danes to fulfil their engagements.[43]

But even the special mission to Denmark in December produced two upheavals, and it is significant that Palmerston and Russell were forced to yield on both occasions. The very choice of a special envoy involved much difficulty. Palmerston recommended Sir Henry Howard, but although Russell and the queen agreed with this nomination, the rest of the cabinet chose Lord Wodehouse – despite Russell's objection that he was too pro-Danish.[44] More difficult still was the preparation of Wodehouse's instructions. It was ultimately decided that he should go to Berlin as well as Copenhagen in an effort to induce both the Prussian and Danish governments to uphold the London Treaty. When the queen objected to Russell's first draft, on the ground that it conveyed an implied threat to Prussia, he appealed to the cabinet.

Russell, however, now found himself opposed by the majority of his colleagues. Wood, for example, urged him not to make any threats to the Germans or to commit Britain in any way before France had declared her hand. Earl de Grey, the secretary for war, voted for the amendment of Wodehouse's instructions exactly as suggested by the queen. The duke of Argyll, lord privy seal, wanted to draw up an entirely new set of instructions as he could not see why Britain should wish to speak strongly either to Prussia or Denmark. Sir George Grey, home secretary, stressed the importance of keeping Britain free to take whatever course her honour and interests required. He advised Russell not to persist in irritating Austria and Prussia if he did not mean to threaten them with war. Earl Granville, lord president of the council, thought that Britain should issue no threats which she did not positively intend to fulfil. He especially objected to an Anglo-German war on the Schleswig-Holstein question, 'leaving France and Russia to take any part in such a war, and at whatever time they thought fit.' W.E. Gladstone, chancellor of the exchequer, stressed the folly of 'quasi-threats on both sides.' Indeed, apart from Palmerston, only the lord chancellor, Westbury, agreed with Russell.[45] The latter's appeal to the cabinet thus resulted in a triumph for the court. He could not now threaten Prussia as he had wished. Wodehouse was eventually instructed to use identical language to both sides, reminding them of the binding force of the London Treaty. Bismarck was to be alerted to the dangers of federal execution at that stage, and Christian IX was to be persuaded to repeal the Constitution of November.[46]

Wodehouse did not have the slightest chance of averting the federal execution. On the very day of his first meeting with Bismarck, the Diet served a week's notice on Denmark. The mission to Berlin, in fact, accomplished nothing. Wodehouse fully admitted his own failure and could only 'regret to be obliged to add that my observations appeared to make little impression on M. de Bismarck.'[47] He fared no better at Copenhagen where Hall not only refused to repeal the constitution but seemed unwilling to make any concessions whatever to the Germans.[48]

Russell had no choice but to resign himself at last to the idea of federal execution, but he did not do so philosophically. He never admitted the justice or the expediency of the measure. Not only did he believe that the dispute could be settled amicably but he remained convinced that the Diet was overstepping its authority. He was sure that federal execution in Holstein was being ordered for the accomplishment of objects relating to Schleswig. Above all, he feared that federal execution would result in a general war which might create opportunities for France. These sentiments prevented him from taking a favourable view of the Diet's policy.

Having failed to avert the federal execution, Russell now tried to control it. He urged Austria and Prussia to make sure that the Diet did not encourage revolution in Holstein or raise a rebellion in any way against Christian's authority. 'Great care,' he felt, 'should be taken that no doubtful or mixed territory at Rendsburg or any disputed part of the frontier is occupied by the Federal troops.'[49] He also asked the two great German powers to dissuade the Diet from occupying the Tête du Pont at Frederickstadt.[50] As for the Glücksburg title, Russell informed all Germany that this was beyond question,[51] and he warned Prussia on 21 December that very serious results would follow any German attempt to overthrow 'the dynasty now reigning at Copenhagen.'[52] Russell also spoke forcefully to the Diet, warning it of the most serious complications which must ensue should the Bund hastily adopt any measures contrary to the settlement of 1852.[53] But these messages apparently produced no impression on Austria, Prussia, or the Diet.

The federal execution gave rise to the very complications that the British government had foreseen. In the wake of the confederate troops the agents of Augustenburg appeared in Holstein, and even the pro-German Ward was obliged to report that the federal commissioners in the duchy were doing nothing to suppress the many demonstrations in the pretender's favour.[54] As Hall bitterly complained, the entire spirit of the federal execution was wrong.[55] The legal procedure was immediately transformed into an act of hostility against Christian IX. The overt encouragement of Augustenburg's banner in Holstein did violence to the king's position there. The federal execution became a naked invasion.

At the end of the year Russell remonstrated with all the German states. He denounced their failure to recognize the validity of the London Treaty, especially since the majority of them had voluntarily assented to it in 1853. He accused Austria and Prussia particularly of bad faith since they had actually signed the treaty in 1852. He failed to see how Prussia could think of defending nationalism in the dominions of Christian IX when, at the same time, countless Poles in Posen were being oppressed by Prussian rule. Prussia, moreover, was sadly mistaken if she believed that by precipitating a war she could absolve herself from her international obligations. She ought long ago to have recognized the title of king Christian IX of Denmark. Russell urged the German states not to destroy the status quo in the duchies, and he expressed a determination to arrange a conference for the purpose of settling the dispute.[56]

Russell had become increasingly pro-Danish in spite of Denmark's obstinacy, and in this respect he was sharing the opinions of the majority of Englishmen. Palmerston, too, was annoyed by the policy of the Germans. Like Russell, he was sure that a strong line would keep them in check. He thought that Bismarck ought to be reminded confidentially that if the Germans repudiated the London Treaty they would thus 'entitle the King of Denmark to deem himself set free from all the engagements he has entered into towards Germany; and Denmark might possibly find effectual support in such a course.' Palmerston considered a German invasion of Schleswig 'an act of war which would in my clear opinion entitle Denmark to our active military and naval support.'[57] The prime minister undoubtedly wished in December 1863 to foil the German plans by the use of force. Equally belligerent at this stage was Argyll who was totally opposed to the federal execution as he believed that the November Constitution had not in fact violated the Danish engagements of 1851-2. At first, Argyll, like Palmerston, wanted Britain to intervene to prevent the invasion of Schleswig, but after Holstein and Lauenburg were effectively occupied by the Diet's troops he began to doubt the wisdom of 'answering those fools according to their folly.'[58] Clarendon was appalled by the 'impudence of Austria and Prussia wanting to set aside the London Treaty.' He considered the federal execution a German folly which was bound to result in dire consequences for Germany and to provide opportunities for Napoleon III.[59] Hammond was also perturbed by the way in which the German states were encouraging Napoleon's plans 'by their insane ravings.'[60] In a public speech early in December, Seymour Fitzgerald deplored the aggressiveness of the Germans and trusted that Britain would not permit them to violate the integrity and independence of the Danish monarchy.[61] Several pro-Danish letters also appeared in the British press towards the end of the year.

The federal execution had thus increased the spirit of anti-Germanism in Britain. It was condemned on all sides, and few Englishmen in December 1863 seemed to doubt that the British government would defend Denmark in the event of an improper federal assault on Schleswig. This, in fact, was the general attitude of the British press at that time.

The *Morning Post* was particularly warlike. It had never acknowledged the expediency of federal execution, and it warned the Diet on 16 December that Denmark would surely find an ally in Britain in the event of an abuse of federal rights. Its language became even more aggressive when the occupation of Holstein promoted Augustenburg's plans. It urged the British government on 30 December to act at once not only to prevent the Diet from arrogating to itself any claims in Schleswig but to ensure German honesty in Holstein.

The *Daily News* denounced German policy in Holstein and described the federal execution as a subterfuge. It asserted on 29 December that Germany intended to detach both duchies from Denmark, and it thought that the results would not be so pleasant for the wayward 'Fatherland' if the French emperor were to follow the German example of repudiating European treaties. The *Daily News* did not think that Britain could possibly remain passive if the federal troops invaded Schleswig.

The *Morning Herald* expressed the view that Denmark had impaired her position in the duchies by adhering too often to the feeble counsels of the British government. On 17 December it prophesied the invasion of Schleswig and criticized Denmark for abandoning Holstein. On 14 December it blamed the 'busybodyism of Earl Russell and the wavering Cabinet' for emboldening the Germans. It felt that if Russell had dealt firmly with Germany from the outset this Schleswig-Holstein nonsense would have been nipped in the bud. The *Morning Herald* on 30 December concluded that Britain had no choice but to declare war against Germany in support of her faithful ally and protégé.

The *Standard* was equally bellicose. On 14 December it argued that federal execution was but the first step to open warfare, and it declared three days later that it was Britain's clear duty to defend Denmark whose plight was mainly the outcome of following Russell's advice. It expressed much disappointment on 21

December over Denmark's decision to withdraw from Holstein and over Britain's feeble policy in the face of patent German injustice. At the end of the year the *Standard* vigorously censured the attitude of the federal commissioners in Holstein who were taking no steps to quell the uprising in favour of Augustenburg.

Many British journalists advocated an Anglo-German war to prevent the Diet from seizing Schleswig and Holstein. Those who did not actually agitate for war at least demanded a strong enough policy to thwart the advance of the Germans. No British paper of repute defended the principle of federal execution. Even the *Saturday Review* could not deny the recklessness of the federal program, although it continued to blame the Danes for precipitating their own embarrassments. But the editors who so ardently clamoured for a warlike policy did not do so with the conviction of truly warlike spirits. Their basic suggestion was that Britain could best preserve the peace by adopting a decided anti-German stand. It was felt, particularly by the leader-writers in the conservative papers, that German ambitions had been encouraged by the timorous and vacillating diplomacy of the liberal administration. Very few of the warlike journalists doubted that Germany would have withdrawn in the face of active British opposition from the start.

The more moderate editors pleaded for a conference, for which indeed the independent whig-liberal *Spectator* had asked since 21 November. *The Times* also advocated a policy of moderation, having assumed a strange attitude of resignation from the time that the order for federal execution was given. It gradually abandoned the warlike tone it had adopted throughout November even though it was no less suspicious of German designs in the duchies. *The Times* did not deny the Diet's right to perform an execution in Holstein but it continued to regard that measure as dangerous and impolitic. The policy of moderation, however, found little support in Britain towards the end of 1863.

The bald fact is that Englishmen were too sympathetic to Denmark to view the federal execution in its proper light, even had it been scrupulously performed. This overwhelming moral support for the Danish cause perturbed the handful of German sympathizers in Britain who could not but fear that the Danophile cabinet might be induced by public opinion to give material support to Denmark. This was the prospect which alarmed the queen more perhaps than anyone else in the country. She had never denied the federal right of execution in Holstein nor had she even questioned the justice of the measure. She did her best now to impress upon Russell the vital necessity for a compromise. She encouraged him to seek a European conference, anxiously remarking that it was no longer a question of upholding the treaty of 1852 but of trying to avoid bloodshed. Russell agreed that some compromise should be reached, but he warned the queen that Britain could not in the meantime consent to the German occupation of Schleswig.[62]

The federal execution had thus brought the Danish crisis one step closer towards its ultimate explosion. The European situation in December 1863 was very critical. In Britain the queen, her ministers and the general public had just cause therefore to be alarmed.

Map III The theatre of war. Reprinted from Ward: *Germany 1815-1890*, by permission of Cambridge University Press.

6
British reaction to the Dano-German war, 1864

After the federal occupation of Holstein and Lauenburg, the smaller German states wanted to seize Schleswig and place it under Augustenburg's control. Impelled by the potent forces of liberal nationalism, they were exerting considerable pressure on the two great German powers to play a more active part in the Dano-German conflict at the end of 1863. This placed Austria in a very difficult dilemma, for although she realized that the national movement represented a serious threat to the very existence of her multi-national empire, she was still too conscious of her diplomatic isolation and too anxious to maintain her supremacy within the Bund, to alienate herself from the rest of Germany. She also knew that any Dano-German war would leave the initiative with Prussia, on whom the heavier military responsibilities would automatically fall. This could serve only to encourage the ambitions of Bismarck, of whom the Austrians were very suspicious. Austria resolved therefore to participate in the German movement in such a way as to frustrate the schemes of both the Prussians and the German liberals. She hoped to avoid complications with the neutral powers by establishing, under a European guarantee, a new Schleswig-Holstein state attached, in 'personal union,' to the Danish monarchy. She concluded that, in the prevailing circumstances, her aims could only be achieved by working in concert with Prussia. Meanwhile Bismarck, who was already contemplating the annexation of the disputed territory by Prussia, also needed the Austrian alliance in order to checkmate the Diet. Austria and Prussia, therefore, for strikingly different objectives, swiftly cemented their alliance early in January 1864.[1]

To prevent the Diet from irritating the neutral powers by illegally extending its jurisdiction to Schleswig, Austria and Prussia resolved instead that that duchy should be occupied as a material guarantee. They argued that it would be better for Germany to claim to hold Schleswig as a pledge for the fulfilment of Danish engagements than to deny altogether the authority of Christian IX. When the Diet defeated this Austro-Prussian resolution, the two great German powers promptly decided to act on their own responsibility and to defy the rest of Germany. On 16 January they presented their ultimatum to Denmark demanding the revocation of the November Constitution within forty-eight hours. As this was obviously unacceptable, it proved to be a declaration of war.[2] The moment was ripe for a bold Austro-Prussian stroke, as it was impossible, at that time of the year, for the Danish navy to operate effectively in the Baltic. Moreover, Britain, France, and Russia had all been left in diplomatic isolation as a result of the Polish revolt and Napoleon III's congress proposal.

Britain was alarmed by the bitter squabbles within the Bund which had eventually propelled the Austrian and Prussian governments to branch out on an independent and aggressive policy. It was well known in Britain that the antipathy between Germany and Denmark had risen to such a peak that friction of any sort was liable to precipitate a violent explosion, and the British people had for this reason condemned the federal execution. Russell had advocated the Danish retreat from Holstein, but he had little faith in the prospects of peace even after the Danes had followed his advice. He was sure that the proximity of German troops and Danish officials was bound to produce conflict. This is why he had stressed, throughout December, the advisability of disavowing the Augustenburgs and keeping clear of all disputed areas. As the Diet refused to follow his advice, the federal execution assumed the character of an invasion and confirmed Russell's gloomiest fears.

Russell sought European help to bring the affair to an amicable solution. He was willing to try any proposal for which European enthusiasm could be generated. On 31 December he addressed himself to all the European courts. He made an impassioned appeal for law, order, and peace. He exhorted both sides to seek an amicable settlement of this dispute by adopting conciliatory courses. He urged the European states to respect the London Treaty, and proposed a conference in either London or Paris to settle the quarrel.[3] Meanwhile he requested an emergency meeting of the cabinet to discuss the crisis.[4]

When the cabinet met on 2 January 1864 it was, as Gladstone recalled many years later, 'indignant at the conduct of the German Powers who ... were scheming piracy under cover of pacific correspondence.' The British ministers decided to take up arms for Denmark should any active help be forthcoming from France and Russia. It seemed clear to them that Germany should not be allowed to encroach further upon Danish soil, but it was recognized by the majority that Britain would need continental assistance.[5] The upshot of this meeting was a proposed letter to Sir Alexander Malet, the British minister at Frankfurt, which would be officially communicated only if France and Russia agreed to send a similar note. The despatch contained a warning to the Diet that Britain would feel herself compelled to give material aid to Denmark should any attempt be made to establish the duke of Augustenburg in Holstein and Schleswig. The Diet was urged to await a definitive and impartial settlement of the case by those who had signed the London Treaty. Should the Diet reject their proposal, then each power would be left free to pursue whatever course it thought best suited its own honour and interests.[6]

In the absence of Palmerston, who was bed-ridden with gout, Russell could not persuade his colleagues to go further. The prime minister had tried vainly to influence the Manchester faction within the cabinet by explaining his views fully to Milner-Gibson, the president of the board of trade, and by writing a detailed memorandum for Russell's use during the discussion. Palmerston's advice was that Britain should invite the parties to the 1852 agreement 'to send instructions to their Representatives in London to concert with us the best means of carrying the Treaty into effect.' He argued that the November Constitution was properly the only question pending between Denmark and the Diet, and that the federal troops should therefore leave Holstein as soon as that constitution was repealed. Palmerston also declared that Britain would make herself 'the laughing stock of Europe' if she permitted the London Treaty to be 'set aside by the violence of such petty princes as Coburg and others.' The prime minister, very bellicose at this point, expressed dissatisfaction with the result of the cabinet meeting of 2 January; he really could not understand why British policy in this crisis should have to depend on the whims of France and Russia.[7]

The cabinet's decision also disturbed the queen who had tried to nip all aggressive notions in the bud by submitting to the foreign secretary a long memorandum on the Schleswig-Holstein question. She had made it clear that, for a variety reasons, she would not 'willingly give her consent to any course which may tend to involve England in war on this question,'[8] but none the less she found the cabinet more defiant than usual; and, as was her custom when faced with combined ministerial resistance, she gave way, albeit reluctantly. She now shifted her ground. She approved the despatch to Malet and hoped that no time would be lost in trying to receive answers from France, Russia, and Sweden, but her approval was made contingent upon the concurrence of the three powers; it was to be 'clearly understood' that she was not consenting to 'single-handed interference by England in support of Denmark.'[9]

Palmerston was so upset by the German tone of the queen's communications that he wrote her a long and impertinent letter. He declared that he could quite understand the queen's reluctance to participate in any active measures against Germany, but he was 'sure that your Majesty will never forget that you are Sovereign of Great Britain, and that the honour of your Majesty's Crown and the interests of your Majesty's dominions will always be the guide of your Majesty's conduct.' He went on to condemn the disgraceful behaviour of the Germans and the 'doubly scandalous' conduct of the Augustenburgs. Referring to the queen's claim that the London Treaty had imposed an unpopular monarch upon the people of Schleswig and Holstein, he asked:

How many of the territories held by the European States under the Treaty of Vienna were assigned to them subject to popular appeal? The answer is *none*. What Sovereign is there in Europe, your Majesty not excluded, in some parts of whose dominions a set of factious demagogues, acting from without as well as within, might not raise a local cry for separation and for transfer to some other authority?

Palmerston agreed that Denmark should revoke the constitution. If this were done, the Diet would have no excuse for the continued occupation of Holstein, and he thought that the king of Denmark should be advised, in the name of peace, to grant a full and complete amnesty. The queen replied that, while she would hesitate to quarrel with Germany, nothing would ever prevent her from defending British honour and interests. She assured Palmerston that 'it is because she feels strongly the responsibility as Queen of these realms that she is anxious to avoid their being hurried into an unnecessary war.'[10]

The Cabinet's decision of 2 January 1864 was, like the choice of Wodehouse to go to Copenhagen, an immediate triumph for the ministers at the expense of Palmerston, Russell, *and* the queen. But, since it left British policy in Schleswig-Holstein at the mercy of France and Russia, it proved to be of inestimable value to the queen in her efforts to preserve the peace. No provision was made for a positive program in the event of a Franco-Russian rejection of the British proposal to send identical notes to Frankfurt. Yet this was the vague and uncertain position into which the cabinet and the queen consistently forced Russell during the rest of the crisis.

As neither France nor Russia showed any enthusiasm for active intervention in the Dano-German conflict, the British project of 2 January failed. Russell could not threaten the Diet with war as he had planned. He still tried, nevertheless, to restrain the Diet by writing forceful despatches to Bavaria, Saxony, and Württemberg despite the queen's objections.[11] He also instructed Bloomfield and Buchanan to express to the major German powers the keen British dissatisfaction with the policies of the Diet, and to call upon them to resist any federal occupation of Schleswig.[12] While he considered using strong language to Germany as a reserve plan, Russell's major objective was to arrange a conference; and yet, at the same time, he was trying to persuade his colleagues in the cabinet to sanction a policy of active British interference. Russell was thus making the error of pursuing several projects simultaneously.

The cabinet met again on 7 January to consider the situation in view of the indifference of all the neutral powers except Sweden. Russell was forced to admit that France was not prepared to defend the London Treaty by force of arms, and his colleagues declined to commit Britain to active interference while France retained her liberty of action. The foreign secretary found the cabinet much more pacific than it had been on 2 January. Granville, acting as the queen's spokesman, dominated the discussion; and since Palmerston's hands were tied by his having assured Granville on the previous night *'that there was no question whatever of England going to war,'*[13] Russell was left without adequate support. He had hoped for a more positive result from the cabinet meeting for he was sincerely anxious to thwart the Prussian designs of which Buchanan had warned.[14]

Russell now decided to apply direct pressure on Bernstorff, the Prussian ambassador in London, by telling him confidentially that Britain could not sit still indefinitely while Christian's enemies overran his kingdom.[15] He then attempted to summarize this conversation in a confidential despatch to Berlin, but the queen complained to Palmerston that such language was in keeping neither with the decisions of the cabinet nor the wishes of the crown. Palmerston defended the foreign secretary as best he could,[16] but it was clear that the two cabinet leaders were being seriously restricted by the refusal of the other ministers to support them. Palmerston was convinced that Germany would relent if she felt that Britain was in earnest,[17] and Russell believed that if Britain took a strong stand, even if in alliance only with Sweden, the Germans would retreat.[18] He regretted that Britain was tending to increase the danger of war by creating the impression that she meant to do nothing at all in any circumstances.[19]

Neither Palmerston nor Russell really wanted to precipitate an Anglo-German war, but they had no doubt that unless the British government adopted a more positive approach, peace could not be preserved in the Baltic. This opinion was also held by many of the leading British ambassadors in Europe. Bloomfield, for instance, privately advocated a more aggressive program.[20] Malet often lamented the German tendency to ignore British counsels since it was felt that she would not 'interfere materially.'[21] Buchanan was sure that 'a little decided language' would induce the Prussian king to 'abstain from military operations.'[22] And Napier went so far as to demand the prompt despatch of British warships to the Baltic.[23]

Russell therefore found himself in the position of having to choose between the peaceful ministers at home and the warlike diplomats abroad. While Palmerston and Russell wished to pursue the line advocated by the British ambassadors, the queen was doing her utmost to thwart them. She succeeded so well in influencing the cabinet through her alliance with Granville and Wood that the two political leaders found it increasingly difficult to make their views on the Danish question prevail. These disagreements between Russell and the queen led to an animated cabinet discussion on 12 January. The foreign secretary wanted to propose that Britain should persuade Austria and Prussia to postpone all unfriendly measures and allow Denmark a reasonable time to rescind the November Constitution. He did not think that Britain could force Denmark to withdraw the constitution and then leave her in the lurch. She must pledge herself to support the Danes if they fulfilled all their engagements.[24] Once again, however, the peace-party, influenced by the court, overruled Palmerston and Russell. A warlike despatch intended for Bloomfield was amended at the queen's instigation and the ministers merely agreed 'to enquire from the co-signatories of the Treaty whether they would agree to declare their determination, in case Denmark cancelled the Constitution of November, not to allow the invasion of Schleswig and the dismemberment of the Danish Kingdom, under the Treaty of 1852.'[25] This was, in essence, a simple repetition of those views expressed by the cabinet on 2 and 7 January. It again left Britain without a policy since nothing was done to provide for the anticipated rejection of the scheme by the other governments. This project, in fact, collapsed at once.

The French reply to this proposal was unsatisfactory. Conscious of the general mistrust in which he was now held, Napoleon III was determined to pursue a circumspect policy in Schleswig-Holstein. Cowley attributed the emperor's indifference to the British project to several distinct causes: the British refusal to accept the congress proposal; the conduct of Britain during the Polish crisis; the waning of French sympathy for Denmark as a result of the Anglo-Danish marriage-alliance and the election of a Danish prince to the Greek throne; the emperor's fundamental interest in the projected Scandinavian union; and, above all, Napoleon's determination to derive some benefit from the impending Dano-German war. Cowley despaired, therefore, of any concrete Anglo-French understanding on this question.[26] The Russian response, as Napier had to admit, was equally discouraging.[27]

There were many sound reasons in fact for the rejection of Russell's scheme by France and Russia, who were reluctant to commit themselves to an undertaking that could lead to war against the whole of Germany, especially since the Polish revolt had demonstrated the unreliability of the British alliance. Napoleon had already concluded that the progressive isolation of France could only be checked by a closer understanding with Prussia. An alliance with Prussia was also favoured by the tsar who was aiming to isolate France completely by establishing a quadruple alliance of the other great powers. Still trying to recover from her Polish exertions, Russia had no desire to participate in a Baltic campaign, even though she wished to uphold the London Treaty.[28]

The Austro-Prussian ultimatum of 16 January alarmed the rest of Europe and left Britain apprehensive and bemused. The British public could not understand the designs of Bismarck and Rechberg, but they were suspicious. It was well known that the major German powers had persevered in their efforts to oppose the Augustenburg candidature and to prevent the Diet from repudiating the London Treaty. But the conduct of Austria and Prussia had not always been consistent. They had never, for instance, acknowledged the title of Christian ix without reserve. They had recalled their own ministers from Copenhagen on 1 January, had persisted in treating the London Treaty as contingent upon the withdrawal of the November Constitution, and now had agreed to a joint occupation of Schleswig as a 'material guarantee.' The Austro-Prussian attitude towards the Danish question was, to the British public, unintelligible at best. Even Palmerston seemed momentarily bewildered. He was glad to see that Austria and Prussia were at last willing to shake themselves free from the shackles of the Diet and to put themselves right in the sight of Britain and Europe.[29] These ideas clearly did not tally with his oft-repeated opinions on Austro-Prussian weakness and dishonesty. This unfortunate confusion of ideas, which was by no means peculiar to Palmerston, made it difficult for the British government to formulate a definitive policy at this stage.

The Austro-Prussian ultimatum rendered the diplomatic situation even more critical, and Russell redoubled his efforts to maintain peace. He began by appealing, on 18 January, to Austria, France, Prussia, Russia, and Sweden to preserve the treaty of 1852 and the integrity of Denmark. He wondered whether these governments would, for this purpose, 'concert and co-operate' with Britain.[30] On the same day, Russell urged the ministers to these courts to seek the co-operation of their colleagues in trying to persuade Denmark to revoke the constitution.[31] He also proposed, on 22 January, that France and Russia should join with Britain in offering their good offices to Austria and Prussia, and making a joint appeal for the postponement of the threatened occupation.[32] And then, four days later, Russell proposed a protocol. He now intended to invite the parties to the London Treaty to sign a protocol based on the repeal of the Danish constitution in return for the postponement of the occupation.[33] Russell thus continued to increase his own problems by making too many recommendations simultaneously, with the result that hardly any one of them was given enough time to work itself out.

All of these projects failed miserably. Prussia summarily rejected Britain's request to delay the invasion of Schleswig,[34] and France and Russia eventually refused to commit themselves to a policy of active intervention. Only Sweden seemed eager to give material aid to Denmark. Russell himself did not spurn the Swedish alliance, but the cabinet could not be persuaded to engage in hostilities without stiffer continental backing. His hopes for a strong European concert to restrain the Germans were finally demolished on 28 January by La Tour d'Auvergne, the French ambassador to London. La Tour explained to Russell that a Baltic war was a far more serious undertaking for France than for Britain. In any European encounter France would have to embark on huge military enterprises; she would have to provide military as well as naval forces in keeping with her dignity; she would have to fight a defensive as well as an offensive war. These were sacrifices which France could ill afford to make. Britain, on the other hand, could view a continental war with equanimity, for she could confine herself to blockading tactics. In view of these considerations the French government had necessarily to be very circumspect.[35]

Russell's appeals to Austria and Prussia fared no better. He warned them that such a 'principle and practice of taking possession of the territory of a State as what is called material guarantee' was a most dangerous weapon which could recoil upon those who used it. He also insisted that a Dano-German war could not absolve Austria and Prussia from their engagements to the other powers who had signed the London Treaty.[36] But in spite of Russell's warnings, Bismarck instructed Bernstorff to declare in London that Denmark must be held responsible for any consequences which her resistance to the Austro-Prussian occupation might bring upon herself and Europe. The German measure was simply intended to secure the arrangement of 1852 which Denmark had so often violated.[37]

Russell thought that if he could hold the Germans to the London Treaty he could prevent them from violating the integrity of Denmark. But the equivocal answer made by Bismarck and Rechberg on 31 January left Britain with no opening for stronger measures against them. They continued to claim that they were not departing from the treaty of 1852, but warned that they would be compelled to do so 'in consequence of complications which may be brought about by the persistence of the Danish Government in its refusal to accomplish its promises of 1851–52, or of armed intervention of other Powers in the Dano-German conflict.'[38] In any case, by the time their official reply reached London on 4 February, the war had already started.

The Austro-Prussian forces reached the southern border of Schleswig on 31 January and within a week the duchy lay at the mercy of the allied troops who had contrived, by 6 February, to capture the Dannevirke, the famous Danish line of fortifications.

The sudden collapse of the Dannevirke came as a severe shock to the British public. The press, in fact, had confidently foretold that it would suffice to keep the Germans at bay. The British government was disappointed but unable to act. Russell had failed to compel Denmark to repeal the November Constitution or to persuade Austria and Prussia to extend the time-limit. A European conference was needed to break the deadlock but it could not materialize so long as Napoleon III continued to sulk. Russia was still too friendly to Prussia. Russell could, therefore, find no substantial support for his proposals to coerce the German powers. Chiefly as a result of her policy in Poland, Britain now found herself isolated on the Danish affair. The circumstances demanded an immediate resolution, and Britain was embarrassed by failing to reach one. On the surface, her problem was simple: she must either conduct herself in the proper manner of a neutral, or defend her protégé to the utmost limits of her power. In practice, however, her foreign secretary had to choose between a number of divergent attitudes. Russell's own instincts, like those of Palmerston, suggested that Britain should not allow any extension of German influence in the Baltic. To thwart the designs of Austria and Prussia, Palmerston and Russell were ready to take a firm pro-Danish line. But the queen refused to contemplate the prospect of an Anglo-German war and insisted that British interests required a passive program. The press and the public were in such a state of bewilderment that it was difficult to tell exactly where they stood. The majority of Englishmen were pro-Danish, but even the Danophiles were divided on the question of peace or war. Caught in this vortex of conflicting passions, Russell vacillated.

The Germans, as a result, had no difficulty in parrying Britain's diplomatic thrusts. Russell weakened his own hand even further by allowing Bismarck to trump his solitary ace: adherence to the Treaty of London. From the outset he took his stand on the arrangements of 1852 and called upon the Germans to do the same. Since these were the avowed principles upon which the occupation of Schleswig was based, Russell could make no headway with this unfortunate line of approach. Lacking a clear-cut Schleswig-Holstein program, he visibly hesitated between the pliant and the defiant course. This conspicuous absence of settled policy undermined his position beyond repair, and his despatches failed to make any impact in spite of their abundance.

While the German soldiers were marching northwards the British ministers assembled again, on 27 January, to discuss the crisis. Anticipating warlike gestures from Palmerston and Russell, the queen tried to counter their arguments by writing a forceful letter to Granville, in which she urged the peace-party to hold fast to the position adopted by the cabinet at the beginning of the year.[39]

Russell meanwhile came to the meeting with a clear and explicit program that was diametrically opposed to the royal advice. He proposed:

1 That Great Britain should offer her good offices to Austria, Prussia and Denmark with a view to the settlement of the pending differences.

2 That Great Britain should offer to Austria and Prussia to obtain from Denmark the revocation of the Constitution of November, and an organization of the Danish Monarchy on the basis of the Royal Proclamation of 28 January 1852. Denmark to promise to fulfil all her engagements of 1851-52, Great Britain guaranteeing their observance by Denmark. The organization of the Danish Monarchy and the engagements by which Denmark is to be bound to be specified in a Convention between Austria, Great Britain, Prussia and Denmark.

3 The integrity of the Danish Monarchy, and the obligations of Denmark to maintain her federal relationships in Holstein and Lauenburg as stipulated in the Treaty of London, to be recognized throughout these negotiations.

4 All military and naval operations to be suspended during the negotiations.

5 If Denmark should not fulfil the conditions here enumerated, Great Britain will interfere no more on her behalf.

6 If Austria and Prussia either refuse to negotiate on these conditions or to stop the march of their troops across the Eyder, Great Britain will make such military and naval preparations as may enable her to assume the attitude of armed mediation or of assistance to Denmark, and will notify such intention to the Governments of Austria and Prussia.[40]

This bold design, justified by Russell's diplomacy in Schleswig-Holstein since 1859, was completely rejected by his colleagues. Inspired by the court, the ministerial rebels defeated Palmerston and Russell for the fourth time in as many weeks.

Lord Stanley of Alderley, the postmaster general, supported Russell's proposal, and Westbury made a strong plea for maintaining the integrity of Denmark as well as protecting British honour and interests, but these views could not prevail against the combined assault of the peace-party. Wood refused to contemplate going to war against Austria and Prussia without the help of France, and he warned Russell that a naval war would be more harmful to British than to German commerce. The duke of Somerset, first lord of the admiralty, placed particular emphasis on the hazardous nature of naval action in the Baltic during the winter months.[41]

As Palmerston and Russell had failed to carry the cabinet with them, they were now hoping that a warlike parliament might bring pressure upon their more timid colleagues. The queen appreciated this danger and set out to combat it. She persuaded Lord Derby, the leader of the conservatives, to promise her that he would not make the Dano-German problem a party issue during the forthcoming parliamentary session. Derby himself was pro-Danish but he was averse to war, and since his party was divided over the issue, he was willing to agree. The queen then supervised the royal address with meticulous care, making sure that it dealt as vaguely as possible with the Danish crisis.[42]

When the parliamentary session opened on 4 February, Palmerston and Russell discovered that both houses were sympathetic to Denmark. The British Parliament was puzzled by the rapidity of the recent events in the duchies, but it did not display any enthusiasm for active interference. There was keen criticism of Russell's foreign policy – particularly by Derby in the House of Lords – but no one came forward with concrete suggestions for checking the German advance beyond the Elbe. In his usual jaunty fashion, Palmerston tried to reassure the House of Commons that '... within the last very few hours we have received information from the Austrian and Prussian Governments, that they are prepared to declare that they abide by the Treaty of 1852, and will maintain the integrity of the Danish monarchy in accordance with the provisions of that treaty.' He expressed himself satisfied that the two German powers were committed to the evacuation of Schleswig as soon as Denmark fulfilled her obligations of 1851-2.[43]

The recent events in Europe had produced considerable excitement and suspense in Britain. The public thought that the government was contemplating an active course and it waited anxiously to hear what direction that course would take. Consequently, the opening of the parliamentary session was attended by much curiosity and speculation. The press added to the tumult by trying to anticipate the royal address from the time it was known that the Germans had crossed the Eider. But the long-awaited speech from the throne was a colourless affair, totally vague and non-committal. Parliament waited to hear what Britain intended to do in the face of the violation of the integrity of Denmark. All it learned was that the government would continue its efforts in the interests of European peace.[44] Hardly a newspaper in Britain, even those professedly liberal, failed to express wrath and disappointment. Even in Europe, the royal address was ridiculed.[45]

It was thus in vain that Palmerston and Russell had sought guidance from Westminster. Parliament had not come to offer a program to the government. It had assembled on 4 February to learn what the government's policy was. The divided cabinet had failed to provide leadership on the Dano-German question, and Parliament was merely prepared to offer scathing criticism. No one could doubt that the British public was becoming restless, but there was so much confusion over the issue that no clear-cut picture could emerge. Even the editors of the leading newspapers seemed, like Parliament, to be seeking ministerial guidance. Some of them were often critical though seldom constructive.

Some publications clamoured for war. The *Morning Post*, for instance, used every conceivable argument to demonstrate why Britain could not afford the price of peace. The *Standard* likewise called upon Russell to penalize the Germans for their misdeeds. The *Spectator* demanded strong measures in January, and later (on 13 February) denounced the attitude of the Manchester School whose members appeared too concerned about commercial interests only. The liberal *Economist* could not see, on 30 January, how Britain could possibly abandon the Danes in the face of German bullying. The conservative *Dublin Daily Express* urged Britain to destroy that illusion of pusillanimity which had lately prevailed in Europe. After advocating a policy of war on 29 January, it lamented the feeble British approach in the weeks that followed. The independent *Glasgow Herald*, on 3 February, expressed the view that since Britain had so often declared her allegiance to the London Treaty, she could not honourably remain at peace while Denmark was being overrun.

These warlike sentiments were shared by Russell, but there were other press opinions which supported the arguments of the court and the peace-party within the cabinet. *The Times*, for example, was directly opposed to a violent policy. It repeatedly argued that Britain had no real interest in such a shadowy issue. Her sole duty was to demand a strict adherence to the London Treaty, mediate between the disputants, and strive for a termination of the conflict. The *Daily Telegraph* also, on 3 February, saw Britain's role as that of an arbiter rather than a partisan. The *Saturday Review* recommended a program of peace, considering Denmark undeserving of British aid. The *Liverpool Mercury*, mainly concerned about possible injury to British commerce in the event of war, was also pacific.

Some liberal newspapers, unsure of the government's intentions, hesitated until the speech from the throne before committing themselves to a peaceful policy. The *Globe*, for instance, meekly supported the government's program despite the violence of its own language in January. The *Observer* also adjusted its remarks to suit the government's needs after 4 February. And the *Daily News*, modifying its earlier belligerence, stated resignedly on 11 February that it was 'idle now to talk about the causes of this wicked war, or to discuss the character of the Austrian and Prussian Governments ... We have allowed the moment of action to pass away, and it will not return.' The *Manchester Guardian* remained non-committal even after the royal address, but seemed, by its general tone, to imply a preference for non-intervention. Many liberal papers, in fact, were prepared to defend Russell's policy rather than to recommend one of their own.

In the early months of 1864, British public reaction to Russell's policy in Schleswig-Holstein was considerably mixed. So confused was press opinion on this matter that the *Globe* and the *Morning Post*, normally staunch supporters of Palmerston, were actually suggesting contrary courses; and some liberal journals were expressing dissatisfaction with Britain's timidity during the crisis. On some points, however, there was unanimity. Whatever their political affiliation, British journalists, almost without exception, castigated the Germans for their hasty occupation of Schleswig; condemned the principle of seizing territory as a material guarantee; and, manifesting their fear of France, prophesied a swift and vengeful retribution for the Germans. Similar ideas were also expressed at several public meetings, during which, significantly, Russell's policy in Schleswig-Holstein came under heavy fire. It was criticized, generally speaking, on three grounds: it was unduly meddlesome, inconsistent, and sometimes too warlike.

In the winter of 1863-4, Britain's policy in the Danish duchies was attacked publicly even by the liberal W.E. Forster who, in addressing his constituents at Bradford on 8 January, denounced the Palmerstonian habit of interference and hoped that Britain would concentrate in future on domestic reconstruction.[46] Bright struck the identical note in two forceful speeches at Birmingham.[47] Milner-Gibson admitted his ignorance of the central facts in the Dano-German controversy, but told the public gathering in the Town Hall at Ashton-under-Lyne on 20 January that arbitration was superior to war. His opinion was that Britain should try to terminate rather than extend the struggle in the duchies.[48] William Scholefield, a liberal MP, told his constituents in Birmingham that the Schleswig-Holstein question was no concern at all of the British government.[49] On 29 January, John Benjamin Smith, the liberal MP for Stockport, expressed himself in favour of splendid isolation when he addressed a political rally at the Odd Fellows' Hall in his constituency.[50] Speaking to his constituents at Oldham, John Morgan Cobbett, an independent MP, declared that Britain should engage in military conflict only when her national honour was at stake.[51] The liberal William Massey gave the opinion, in the presence of his constituents in the Town Hall at Salford, that Britain should adhere to the London Treaty and strive to preserve the peace. He could not but feel that the Dano-German war was essentially a foreign affair.[52] A conservative MP, Mowbray, told a vast audience at Reading on 1 February that the government had made a mess of the whole Danish affair and must explain to Parliament why it had found itself in such a quandary.[53] All of these speakers had criticized the government and had been well received. Considerable applause had greeted their appeals for peace. Their listeners seemed reasonably pacific although they had remained pro-Danish.

Meanwhile, two important events occurred. On 26 January, Russell was presented with a memorial by the Peace Society, whose members praised the foreign secretary for his untiring efforts to maintain peace and strongly urged him to stay clear of the Schleswig-Holstein war.[54] On 11 February, an immense crowd gathered in the Town Hall at Manchester to support a petition for non-intervention in Schleswig-Holstein. When Alderman Heywood moved the adoption of a memorial to Palmerston and a petition to Parliament, there was only *one* dissenting voice. This Manchester meeting was actually called together by the conservative J.M. Bennett, the mayor of the city, in compliance with a petition that had been 'numerously signed.' The main resolutions were vigorously supported by some of the leading citizens of Manchester, notably Ernest Jones, R.N. Phillips, T.B. Potter, and Dr John Watts. Even Thomas Bazley, the liberal MP for Manchester, gave the petition his 'cordial approval and support.'[55]

The city of Manchester, it is clear, was not in favour of a warlike program. The north of England, in fact, was solidly for peace and, although London at this point was perceptibly restless, it would surely have been risky for Palmerston and Russell to appeal to the electorate in an attempt to coerce the cabinet and the court.

Faced with an anti-Danish court, a divided cabinet, a baffled Parliament, and a confused public opinion, there was not much that Russell could do even after the Austro-Prussian invasion of Schleswig. The government's position was not noticeably shaken, even by Derby's frontal attack, but the debates of 4 February seem ultimately to have weakened Russell's position within the cabinet. At the very time when he most needed his help, Palmerston resigned himself to the parliamentary will and left the foreign secretary virtually alone to combat the influence of the pacific faction. For several weeks after the opening of the parliamentary session, Palmerston appeared perceptibly less warlike. Apart from the peaceful disposition of Parliament, this change in his attitude was probably due to the impact of the Austro-Prussian note of 31 January, in which the two powers indicated their willingness to adhere to the London Treaty. He seemed to believe that Austria and Prussia were trying to uphold that settlement in defiance of the minor German states, although Russell himself was much less optimistic.[56]

When Austria and Prussia invaded Schleswig in February, Denmark appealed directly to Britain and the other neutral powers for material aid. Russell, now more belligerent than ever, suggested that Britain should try once more to concert with France for the purpose of compelling the Germans to accept mediation. He added that

If Austria and Prussia refuse mediation, decline to accept the bases proposed, or insist on terms which are, in the opinion of France and England, inconsistent with the integrity and independence of Denmark, Great Britain will at once despatch a strong squadron to Copenhagen, and France will place a strong corps of troops on the frontiers of the Rhine Provinces of Prussia.[57]

Palmerston, however, still thinking in terms of preserving peace, completely discouraged Russell's scheme. He pointed out that a British naval expedition to the Baltic, even if it were possible before spring, would hardly serve to deter the Germans, and he was most reluctant to commit the small British army to a direct confrontation with a quarter of a million German soldiers. He particularly questioned the wisdom of encouraging the French to perform military exercises in the Rhineland area.[58] Palmerston was not averse to using strong language but clearly he was averse to war. He did not think that Britain should fight merely to restrain the Germans and thus encourage Napoleon III to disrupt the balance of power. He was still governed by the early Victorian attitude towards France: nothing, in his opinion, could be worse than French expansion on the Rhine.

With Palmerston in this frame of mind, Russell could not persuade the cabinet to accept his warlike suggestions on 13 February. The peace-party therefore triumphed again, supported as it was by the queen who, on 12 February, told Granville that Denmark was 'after all of less vital importance than the peace of Europe, and it would be madness to set the whole Continent on fire for the imaginary advantages of maintaining the integrity of Denmark.'[59] Russell was thus forced to announce 'his adherence today to what he believed to be the doctrine of the Cabinet, viz., that there is no question of our going to war single-handed.'[60]

After suffering another rebuff on 17 February when the cabinet vetoed two more of his proposals that the queen had refused to sanction, Russell had to send a disappointing reply to the Danish appeal for military assistance, stating that 'Her Majesty's Government can only say that every step they may think it right to take in the further progress of this unhappy contest can only be taken after full consideration and communication with France and Russia.'[61] This was the best that Russell could do, although, on 15 February, he had expressed the conviction that 'the only way to save Denmark from very harsh, and indeed intolerable terms on the part of Austria and Prussia is to make some demonstration of support.'[62]

Hardly had Russell rejected the Danish appeal for help when news of the Prussian invasion of Jutland reached London. After overrunning Schleswig the Prussian commander disobeyed his instructions and occupied Kolding on 18 February. Bismarck and Rechberg accepted Wrangel's disobedience as a *fait accompli*, revised their January compact, and explained that Jutland had to be invaded as a necessary reprisal for the seizure of German ships by the Danes.[63] Bismarck was determined to humble Denmark while the diplomatic situation was still favourable, and Rechberg had become too deeply involved in the Baltic adventure to withdraw in mid-stream.

Coming as it did upon the frequent assurances of the German powers that they intended to abide by the London Treaty, the invasion of Jutland outraged

British public opinion. The British people, who had never favoured the German cause, became dangerously excited. Widespread rumours that Austria intended to send a squadron to the Baltic also increased the tension. Bloomfield and Buchanan were promptly instructed to impress upon Rechberg and Bismarck that the British government viewed the extension of the war 'in a very serious light.'[64]

Even the cabinet, which had so often insisted on feeble courses, was perturbed by the turn of events. It agreed that the Channel Fleet should be ordered home.[65] This action was instigated by Palmerston who was temporarily jolted from his unusual attitude of cautious reserve by the brazen temerity of the Germans. He told Russell that it was Britain's duty to prevent any German occupation of Copenhagen, and he urged the foreign secretary to speak firmly to Austria.[66] Palmerston also wrote a violent letter to Somerset advising the despatch of a British squadron to the Baltic.[67] In his view, an occupation of Schleswig on the basis of the Austro-Prussian note of 31 January was an entirely different matter from an invasion of Jutland or an attack upon the Danish capital. The Prussian occupation of Kolding made Palmerston much less patient than he had been for some weeks.

The queen approved the decision to recall the Channel Fleet to patrol British waters and be prepared for any emergency, but she trusted that 'no further important orders' would be given this fleet 'without her previous sanction.'[68] She was evidently not prepared to brook any of the drastic suggestions just made by Palmerston. Nor did Somerset have any enthusiasm for a Baltic expedition. He could see nothing but obstacles in the path of the prime minister's proposal. As he explained, 'there is some difficulty in protecting Copenhagen from attack, while the Danes pursue and seize all German ships at sea. Again, if we get into a naval war with the German Powers, we must expect Alabamas will be fitted out in America and elsewhere to prey upon our commerce. These and other questions must be carefully considered.' Somerset was merely repeating the arguments he had employed in January to discourage Russell's warlike intentions.[69]

With Somerset and the queen unwilling to support the aggressive measures recommended by Palmerston and Russell, it is not surprising that the cabinet simply agreed on 21 February to recall the British ships of war. Russell, nevertheless, sent telegrams to Cowley and Napier, requesting the French and Russian governments to join Britain in a naval demonstration to defend Copenhagen and to prevent new complications.[70]

The queen was much annoyed by these warlike telegrams which Russell had sent off on his own responsibility. She agreed that an attack upon the Danish capital would require 'the most serious attention of her Government,' but as this was not being contemplated by the Germans she did not see why Britain should now change her policy.[71] Russell warned the queen that the Germans seemed likely to invade Copenhagen itself unless someone decided to stop them. He added, however, that so long as Austria and Prussia did not attempt such an outrage the best course for Britain was one of mediation.[72] Palmerston came to Russell's defence by explaining to the queen that the idea of the Baltic expedition was the result of warnings from Vienna that the Austrian government had decided to despatch warships to the Baltic. He now advised the queen not to be alarmed since the Austrian government had denied all intentions of sending ships into that sea.[73] In their efforts to appease the queen, Palmerston and Russell had both retreated from their original stand. The idea of the Baltic excursion had sprung mainly from the news of the occupation of Kolding. Now they both pretended that the proposal had been based on the supposition that Austrian ships were on their way to the Baltic and that the allied forces intended to attack Copenhagen. It was simple for the queen to point out that there was insufficient ground for either supposition, and as the German powers disavowed these alleged designs the telegrams to Cowley and Napier had to be recalled.[74]

With the exception of Palmerston and Westbury, the British ministers supported the queen. They claimed that Russell had misrepresented their views and they condemned the unauthorized telegrams. Gladstone 'declared his opinion with great warmth,' and Somerset was particularly irritated. Once again Russell was forced to submit to the will of the cabinet. All that he could salvage from his bold plan to combat the invasion of Jutland was the recognition on the part of his colleagues that it would be necessary to review Britain's policy in this matter should Copenhagen be attacked; and even this concession might not have been made had the peace-party not believed that a German assault on the capital of Denmark was 'about the most improbable occurrence it is possible to imagine!'[75]

The immediate result of this cabinet meeting was a feeble telegram to Cowley and Napier announcing that there was 'no case at present for sending a fleet to the Baltic, and the question may drop until a fresh danger arises.'[76] France and Russia, in any case, had already refused to participate in the projected naval demonstration.[77] It is, of course, impossible to tell how successful the Copenhagen expedition might have been, but the significant aspect of the ministerial quarrel of 24 February is that the British cabinet saw no need to formulate a positive policy to check the allied invasion of Jutland which was obviously contrary to all the laws of Europe as well as the earlier declarations of the Germans themselves. Austria and Prussia had professedly set out to occupy Schleswig as a material guarantee for the purpose of thwarting the reckless designs of the Diet and upholding the arrangements of 1852. Now they were in the process of violating Jutland, a totally Danish province outside any possible German sphere of jurisdiction. And yet the British cabinet could vote with equanimity to return to the non-policy that Britain had so colourlessly pursued since 2 January.

No course was left for Russell but to persevere with his proposal for a conference which had languished ever since December because of the minor objections which were being made on all sides. Russell himself added to the difficulty by working on the premise that an armistice was a vital prerequisite. The failure of the antagonists to agree to any conditions for a truce forced Russell to give up this idea by the end of February. It was impossible for Britain to compel the allies to accept reasonable terms since France and Russia gave her no support. It was not, in fact, before the end of March that Russell could persuade all the parties to agree to the principle of a European conference 'sans bases et sans phrases' (as Bismarck put it).[78]

The German preparations, however, were deliberately drawn out by Bismarck who was determined to capture Düppel before the first meeting of the conference.[79] The first full session of the London Conference did not take place therefore until 25 April, a week after the fall of Düppel. The delay distressed Palmerston who suggested to Russell that a British fleet should be sent to the Baltic to expedite an armistice. 'If the French, Russians and Swedes would agree with us,' he wrote,

we might say to Austria at the meeting of the Conference ... that, unless the German Powers agree to an immediate armistice on the basis of present occupation, our fleet is under orders and will go at once to the Baltic to execute such orders as we may think fit to give it. Public opinion in this country would be much shocked if we were to stand by and see the Danish army taken prisoners, and Denmark thus laid prostrate at the feet of Germany.[80]

Russell agreed with Palmerston's proposal, but it was promptly vetoed by the queen who argued that it could 'only have the effect of irritating the German Powers and embittering the future course of the discussions.'[81] Russell and Palmerston withdrew their proposal as it was also vigorously opposed by Clarendon who had just entered the cabinet as chancellor of the duchy of Lancaster.[82] They needed Clarendon's help in the forthcoming conference.

Palmerston and Russell continued to promote the idea of a Baltic expedition now that the season was more favourable. Palmerston felt that, if the Germans would not consent to an armistice unless the Danes raised their blockade, then Britain should insist upon the German withdrawal from Jutland and upon their abstention from any military operations during the conference. He also advised Russell to inform the Austrians confidentially that, if they violated their assurance and sent ships to the Baltic, they 'should not be surprised if a British squadron should follow them, and watch and control their proceedings.' But when the cabinet met on 30 April it rejected Russell's proposal (in concert with France and/or Russia) 'to send a small squadron of ships of war into the Baltic with instructions not to fire except in the two cases of an attempted entrance of Austrian men-of-war or of an attempted attack on the Island of Zealand.'[83]

Palmerston was so dissatisfied with the cabinet's decision that he decided to act on his own and inform Apponyi (the Austrian ambassador in London) confidentially that Britain could not let Austrian ships pass unmolested through British waters for the avowed object of harassing Danish vessels. He warned Apponyi that war could possibly result from this situation,[84] wrote a memorandum on the interview and placed it before the cabinet on 2 May. Palmerston's 'weak and timid' colleagues were thus left to reflect upon this 'notch' off his 'own bat' after it was a *fait accompli.*

The result was another ministerial squabble. When Russell decided to embody the prime minister's memorandum in a despatch to Bloomfield, Granville protested that the cabinet had not approved Palmerston's language to Apponyi. Russell's response was that 'in the event of the Austrian fleet going into the Baltic, the event must not find the Cabinet unprepared. They must make up their minds one way or the other.' He told Granville that the cabinet must either sanction Palmerston's conduct or repudiate it completely. He himself would refuse to participate in any such condemnation of the prime minister's behaviour. The queen objected to the warlike attitude of Palmerston and Russell, and the cabinet refused to endorse the confidential threat to Austria.[85] The Austrian government then helped to put an end to the quarrel by again denying all intentions of sending its fleet to the Baltic.[86]

Considerable excitement was created in Britain not only by the naval activity of Austria but also by the frequent acts of brutality committed by the Prussians in Jutland and Schleswig. The most barbarous of these was the bombardment of Sonderburg on 2 April in which a number of civilians were slain.[87] This evoked much indignation in Britain, but Russell's remonstrance to Prussia produced only scathing comments from Bismarck.[88]

Reports of Austrian naval threats and Prussian cruelties, which were given so much prominence in the British press, not only kept alive public interest in Schleswig-Holstein but intensified the anti-German feeling throughout the country. Many newspapers resigned themselves to the idea of British inaction, but they continued their attacks on German injustice and British timidity.

The conservative papers were naturally critical of Russell's policy in this crisis, but many liberal journals also failed to support him. The *Morning Post*, for instance, was too warlike to understand Russell's shilly-shallying; and even the *Daily News* repeatedly demanded a recognizable and intelligible program in the duchies. It claimed that Britain should either intervene effectively or withdraw altogether from the struggle. The *Daily Telegraph*, the *Globe*, and the *Observer* continued to follow the government's lead, and applauded its efforts to arrange a conference. It was *The Times*, however, that provided Russell with his strongest defence after the occupation of Holstein; and it even began in February to criticize the obstinacy of the Danes while disparaging all the government's detractors in Parliament and elsewhere. Even so, it is clear that the government found only a minority of journalistic supporters for its policy in the Schleswig-Holstein crisis after the invasion of Jutland.

However the British editors quarrelled among themselves as to the merits of a warlike policy, and whatever the measure of their individual inconsistencies, the press, as a body, entertained no two notions respecting the invasion of Jutland. This was seen as an unspeakably shameless outrage perpetrated on a small country by two great powers who had begun the war on one pretext and were extending it on another. The British press found the German behaviour all the more galling since Her Majesty's government could apparently do nothing about it. It was in fact this keen sense of futility that alarmed and frustrated Englishmen while Austria and Prussia were ruthlessly carrying all before them.

Britain, as a whole, considered the Dano-German war unnecessary. But while her people now accepted that it could perhaps only be terminated by an international congress, they approached Russell's conference in the spring of 1864 with mingled feelings. Some Englishmen, particularly editors of liberal newspapers, saw the London conference as a fine stroke for Russell's diplomacy and expected it to produce an amicable settlement. Many others, however, regarded the conference with misgiving; to them, it was merely another step in this relentless humiliation of Britain.

British public opinion had thus remained confused and divided throughout the Dano-German war. Even the liberal journalists were opposing each other in an unusual fashion on the Schleswig-Holstein question. This strange spectacle led the London correspondent to the *Manchester Guardian* to observe, early in March, that 'from such discrepancies in the tone of journals all considered in some way ministerial, many people infer great differences of opinion in the Cabinet, and insist upon it that there are attempts in progress on each side to rig the market of opinion against the other.'[89]

7
The British withdrawal

By the end of February 1864 Britain had resigned herself to the idea of settling the Dano-German conflict by means of a conference since the other great powers had refused to join with her for the purpose of compelling the Germans to withdraw from Danish territory. The Germans were so determined to seize Schleswig and Holstein from Denmark that only the closest co-operation of the neutral powers could thwart their schemes. Russell's conference therefore could hardly produce an amicable settlement unless Britain, France, and Russia reached a solid agreement among themselves. But Gorchakov was too anxious to co-operate with Bismarck to follow Russell's lead in Schleswig-Holstein, and there was thus no hope of an Anglo-Russian alliance to coerce Austria and Prussia even though Russia was far more friendly towards Britain in the spring of 1864 than she had been for some years.[1]

France was no less reluctant to co-operate with Britain on the question of the duchies. In fact, as early as 12 March she began to create difficulties for the London conference by proposing a plebiscite to decide whether the Schleswig-Holsteiners should remain within the Danish kingdom. None of the other parties to the London Treaty, including Britain, showed any enthusiasm for this project. Palmerston and Russell did not deny its possible utility in dealing with the mixed districts in Schleswig, but they emphasized the obstacles in the way of consulting the people at a time when German troops were occupying both duchies.[2] It was agreed eventually that the idea of a plebiscite, lest it tended to paralyse the impending deliberations, should only be discussed when all other avenues had failed.[3]

Having opposed the French plan without offering an alternative, the British government decided to send Clarendon to Paris, early in April, in the hope of establishing an Anglo-French alliance to counter the aggressiveness of the Germans. Russell instructed him to propose the partition of Schleswig as the remedy to be prescribed by the western powers during the conference. Russell's idea was to join the northern portion of the duchy to the kingdom of Denmark while still leaving it with its local representation; to attach the southern portion to Holstein; and to leave the middle area, known as the mixed districts, to be dealt with by the conference. Russell also suggested that Holstein and the German part of Schleswig thus united should enjoy an independent Diet with the exclusive right to pass laws and vote taxes for provincial purposes. He felt that France and Britain should withdraw altogether from the controversy if the Danes refused this plan; and if the Germans rejected it, then 'it would be desirable to establish a concert between France, England, Russia and Sweden – France, England and Russia, or England and Russia only engaging to defend Zealand, and Sweden engaging to assist in the defence of Jutland and Fünen.' Russell admitted, however, that in making this last proposal he was exceeding anything that the cabinet had as yet authorized.[4]

But Palmerston, who was still most reluctant to abandon the London Treaty, raised serious objections. He declared himself in favour of a settlement 'less prejudicial to the Danish interests.' He drew attention to the prospect of a federal fortress being erected at Rendsburg and warned Russell that any such scheme might militate against the independence of Denmark. The queen, too, was opposed to any understanding with France although she admitted the prudence of Napoleon's proposal for a plebiscite. This conflict of ideas prevented the British government from deciding on a definite set of instructions for Clarendon,[5] and even he seemed from the outset to have resigned himself to the futility of his mission.[6]

In Paris Clarendon was warmly received but, since he had to admit that Britain was not yet prepared for war, nothing came of Russell's proposed threat to the German powers. Napoleon seemed sympathetic enough to Clarendon's projects, but he was clearly determined to avoid a 'gros soufflet' such as the one he and Russell had suffered at the hands of the tsar over the Polish affair in 1863. The emperor denied that the Danish question was important to France and, since his country merely wanted peace, he could not commit himself to a serious military undertaking against Germany. He explained that, if he were to join the fray, his subjects would expect suitable compensation on the Rhine and that would then set all of Europe against France. Furthermore, 'the policy of nationalities' appealed both to him and to his people and he was therefore very unwilling to be 'party to replacing the Holsteiners under the rule of Denmark, which they detested.' As Clarendon knew, one of Napoleon's pet projects was the restoration of Venetia to Italy, and he was consequently not prepared to 'lay himself open to the charge of pursuing one policy on the Eider and a totally different one on the Po.'[7]

As Russell had failed to revive the Anglo-French concert, the Germans could not be restrained even after the opening of the London conference. They refused for two weeks to accept reasonable terms of truce, and as a result an armistice could not be arranged before 12 May; and even then its stipulations were patently one-sided. For, whereas Denmark was forced to loosen her grip on the German seaports, Austria and Prussia were permitted to retain their hold on Holstein, Lauenburg, Schleswig, and Jutland. This truce was to last for one month.[8] The Germans also insisted, early in the conference, that the London Treaty was no longer valid.

The refusal of the cabinet to permit Russell's strong line meant that Britain could exert little influence over the Germans during the conference. Russell, therefore, had to give up the London Treaty and aim at the partition of Schleswig. The cabinet readily admitted on 13 May that the arrangements of 1852 could hardly be upheld in the prevailing circumstances.[9] Accordingly, on 18 May, Russell and Clarendon drew up a definitive proposal for the consideration of the conference. They proposed that Lauenburg should be ceded to the German confederation and annexed to Holstein; Denmark, as a compensation, should be allowed to attach the mixed districts of Schleswig to the Danish kingdom. The people of Holstein, Lauenburg, and Schleswig were to be consulted through a Diet 'in the most formal and authentic' manner on the choice of their future sovereign.[10] The queen expressed satisfaction with this scheme, and Clarendon suggested that Britain should coat this Danish pill by promoting the idea of a European guarantee to forestall future German encroachment.[11] But the obstinacy of the Danes and the Germans over the all-important question of the frontier eventually killed the British proposal even after all sides had more or less accepted the principle of partitioning Schleswig.[12] The queen herself earnestly entreated the king of Prussia 'in the interest of the world and of Peace, to consent to such concessions as Denmark would probably accept.'[13] The king replied that the London conference should not even have attempted to impose such humiliations upon a triumphant nation.[14]

The arrogance of the Germans emphasized the need for Anglo-French cooperation. Russell, who believed that his colleagues' timidity was mainly responsible for the excessive caution of the French in this matter, warned the queen that, even if France would not support an aggressive British policy by force, the cabinet still had to show Parliament that an honest effort had been made to secure French aid.[15] This topic was discussed by the British ministers on 11 June when, in the face of the dying conference, they displayed much more spirit than formerly. Gladstone observed that the discussion was 'very stiff,' while Granville sadly reported that the 'majority of the Cabinet is not as compact as it was.'[16] Obviously the peace-party had relented somewhat. Apparently, however, no positive decision was taken. Russell, nevertheless, told the queen that her ministers had resolved 'that the plan of arbitration for a line to be traced between the German and Danish proposals should be favoured by your Majesty's Government. That, in case this plan should be accepted by the Danes and rejected by the German Powers, in the event of the resumption of hostilities, material aid should be afforded by Great Britain to Denmark.' Russell also submitted to the queen his *Pro Memoria* of 12 June wherein he stated that, though France and Russia were apparently reluctant to give active help to Denmark in any contingency, Britain should fight to enforce a line drawn north of the frontier indicated by Denmark and south of the line demanded by the Germans.[17]

When the queen disapproved of this resolution and asked the cabinet to reconsider it, the peace-party hastened to deny that Russell's conclusion was a fair expression of the ministerial views.[18] Consequently, the cabinet had to meet again on 15 June to clarify its stand on this business of defending Danish boundaries by force of arms. But by this time the temporary zeal of 11 June had abated. The ministers now indulged in 'much desultory conversation on war and peace,' and Russell's warlike language was once more disavowed. Curiously enough, even Palmerston supported the peace-party on the ground that 'this question was not yet ripe for decision.'[19] Thus the cabinet overruled Russell once again without substituting any specific program of its own. It was this lack of a clear policy, more than anything else, which severely hampered Russell's manoeuvres during the London conference.

Even Russell appeared much too uncertain in the month of June. He made out a strong case for British intervention on 8 June, when he argued that the 'utmost in point of concession which Denmark can be asked to accept' was a line drawn from Kappeln on the Baltic to Husum on the North Sea, including the towns of Flensburg and Husum in the Danish dominions. If Denmark could be urged to accept this line, Russell was ready to support her in the event of a German refusal. He felt that Britain should, in such a case, despatch a squadron to the Baltic with, or without, French co-operation since she could now use her navy far more effectively than in the winter months.[20] Yet, only two days later, he told Palmerston:

Taking into account the unwillingness of France and Russia to enter into hostilities against Germany, the indisposition of the Cabinet to undertake any vigorous measures, the necessity of our being united, and the great danger of a war with America supervening upon that against Germany, I have come to the conclusion that we cannot press the Cabinet to come to any resolution to act by force against the Germans in the Danish question.[21]

This was Russell's view on the eve of the cabinet meeting of 11 June when he tried so hard to persuade the peace-party to support a policy of active intervention. It is remarkable that this admission of the difficulties involved in British action in the Baltic was made only two days before Russell produced his notorious *Pro Memoria* in defiance of ministerial opinion. Still bellicose on 13 June, he was once again suggesting that Britain should blockade the German ports in the North Sea and the Adriatic if Austria and Prussia refused his intended arbitration; he was now sure that such a threat would compel Austria to seek peace.[22]

The aggressive measures proposed by Russell in mid-June were frustrated not only by the fierce resistance of the queen and the peace-party within the cabinet, but also by the indifference of Palmerston himself. For the prime minister was much less warlike than the foreign secretary at this stage and was, in fact, endeavouring to preserve the peace by an entirely different approach. Palmerston now concentrated on warning the Danish envoys that external help had become so problematical that they might find it beneficial in the long run to accept a frontier north of the Schlei (at which point they seemed determined to draw the proverbial line). On 4 June he interviewed George Joachim Quaade, the Danish foreign minister, and emphasized the futility of British intervention which, in any case, had become improbable. He also stressed the impossibility of British intervention if *both* antagonists rejected Russell's propositions.[23] Now that Palmerston was so much less bellicose than Russell, the latter had no hope at all of inducing the cabinet to adopt stronger measures; and Russell's own uncertainty meant that he did not perhaps feel strongly enough on this issue to tender his resignation.

Russell's *Pro Memoria*, in actual fact, was not only wrong in an ethical sense (since it was clearly a misrepresentation of the cabinet's feelings), it was also a tactical blunder. Its immediate effect was to re-unite the cabinet against him. On 11 June the peace-party had lost its former cohesiveness and seemed on the verge of collapse, but it regrouped swiftly to denounce his ill-advised memorandum. When the queen demanded an explanation of Russell's reports, the waverers returned to the fold. Russell had thus played straight into the queen's hands.

When it was clear, in mid-June, that the London conference was failing, Russell tried harder than ever to persuade his colleagues to decide on a concrete program in Schleswig-Holstein. He now suggested that, since the line of partition in

Schleswig was the main bone of contention, Britain should urge the conference to renew and guarantee some of the conditions agreed upon in 1852. But the cabinet rejected this proposal on the ground that such a guarantee might lead to an embarrassing situation in which Britain would have to choose between diplomatic humiliation and war. Even so, the results of the meeting of 19 June were so inconclusive that, while Russell could leave it with the impression that the ministers favoured a strong pro-Danish line, Granville could once again accuse him of misinterpreting the will of the majority. As usual, Russell retreated.[24] His position was somewhat undermined by the news of the recent quarrel between himself and Quaade. Russell had to explain to his colleagues that Quaade's bitterness sprang mainly from purely personal observations which he (Russell) had made to the effect that Britain might, in the event of the German rejection of the British proposals, consent to afford naval assistance to Denmark. These improper comments were heartily disavowed, especially by Wood and Sir Charles Villiers, the president of the poor law board.[25]

Despite these constant rebuffs Russell did not give up the idea of assisting Denmark. Nor did he abandon hope of reviving the Anglo-French concert. He now thought that Napoleon had grown so impatient at waiting for a concrete British offer that he was ready to state the French price himself. Russell's opinion was that 'the Adriatic provinces of Venetia for Italy, and a bit of the Rhenish frontier are not extravagant terms, and if the German Powers refuse our proposal, I should not be obstinate in rejecting them.'[26] Cowley, who suspected that France was still not anxious to help Russell out of his Danish difficulties, discouraged the idea in a private letter to Clarendon. It is clear, Cowley thought, 'that the French alliance is to be bought, but the price will perhaps be more than it is worth.'[27] The queen also warned Russell against falling into the trap which Napoleon was preparing for England. The emperor, she said, did not intend to play an active role in the conflict but was merely determined to persuade Britain to commit herself irrevocably to a policy of war.[28]

Russell's aggressive projects floundered in June, however, mainly because even Palmerston was not interested in them. The prime minister continued to take a more practical view of the situation than Russell. He advised the foreign secretary to explain carefully to the Danish envoys that Britain was in no position to help Denmark expel the invaders from Jutland and Fünen. Even if Britain could send effective naval help in June her largest warships would be forced to quit the Baltic at the end of autumn. He told Russell that, apart from the fact that British opinion had grown much less warlike than it had been, Napoleon III could not be trusted. The French emperor, Palmerston thought, was only hoping to see Britain engaged in war before coming forward boldly and stating the real price of French co-operation in the midst of Britain's complications.[29]

Palmerston indeed had gravitated towards the royal camp by the third week in June. When the queen held a long conversation with him on 21 June, she was delighted to find that for the first time the two of them could agree on the Danish question. She was pleased to hear him admit that Britain could not interfere effectively. They both felt that in this case it would be less humiliating to stay clear of the struggle. The prime minister declared that he had done his utmost to dissuade the Danes from their obstinate course, but he feared that they were 'not an intelligent race, and very *borné*.'[30]

Faced with the inevitable failure of the conference, the British ministers were now compelled on 24 June to avow a Schleswig-Holstein policy of some kind. This they had steadfastly refused to do despite Russell's urgent prompting. He confronted them with four options: '1. To send a fleet to Copenhagen to take part in hostilities. 2. To prepare for war by making an alliance with France. 3. To give up all concern in the war. 4. To resume our former attitude.'[31] The members of the peace-party, who did not trust Napoleon at all, were quite opposed to Russell's warlike attitude. They vetoed the suggestion of going to war against Germany single-handed or even in conjunction with France. The greatest difficulty arose over the question of sending a fleet to Copenhagen if the Austrians threatened to do the same. The peace-party opposed this course on the ground that it could conceivably lead to disastrous complications. Gladstone, Granville, Milner-Gibson, and Wood were Russell's leading critics on 24 June and they hoped that something would emerge from the final meeting of the conference to strengthen their position.[32]

This cabinet meeting was resumed on 25 June when it was already known that the conference had finally collapsed and that the war would definitely be resumed on the next day (the original truce had been extended for only two weeks on 12 June). In the light of this the cabinet decided on a policy of non-intervention. Clarendon remarked that the ministers were 'united and pacific.' General Grey, the queen's private secretary, was sent to 'lobby' them, but royal intervention was probably no longer necessary.[33] Gladstone dominated the debate by skilfully demonstrating the futility of British naval action at that point in the war. He rejected the idea of a Baltic expedition on the ground that it was at once 'too much and too little'; for while it involved all the liabilities of the war it could not adequately guarantee the protection of Denmark.[34] Gladstone's arguments prevailed to such an extent that it was only with the greatest difficulty that Russell persuaded his colleagues to vote for a reconsideration of their decision to stay clear of the struggle in the event of an invasion of Copenhagen. It was ultimately resolved by the slim majority of eight to seven that 'we do not propose to engage in a war for the settlement of the present dispute, so far as the Duchies of Schleswig and Holstein are concerned; but if the war should assume a new character and the safety of Copenhagen or the existence of Denmark as an independent kingdom should be menaced, such a change of circumstances would require a fresh decision on the part of the Government.'[35] Palmerston, Russell, Grey, Argyll, Somerset, Westbury, de Grey, and Stanley of Alderley voted for the idea of reconsidering the policy of non-intervention in the event of a threat to Copenhagen's security. The prudence even of this reservation was questioned by Cardwell, the secretary of state for the colonies, Clarendon, Gladstone, Granville, Milner-Gibson, Villiers, and Wood.[36]

The cabinet thus remained divided to the end. Even when, at long last, it emerged with a recognizable resolution, the decision still left British policy in the duchies dependent upon the behaviour of the German powers. The reference to Copenhagen kept alive that painful sense of uncertainty under which Russell's diplomacy in Schleswig-Holstein had laboured since 2 January. Notwithstanding the qualifying clause, against which the peace-party had argued vainly, the resolution of 25 June was primarily a triumph for the court. This was instantly recognized by General Grey who hastened to congratulate the queen. 'Your Majesty,' he proclaimed, 'may justly take to yourself a principal share in the maintenance of peace ... General Grey believes with your Majesty that it is only *justice* that will now be done. And it is a gratifying and inspiring thought to him, that he has been permitted in a very humble way to assist your Majesty in giving effect to the policy which the beloved Prince had always at heart.'[37] The queen joyfully approved the cabinet's decision, which she considered 'the only true one for the *safety* and *dignity* of this country.'[38] She expressed the hope that all menacing language would be given up for the future and she asked Clarendon to work unofficially with Apponyi and Bernstorff to prevent further complications. She did not doubt that the Danes would shortly submit so long as Europe made it clear that they would receive no help.[39]

The collapse of the conference on 25 June created much alarm in Britain. The conference had been the only result of British diplomacy in this issue and its failure meant that this policy would have to be reconsidered and some new and positive program announced in its stead. The press and the public had followed the conference with keen interest, and the very presence of the envoys in London had added to the tension. But the conference seemed to have accentuated the discord and confusion which afflicted the public mind. If Russell had sought guidance from the British press during the conference, he would have found it even less helpful than the cabinet.

Even on the subject of the conference itself there was editorial discord. Although it had been welcomed as the most likely method of producing an amicable settlement by such newspapers as *The Times*, the *Manchester Guardian*, the *Daily Telegraph*, the *Globe*, the *Liverpool Mercury*, the *Observer*, and the *Illustrated London News*, its utility had been questioned consistently by the *Morning Herald*, the *Standard*, the *Economist*, the *Examiner*, and the *Spectator*. The latter group doubted the wisdom of arranging a conference without concrete bases, as Russell had been forced to do, and they found support for this opinion even from the liberal *Daily News* and the *Morning Post*, whose editors were known to be on friendly terms with Palmerston and Russell.

The conservative newspapers persisted in regarding the conference as a liberal device to escape parliamentary censure. This was the specific charge laid by the *Morning Herald*, for example, on 16 March. The *Standard* unceasingly ridiculed this 'mockery of deliberations' and finally dismissed it on 25 June as a grotesque form of 'carnival.' The *Spectator*, despite its whig leanings, was no more sympathetic to Russell. It observed, on 30 April, that the conference was 'a sedative for the sufferings of Denmark and the restlessness of Lord Russell – not a stimulant to action of any kind.' The liberal *Examiner* had never been any more sanguine than the *Standard*, and it derided the conference throughout its sessions. Although the *Economist* had wished for a peaceful ending to this protracted dispute, it gloomily prophesied the failure of the conference at the end of April and continued to question the wisdom of Russell's diplomacy in the Baltic.

When the conference finally broke down on 25 June, Russell was exonerated promptly and completely by the *Liverpool Mercury* on the one hand, but was bitterly criticized by the *Dublin Daily Express* on the other. There was thus much disagreement over the value and purpose of the conference as well as Russell's role in these futile discussions. As very few liberal journals applauded British policy during the conference, *The Times* proved to be Russell's main source of comfort in May and June. Only on a few points were the British journalists united. They were, for example, disappointed by the failure of the negotiations which they rightly interpreted as a diplomatic defeat for Britain. They also recognized that the Germans had utilized to the utmost their military and diplomatic advantages. This made them even more hostile to Germany than they had been at the start.

The British Parliament, like the country in general, had remained dangerously anti-German, and this had been one of the major considerations in the formulation of policy. The pro-Danish temper of the Lords was actually thought by Clarendon to have occasionally governed the pugnacious attitude of the two cabinet leaders. Clarendon himself supported a policy of non-intervention because he considered that Britain had not made any material pledges to the Danes, who had, in any case, been unduly stubborn and narrow-minded. But he anticipated difficulties for the ministry in Parliament although he felt that the liberals could make much capital out of their peaceful program since both Houses had gradually become less warlike towards the end of June.[40] Indeed, all the ministers feared a wholesale attack and did not expect the decision of 25 June to appease the opposition. Therefore no one was surprised when, on 27 June, the conservatives in both Houses gave notice of an imminent motion of censure after Palmerston and Russell had announced the ministerial resolution to withdraw from the Schleswig-Holstein conflict.

The cabinet's fears were based mainly on the fact that it could not then be stated with any certainty where the public or Parliament stood on this question. This, in fact, had been the chief reason for Palmerston's hesitancy ever since February. The pro-Danish bias could not be mistaken, but the business of war or peace was more complicated. Like the British public, Palmerston vacillated until the end of June although Henry Brand, the liberal chief whip, had strongly urged him to adopt a more aggressive policy.

On 10 June Brand warned Palmerston that the inevitable failure of the London conference could lead to a host of misfortunes for the liberals. He urged the cabinet to decide immediately on a concrete program and to avoid a passive course which was likely to result in political defeat. He predicted that the conservatives would move a straightforward vote of censure upon Russell instead of committing themselves to a policy of their own. Such a tactic, he believed, could possibly succeed since both the country and the Commons were 'undoubtedly Danish.' He anticipated that the members of the House of Commons were likely to vote with an eye on the hustings and support Denmark in order to preserve their seats. In such an event he did not think that the electorate would then reverse the verdict of Parliament. A dissolution after Russell's defeat would therefore be disastrous for the liberals. To forestall these hazards, Brand advocated a bold plan which the electorate could be persuaded to buy. 'The question,' he asked, was 'would the House of Commons vote the supplies for carrying on such a war? I believe it would, although no doubt there would be a serious dislocation of parties. We should lose Cobden and Bright, and their following, which, however, is not large. We should, on the other hand gain, as I think, an equivalent set off from the Independent Members of the Opposition.' Such a policy, Brand concluded, would prevent the conservatives from adopting a warlike program and appealing to the country. An efficient campaign might induce the electorate to sanction material help to Denmark. Taking all these factors into consideration, Brand advocated a policy of war as at once an offensive and defensive political strategy.[41]

Palmerston admitted that there was much good sense in Brand's observations. 'For my part,' he confided to Russell,

I should very much prefer appealing to the country, or retiring into the country for having taken a manly line consistent with our national engagements and consistent with our national honour and position in Europe, rather than to do so for having abandoned everything and everybody we ought to have stood by. My firm belief is that if we stood forward boldly and made Austria and Prussia understand that we are in earnest and are resolved to employ the means we have at our disposal, they would agree to a reasonable arrangement, namely the line from Kappeln to Husum. Brand suggested another consideration which he did not like to put on paper, namely, that our abandonment of Denmark would be ascribed to the Queen, and would annoy public feeling against her personally.[42]

But this spasm of the old Palmerstonianism vanished quickly. Taking his cue from the gallery, Palmerston returned to his pacific attitude towards the end of June. Parliament had also become increasingly pacific despite its antipathy towards the Germans. Palmerston and Clarendon came out on the side of peace and determined to carry the whole nation with them.[43]

Britain thus decided on 25 June to withdraw from the Dano-German dispute in which she had played a prominent but undignified role. Her decision was based partly on simple political considerations. Palmerston did not think that the liberal ministry could long preserve itself in office by embroiling the country in a European war at that point. The majority of the cabinet agreed with him and the chief whip's views were therefore set aside. The decision was also based on considerations of the national interests. Granville and Wood did not believe that it was in the real interests of Britain to fight single-handedly to uphold a treaty which many other European powers had also signed. There were no equivalent boons to be derived from the immense sacrifices involved in an Anglo-German war. The opinions of the foreign secretary were therefore vetoed. The resolution of 25 June was partly dependent on military considerations also. When Palmerston was trying to discourage Russell in February, he estimated conservatively that Britain could afford to send no more than twenty to thirty thousand men to fight in Europe. With an aggregate of almost 100,000 British soldiers stationed at this point in India and on the Canadian frontier, it is unlikely that Britain could have provided more than 50,000 seasoned troops to help the Danes. Gladstone's budget, so obviously prepared in anticipation of peace, could not stand the strain of war. And, above all, the queen refused to contemplate an Anglo-German war and was prepared to go to any length to avert it. In these circumstances Britain decided after all that involvement in the struggle would only serve to promote the interests of the French whom she still regarded as her most dangerous rivals.

After the failure of the London conference the Dano-German war was renewed. On 29 June the Prussians broke the Danish resistance by capturing the strategic island of Alsen. Denmark was compelled to sue for peace and hostilities ended on 20 July. She was now forced to cede Holstein, Lauenburg, and Schleswig to Austria and Prussia who were to administer them jointly until definitive arrangements could be made. Denmark and the duchies were required to pay the cost of the war and the Diet was forced to withdraw its troops from Holstein. The duchies eventually had to pay 29,000,000 Danish dollars as their share of the indemnity, while their claim for self-government was ignored. The Dano-German war thus finished disastrously not only for Denmark but for Schleswig, Holstein, Lauenburg, and the Diet as well.[44]

Denmark's humiliation was a moral defeat for Britain also. Russell had based much of his policy on the validity of the London Treaty. He had several times reproached the Germans for threatening to repudiate it and he had often urged the neutral powers to enforce a strict adherence to its terms. Yet, during the conference, Russell could do nothing to save that treaty. The whole conference, in fact, was a diplomatic disaster for Britain. Her proposals were thwarted at every turn. Even the Danish blockade, a reasonable equivalent in return for the German occupation of Holstein, Lauenburg, Schleswig, and Jutland, could not be successfully defended by Russell in the opening days of the conference. He managed to induce the envoys to accept the principle of partitioning Schleswig, with its 147,000 Germans, 33,000 Frisians, 85,000 'mixed' inhabitants, and 136,000 Danes, but he could not prevent them from quarrelling over the line of demarcation. His own preference was for the Schlei-Dannevirke line, but nobody was prepared to follow his lead and impose it on the Germans. The line from Kappeln to Husum which he proposed in order to pacify the Germans proved acceptable to neither party. His plea for mediation fell on deaf ears. The conference, behind which Russell had been the creative force since early in 1864, broke up in confusion without solving any of his problems. Moreover, by yielding repeatedly to the German pressure, he incurred the odium of Denmark without improving relations with Germany. He considered the German claims inadmissible but could not enforce a just compromise without the help of the neutral governments. To make matters worse, Russell entered the conference without any policy at all, as his colleagues consistently rejected his suggestions and provided no clear-cut alternatives of their own. He therefore had to improvise from session to session and was thus placed at a considerable disadvantage. His own inability to cope with the French language nullified whatever benefit might have accrued to him from the position of president of the conference. The unfortunate Clarendon was consequently much overworked albeit in vain.

Russell had hoped that the London conference would put an end to the Danish problem, but its failure made it more than ever necessary for the British government to declare its hand in a more positive manner than it had previously done. The cabinet emerged with its feeble resolution of 25 June which was shortly to be sanctioned by the House of Commons. Thereafter Russell could state far more clearly what Britain's policy was in Schleswig-Holstein. When Denmark again appealed to Britain for material support on the resumption of the war, Russell instructed Paget to inform the Danish government that Britain had never pledged herself to defend the Danish cause by force of arms and she was certainly not in a position to do so now. It was regrettable that the neutral powers had failed to terminate the conflict but Denmark was not justified in expecting them to enter the war on her account.[45] Russell's language on this occasion stood out in sharp contrast to his earlier tergiversations on the same subject. On 21 July he repeated the message: since no foreign aid was forthcoming Denmark should yield and avoid the unnecessary effusion of more Danish blood.[46]

Although the British withdrawal was complete, some of her ministers abroad (particularly Paget in Copenhagen) continued to regret her feebleness of spirit.[47] Russell, too, was annoyed by the German behaviour in July and August and had to be restrained, at least on one occasion by Palmerston, from registering a formal protest. The prime minister wisely advised the foreign secretary that it would be more dignified if Britain stood entirely aloof from the Schleswig-Holstein dispute.[48] Britain was resolved to pass no judgment on the one-sided Dano-German negotiations in early August, but Bismarck provoked Palmerston by sending a despatch to London claiming support for the 'moderate' terms with which the victors had decided to be content.

Palmerston's rejoinder to Berlin was a scathing indictment of the German policy throughout the crisis. He stated that the British government still regarded the occupation of Schleswig as unjust and unnecessary and could not doubt that the whole question had been ruthlessly settled by the superiority of arms. Britain therefore considered it 'out of place' for Bismarck 'to claim credit for equity and moderation.' It was truly lamentable that some 300,000 loyal Danes were being transferred to German rule. The only satisfaction that Britain could find in the entire proceedings was the implicit admission of Christian's right over the duchies since he could otherwise have had no authority to sign them away by treaty to Austria and Prussia. Britain could only trust that the wretched dispute was finally settled, although she had hoped that 'at least the districts to the North of Flensburg' would have been left under the Danish crown. Her main desire was 'to see the wishes of the people of these Duchies consulted on the choice of their future Sovereign, and to see the Duchies receive free constitutional institutions.' In Palmerston's view this was the only type of liberal and generous settlement that was likely to endure. Otherwise he feared that the new arrangement 'would only be a new source of disquiet and disturbance in Europe.'[49]

Britain remained querulous to the end. She could no longer influence the fate of the duchies but still found it prudent to deliver a didactic lecture to Bismarck. Even the queen approved the haughty despatch of 20 August. She thought that it was only 'quite right that we should not now mix ourselves up in the question, and that Prussia should at least be made aware of what she and her Government, and every honest man in Europe, must think of the gross and unblushing violation of every assurance and pledge that she had given, which Prussia has been guilty of.'[50]

After the despatch of 20 August Britain consistently kept clear of the Schleswig-Holstein question. Russell informed Paget at the end of August that Britain could play no part whatever in the Dano-German negotiations, and finally, in October, declined Denmark's request for Britain's good offices in obtaining a speedy evacuation of Jutland. He now readily admitted that the question was far beyond British control.[51]

The cabinet's decision to withdraw from the controversy inspired a mixed reaction from the British press. On the whole, however, there was an underlying feeling of relief at having escaped the horrors of war. Thus, once the ministers had finally made up their minds to take no further part in the Baltic dispute, they found support from various quarters. The fact is that the country was tired of suspense and seemed willing to accept any ministerial decision that would remove the sense of uncertainty that had prevailed since December. A fair section of the press was evidently prepared to adhere to any definitive program announced by the cabinet. There were, in fact, a number of liberal journals awaiting ministerial guidance. The most conspicuous of these perhaps was the *Observer*. After equivocating on 26 June (before it had heard of the government's verdict), it ardently supported the official policy of withdrawal.

The cabinet's resolution of 25 June was supported also by *The Times* which continued to deny that Britain had any interests at stake in the struggle or that she was under any obligation to assist Denmark. This example was followed by the *Globe* which had never really been convinced of the wisdom of a warlike policy. Notwithstanding its own belligerence immediately before the cabinet declared its hand, the *Daily Telegraph* accepted the doctrine of non-intervention with remarkable zeal. It coldly announced on 28 June that Palmerston was quite right to refuse 'to pledge the strength of England for sixty square miles of swamp, grassland and beechwood.' The *Manchester Guardian*, on 29 June, supported the liberals on the ground that though their Schleswig-Holstein policy had failed they had obviously tried to satisfy British public opinion, and there was, in any case, no indication that the conservatives would have done any better. After deserting the liberals on the Danish question during the first half of 1864, the *Daily News* acquiesced in the British withdrawal. The *Liverpool Mercury*, whose pacifism had always been based on a narrow-minded concern for British commerce, naturally applauded the ministerial decision. The *Illustrated London News* also agreed with the government's determination to keep the peace. On 2 July, even the *Examiner* decided that this was after all the most prudent policy in the circumstances. With these pacific sentiments the *Saturday Review* readily agreed, regretting (on 18 June) that Britain had not conducted herself from the beginning in the same circumspect manner as France and Russia.

All of these papers gave varying degrees of support to the policy of withdrawal. The London correspondent of the *Manchester Guardian* described the feeling of perplexity that pervaded the capital throughout the conference, and often spoke of the widespread sense of humiliation resulting from Russell's approach to the Danish crisis. He reported on 24 June that London would welcome active intervention on Denmark's behalf. But only a few days later he remarked that the tumult had subsided and the public was beginning, almost too late, to consider the full implications of a war with united Germany. Even the war-party, the correspondent noticed, had begun to appreciate the enormous difficulties in the path of active interference. Apparently it was only with the greatest reluctance that Londoners finally resigned themselves to a passive policy in Schleswig-Holstein.

Some of the more warlike editors, however, continued to protest against the government's feeble program. As late as 27 June, the *Morning Post* was calling unequivocally for a British declaration of war. The *Economist* also asserted on 25 June that the policy of inertia could no longer suffice. The *Spectator*, too, believed that British honour demanded a more aggressive approach.

But these warlike notions were clearly in the minority at the end of June, for even the conservative newspapers that had criticized Russell's spinelessness in previous weeks hesitated now, on the eve of the conservative motion of censure, to recommend war. Instead of attacking Russell for pursuing a timorous policy in the duchies, the *Morning Herald* now charged him, on 25 June, with having so completely mismanaged Britain's foreign policy that she found herself in a sorry pass from which neither war nor peace could provide a safe escape. As most of the British editors agreed with the government's resolution, their attacks on Russell at the end of June were based not on the decision to preserve the peace, but more emphatically on the manner in which that peace had been maintained.

The British press as a whole soon resigned itself to the spectator's role, and united after mid-July to condemn the behaviour of the Germans whose eventual claims upon Denmark were considered exorbitant. The *Daily News*, for example, lamented (on 1 November) that the public law of Europe which had once acted as a shield for the smaller states had now failed to operate in Denmark's defence. It feared that this new spirit of lawlessness would inevitably lead to a sense of insecurity and chaos on the continent.

Britain could do nothing now to alter the course of events in the duchies, but the British public confidently expected a swift and violent nemesis to overtake the Germans. Almost to a man, the British journalists, for instance, insisted that the Schleswig-Holstein question, far from being settled, was just about to enter a more acute phase. Austria and Prussia had successfully defied a European conference, it is true, but that could only have been the result of some secret understanding between themselves and France. Sooner or later the question of compensation for Napoleon III was bound to arise. Many Englishmen believed that the dispute was liable to redound eventually to the profit only of France and they were therefore amazed at Germany's blindness to her impending calamity. They consoled themselves with the reflection that the pirates must surely quarrel over their ill-gotten booty.

The British public, in short, resigned itself to Britain's helplessness in this matter while waiting eagerly for a divine providence to mete out poetic justice in Schleswig-Holstein. The mid-Victorian mind was as yet incapable of conceiving of the ultimate triumph of flagrant injustice. This robust faith in the omnipotence of moral right and public law must doubtless have been shattered by the subsequent successes of the amoral Bismarck.

8
The motion of censure

When, on 27 June 1864, Palmerston and Russell announced in Parliament the British decision to withdraw from the Schleswig-Holstein dispute, the conservatives immediately gave notice of a motion of censure. Brand had anticipated a simple want of confidence in Russell's diplomacy in the duchies but the opposition eventually decided on a broader resolution. The final form of this motion might have come as a surprise to the liberals, but no one had had any doubt by the end of June that Russell would be called upon to explain the failure of British policy in Schleswig-Holstein. All evidence pointed to the fact that Parliament was dissatisfied. The members not only suspected that Britain had failed to fulfil her obligations to Denmark but that the government's program had not been guided by any clear-cut plan or principle. In fact, had it not been for a variety of extenuating circumstances, the conservatives would long ago have squarely challenged the government's competence in its treatment of the Danish question.

The conservative challenge was deferred until July mainly because the conservatives themselves were divided over the issue. Some of their younger supporters, notably Lord Robert Cecil, were eager to engage in war on Denmark's behalf. Cecil had written a number of letters to the daily press and some long articles in the *Quarterly Review* calling for a British defence of the integrity of Denmark.[1] Derby and Disraeli, however, were most uncertain, for while they were pro-Danish they were not convinced that British interests demanded a warlike program.[2] The conservatives therefore could do little more than watch patiently while the government fell further into its diplomatic morass. At the end of January a 'much puzzled' Derby promised an uneasy Queen Victoria that he would not make Schleswig-Holstein a party-question during the session. He kept this pledge not so much because he felt himself bound by it, but because he could not see his way clear to break it.[3] The conservative plan, therefore, was to taunt the liberals until their Danish policy had collapsed and then come forward to demand the overthrow of the ministry.

The government was by no means proud of its own policy in the duchies and was naturally reluctant to provoke a debate on what would clearly have been an embarrassing subject. The liberals, in fact, tried deliberately to stifle all discussion of the British role in the Dano-German conflict. In this they succeeded, first by delaying the publication of the relevant papers and later by appealing to both Houses not to undermine the position of the government while negotiations were being conducted in London. These appeals were permitted to bear fruit since the opposition had no alternative schemes to promote.

The hesitant tactics of the opposition were bitterly criticized by the liberal newspapers which repeatedly challenged the conservatives to state their views on the Schleswig-Holstein dispute with greater clarity. An angry *Globe*, for instance, scathingly remarked on 21 June that Derby and Disraeli could avow no policy of their own because they had none, but were merely hoping to win political capital out of whatever might transpire. It bluntly accused them of waiting upon a divine providence, while 'in the meantime they are equally ready to take advantage of the war-trumpeting of Lord Ellenborough in the Lords, and the peace-piping of Mr. Osborne in the Commons.' There was, undeniably, a great deal of truth in these remarks.

Neither the Fabian tactics of the opposition nor the evasive attitude of the ministry could prevent Parliament from maintaining a keen interest in the fate of the duchies and pronouncing its opinions, from time to time, on the happenings in Schleswig and Jutland. The British Parliament was too anti-German, too deeply interested in the Dano-German struggle, to be entirely silenced by its leaders. Although the great explosion was postponed until July, there were nevertheless several spasmodic outbursts which definitely embarrassed the administration.

The Schleswig-Holstein question, in fact, dominated the parliamentary session of 1864. It was so constantly in the foreground of British thought that, apart from the budget, everything else appeared secondary. From the outset there was a good deal of excitement. The royal address was impatiently awaited for some clue to the government's reaction to the occupation of Schleswig. Parliament was anxious to know whether Britain was on the verge of war or whether she was planning to abstain from acts of violence. The acute sense of disappointment evoked by the ambiguity of the queen's speech created an atmosphere of tension. The members were pacific enough but, like Derby, they much feared that the 'meddle and muddle' of 'Snug the Joiner' had purchased peace at too high a price. This was the underlying suspicion that prompted both Houses to tease the government throughout the session.

Questions were frequent and incisive. As early as 9 February, Malmesbury emerged with three vital queries. He wondered whether Britain had obtained any guarantee from the allies that they would evacuate Schleswig as soon as the November Constitution was withdrawn; whether the rest of Europe would still regard the London Treaty as valid in the event of its abrogation by Austria and Prussia; and whether the British government still held Austria and Prussia bound by their treaty with Britain to maintain the integrity of the Danish monarchy. Malmesbury himself was particularly interested in the London Treaty because it was he who had signed it in the name of Britain in 1852. He outlined his role on that occasion and explained the main aspects of the agreement. What now bothered him most was that no papers had been laid upon the table, and Britain did not know precisely where her government stood in relation to this Danish question. He was also alarmed by the aggressive spirit of the Germans. Unfortunately for the government, Russell made a feeble reply. He could give no indication of the government's current or likely action, and he could only trust that the allies would withdraw from Schleswig as soon as the constitution was repealed since they had based their occupation on the engagements of 1851-2. He was compelled to admit that Britain had received no guarantee from Austria and Prussia. This was regretted by Derby who thought that the government should have pressed for an Austro-Prussian guarantee. The conservative Lord Carnarvon – arguing, as he confessed, largely in ignorance since there were as yet no papers to consult – felt sure that Britain was failing to fulfil her obligations towards Denmark.[4] It is clear that the government would have been attacked then and there had the papers been available. The House of Lords, however, held its peace for the moment.

Less than one week later Lord Campbell, without notice, criticized the government for remaining silent on the issue and hoped that every effort would eventually be made to restore Schleswig to Denmark. He denied that Denmark had broken her pledges to Germany and insisted that Britain had given Denmark too many guarantees to permit the violation of Danish soil. He adverted to the treaties of 1720 and 1852 and concluded that Britain had no alternative but to give effective aid to the Danes. Russell made no attempt to refute Campbell's arguments. He merely declared that Britain could do no more in the present circumstances than offer mediation, and since her mediatory proposals were then under contemplation he felt it improper to encourage any lengthy debate on the question.[5] His speech was so vague and unsatisfactory that the House of Lords could hardly have escaped the feeling that the cabinet was baffled by the problem.

On 25 February, Malmesbury made an indignant little speech on the subject of parliamentary papers. Already the House had waited longer than was necessary and still no papers had been tabled to enlighten the members on the Dano-German correspondence prior to 1863. He maintained that it was impossible to understand the present impasse without some knowledge of the earlier negotiations. The result of the government's laxity in this regard, Malmesbury felt, was that the British press was being led astray by the inaccurate reports in the European journals.[6]

On the very next day Malmesbury and Ellenborough expressed alarm over the reports of the invasion of Jutland. They wanted to know if the rumours were well-founded and whether the government had as yet received explanations from Austria and Prussia if indeed they had been so bold as to advance into the town of Kolding. Russell thereupon pacified the Lords by spiritedly denouncing the policy of the German allies.[7]

The House of Commons was equally restless in February. Cecil wanted to know where exactly the government stood with respect to the invasion of Schleswig. On the 8th he asked Palmerston whether the government had sought proper guarantees from the invaders, and what was the nature of the Austro-Prussian demands. Palmerston declared that Britain had remonstrated against the conduct of the allies. He said that, though the Germans still remained on friendly terms with Britain and still professed adherence to the London Treaty, their invasion of Schleswig was a deplorable measure.[8] On the following day, when pressed for a more explicit statement, Palmerston admitted that Britain had received no such guarantee as that mentioned by Cecil and Disraeli; but the Germans, he said, had already reassured the government that Schleswig would eventually be evacuated. Palmerston also remarked that no Dano-German war could release the belligerents from a European treaty in which several other countries had been involved.

The conservatives were so dissatisfied with Palmerston's assurances on 9 February that they demanded the publication of the relevant papers. When Layard announced that these documents could not be presented in less than three weeks there was a general storm of protest. Fitzgerald accused the liberals of avoiding a debate on the Danish question, while Disraeli declared that papers of such importance ought to be placed on the table within two days and that the members should insist upon it. Another conservative, Lord John Manners, expressed the hope that the diplomatic correspondence relating to the Dano-German war would be presented to Parliament much sooner than the government had indicated. It was in vain that Layard and Palmerston explained all the technical difficulties involved in publishing such a huge volume of correspondence.[9]

The conservative efforts to expedite the presentation of the papers culminated in a long debate on 22 February, when the government was attacked on all sides for its delaying tactics. Disraeli led the assault in an able speech in which he re-ferred to parliamentary duties and parliamentary rights in making enquiries and receiving information. He claimed that papers had been tabled in the past some-times before negotiations had even been completed. Gladstone successfully answered Disraeli's appeal to precedent but he was so obscure as to the govern-ment's intentions that he elicited a bitter harangue from Cecil and Bernal Os-borne, the liberal member for Liskeard. Cecil could not understand how Britain could remain idle while Denmark was being overrun, while Osborne moved a resolution for postponing the debate on the navy estimates until the Schleswig-Holstein situation had been cleared up. The secrecy of the government, Osborne claimed, was intolerable. He did not think that the House should vote on a reduc-tion of Britain's naval strength while there was yet a possibility of war. The motion was seconded by Sir John Hay, a liberal conservative, and it inspired an animated discussion. James Roebuck, the unpredictable left-wing liberal, con-strued the motion to imply a vote of censure on the government's foreign policy. When Gladstone declared that this was also his own interpretation of the motion, members found themselves in an odd dilemma. They wanted a postponement of the debate on the estimates but did not wish to condemn the government's for-eign policy before they had studied the diplomatic correspondence. Osborne eventually withdrew his motion when assured that the debate on the navy esti-mates would be postponed.[10]

With the government persisting in its attitude of secrecy, no solid debate on the Schleswig-Holstein question could take place. The annoying silence of which Dis-raeli complained was rendered all the more irritating by the conflicting excuses offered by Palmerston, Russell, Gladstone, and Layard for the delay in producing the papers. This gave rise to the suspicion that the government was deliberately trying to conceal its errors. The longer the delay lasted the greater became the general feeling of dissatisfaction. It was undoubtedly a tactical blunder on the part of the ministry, for it inevitably drove the independents and the waverers into the camp of the opposition. Clarendon, who had not yet been drawn into the cabinet, considered the undue delay 'unpardonably stupid.' He complained to Cowley that such a course was bound to increase the government's difficul-ties. 'Layard,' he said, 'who knows what it is to deal with a rabid House should have seen to this, but I believe the chief culprit is Hammond who has a profound contempt for the House of Commons.'[11] At all events the liberal conduct was a real boon to their opponents who thus found a weapon for harassing the govern-ment without committing themselves to any specific line.

On 29 February, even after the first batch of Schleswig-Holstein papers had been tabled, Disraeli continued to ask for the missing links. He feared that there was some secret understanding between Britain and Denmark which, if revealed, could go far to explain the attitude of both countries. He therefore told the liberals that it was their duty both to Parliament and to the nation to divulge this information so that British policy in the crisis could more easily be understood. He emphasized the various failures of the British propositions and prophetically warned that any attempt to convene a conference without an armistice would produce no positive result. Disraeli was convinced that the critical circumstances in which Britain found herself had sprung from her own mistakes in the Polish affair. Palmerston replied in a brilliant little speech which ignored all the concrete points raised by Disraeli. 'What,' he asked, 'are the circumstances in which we have placed the country? Why, we are at peace; we are prosperous; we have been occupied in communications with all the Powers of Europe in endeavouring to settle differences without war.' But his sortie did not save the beleaguered cabinet. Fitzgerald delivered a powerful speech in which he observed that Palmerston's recent pretence of pacifism was by no means compatible with the belligerent attitude he had been known to strike upon this very question.[12]

The impromptu debate of 29 February, like the strange wrangle of the 22nd, showed clearly that Parliament was deeply concerned over the future of the Danish monarchy as well as the future of Britain's reputation. Numerous questions were asked almost from day to day about the proposed conference, the conduct of the war, and the government's designs. But the government seldom made a satisfactory response. On 22 February, Milner-Gibson could provide no information on the alleged Prussian extinction of the Baltic lights.[13] On 25 February, Layard feigned ignorance of the Dano-German blockades, while Palmerston refused to comment on the legality of Prussian action in Gravenstein.[14] In short, the ministers enhanced Parliament's anxiety by studiously evading all its queries. Only in one instance was there any impression of governmental firmness or prudence: the detention of the Danish warship built in the dockyards of the Clyde. Profiting no doubt from the cases of the *Trent* and the *Alabama*, the government refused to allow the *Pampero* to sail after it had been fitted. Its successor was also taken from the stocks to placate its builders, but it was not permitted to leave the country. Layard explained to the inquisitive Commons on 29 February that these measures had all been taken in excellent spirit by the Danish government.[15]

The liberals were determined to suppress all discussion of the Danish crisis until after the Easter recess. Even as late as 7 April, Russell was pointing out to the House of Lords that since a conference was about to meet in London the threatened debate should be deferred until after the negotiations had ended.[16] His own hesitancy, however, led to many expressions of concern in the upper house which was ardently pro-Danish. Its bias indeed was being daily strengthened by the lop-sided reports of the brutal conduct of the Prussians. Malmesbury and

Shaftesbury, an independent with conservative leanings, gave articulate expression to the general feeling of anti-Germanism during the month of April – especially after the bombardment of Sonderburg.[17]

This overwhelming prejudice in favour of the Danes pervaded all the spontaneous and abortive discussions that occurred in the House of Lords during this period of suspense. It was betrayed, for example, in the words of anguish which fell from Malmesbury and Lord Stratford de Redcliffe on 21 April. These two conservatives saw in the constant postponement of the conference a definite German conspiracy to gain advantages from their military operations in Denmark. Russell tried to moderate the Danish temper of the peers by explaining that it was Denmark who had originally postponed the conference when Austria and Prussia had declared their readiness to attend.[18] The lords tended to blame British diplomacy for the sufferings of the Danes and Desart undoubtedly spoke for the majority when, on 18 March, he harshly criticized Russell's foreign policy.[19] The third Earl Grey, a rather independent liberal, expressed his total disagreement with the government's policy on 7 April when he told Russell not to construe enforced silence as acquiescence in governmental weakness.[20] The Danophile lords feared, in these weeks of waiting, that the debates on Schleswig-Holstein would be postponed until they could no longer serve a useful purpose.

Pro-Danish speeches were also made in the House of Commons where, on 8 April, a sharp debate resulted somewhat accidentally from an innocent enquiry about the bombardment of Sonderburg. The government was criticized by liberals as well as conservatives for having exasperated the Germans without placating the Danes. Osborne made himself conspicuous by denouncing the London Treaty, while Dillwyn, another liberal, advocated a Baltic expedition. Palmerston sought refuge in evasion and ridicule, for which he was soundly rebuked by the conservative General Peel who believed that the reasonable questions asked by the House ought to be answered in the proper spirit. The liberal Sir Harry Verney made a sober speech in favour of the government but even he was moved to regret that so far all the necessary information had not been placed before Parliament.[21]

On 11 April Lord Campbell also precipitated a debate in the House of Lords to the consternation of the ministry. He proposed to resolve

That, in the opinion of this House, if the Demand made by Denmark for Mediation, according to the Principle laid down in the Protocol of Paris, 1856, had been more decidedly supported by Her Majesty's Government, the Bloodshed and the other Evils already occasioned by the war in Denmark might have been prevented, and there would have been less Danger than there now is of a more extensive Disturbance in the peace of Europe.

That, in the opinion of this House, a Conference upon the Danish Question, in order to lead to a practical Result, ought to be accompanied by such Steps as may convince the Powers of Europe that Her Majesty's Government adhere to the Treaties in which the Duchy of Schleswig has been guaranteed to Denmark by Great Britain.[22]

Lord Grey seconded these resolutions and a serious debate ensued, in which the lords vigorously expressed their pent-up views on the Danish question although there was little likelihood of a division on the motion. In the end these resolutions were withdrawn with the leave of the House, and the government was given a clear opportunity to carry out its negotiations.

All the speakers condemned the policy of Austria and Prussia, but the liberals were careful to add that Denmark had not been altogether blameless. This was the main theme of Wodehouse's speech. He denied that any material guarantees had been offered to Denmark and he blamed her for her own calamities. He admitted his pro-Danish bias but felt compelled to acknowledge that the Danes were too stubborn and indiscreet. Although he deplored the German behaviour in Schleswig and Jutland he did not think that the Schleswig-Holstein quarrel warranted an Anglo-German war. Wodehouse defended Britain's peaceful policy, but added that Russell had blundered in the Polish crisis and had generally meddled too much in European affairs. The government's best defence was made by Granville who derided the opposition for adhering to a warlike program when they had hitherto been consistently pacific. He could not agree that the threat of war would have thwarted the German schemes, and he regarded Russell's policy of mediation as the best one in the circumstances. He defied the conservatives to produce any tangible criticism as to detail, and he urged them to give British diplomacy a fair chance to justify itself. The liberals tended on the whole to attack the opposition on the periphery rather than at the centre of its argument. Simply to ridicule the resolutions as too bellicose was to overlook the fundamental criticisms of Campbell, Grey, and Derby: that the government's policy in Schleswig-Holstein was too feeble to be effective; that Russell was depending too much on despatches which had lately become the object of European scorn; that the British conduct in the Polish crisis was largely responsible for the collapse of the western alliance; and that, in the present situation, it seemed increasingly difficult for Britain to protect her own interests in the Baltic.[23]

In the main, the opposition believed that the obligations promised to Denmark were so strongly implied as to have been binding; but this was strenuously denied by the government. The opposition contended that if Russell had meant from the start to remain inactive he should have refrained from so much counsel and remonstrance. The government replied that it could hardly have failed to react in some positive manner to the recent events in the Baltic area since the British Parliament and public had taken so keen an interest in them. The main liberal argument was that Britain could not have remained passive when Germany invaded Denmark, nor could she have possibly gone to war single-handed to preserve the London Treaty – even disregarding the Danish indiscretions. The opposition felt that British diplomacy had suffered so many reverses of late that Parliament could hardly have remained complacent. In the final analysis the issue was clear-cut: the government, faced with problems of extraordinary difficulty, had failed to solve them; the opposition, though quick to perceive this failure, could suggest no remedy of its own.

In the House of Commons also the government continued to plead the propinquity of the conference as an excuse for suppressing critical observations on its Schleswig-Holstein policy. But, on 19 April, in spite of the objections of Palmerston and Layard, Osborne moved: 'That it is both unjust and inexpedient to insist on the provisions of the Treaty of London, 1852, so far as they relate to the order of succession in the Duchies of Schleswig and Holstein, as a basis for the settlement of the Dano-German dispute.' Regarding the treaty as the root of all the recent evil, Osborne called upon the House of Commons to repudiate it. He did not think that peace could be restored if the conference tried to revive that arrangement. He also impressed upon the House the validity of some of the German claims, to which it had previously blinded itself. He then weakened the government's position by focusing attention on the fact that, while it had stated in the royal address of 4 February that it was attempting to preserve peace, it had actually been seeking an offensive alliance with France and Russia at that very time.[24]

The ensuing debate was inferior to that witnessed in the House of Lords in the previous week. There was much rhetoric but little substance. The motion had obviously caught the government unprepared. Palmerston merely repeated the charge that the conservatives lacked a policy of their own, while Layard simply besought the House not to embarrass the government on the eve of the London conference. Nor did Disraeli show much enthusiasm for the skirmish. He spoke in general terms about his dissatisfaction and reserved his ammunition for another day. Clearly the conservatives were neither ready nor able to carry a motion of censure at that stage. The debate therefore seemed strangely artificial. The most interesting speech was delivered by Newdegate who touched the root of the matter when he argued that it was not Britain's habit to fight for an *idea*. He demonstrated that the link between her principles and her interests was a very close one indeed, and he cited statistics to show that commerce was the basic motive for Britain's anxiety over the duchies. But just when he seemed to be developing a good case for British intervention to ensure the integrity of Denmark and the survival of British interests in the Baltic, he suddenly veered round to the side of peace.[25]

This debate, dull as it was, did not lack significance. It revealed the gradual change that had come over the lower house since the opening of the session. Its members in mid-April were less anti-German and less warlike than they had been in February. The majority of the speakers clamoured for peace, and the opposition's only charge now was that the government had failed to fulfil promises to Denmark that should not have been made in the first place.

The gradual shift in parliamentary opinion was due mainly to an increasing awareness of the fundamental issues at stake in the Dano-German controversy. Despite the popularity of the Eiderdanish *Denmark and Germany since 1815*, published by Carl Gosch in 1862, a closer study of Denmark's policy revealed that she had not always adhered faithfully to her engagements. Although the majority of British politicians still failed to grasp the more intricate facets of this Schleswig-Holstein riddle, at least they had begun to understand that the German case was not as irrational as they had previously supposed. The gradual change in their attitude was partly due to political and practical considerations also. Not only had it become clear that British naval action in the Baltic, without the military support of France and Russia, would produce no positive result, but the general tone of public meetings early in 1864 seemed to indicate a peaceful disposition on the part of the electorate – particularly in the midlands and in the north.

Once the conference had assembled in London both Houses adopted an attitude of vigilance. They restricted themselves mainly to harmless questions with respect to the armistice, requisitions in Jutland, and the movements of the Austrian fleet. Only Ellenborough seemed inclined to be impatient. He delivered three vehement speeches in May and June which again betrayed his pro-Danish bias.

On 13 May Ellenborough spiritedly criticized the German treatment of Jutland.[26] Two weeks later he chose to attack the queen for allowing her German emotions to prevent the government from pursuing a British policy in Schleswig-Holstein.[27] Russell defended the queen by explaining that she had never overruled the judgment of her ministers who were entirely responsible for Britain's foreign policy.[28] The queen was deeply offended and could hardly have been consoled by Russell's letter of 31 May. He told her that the German bias of the court was so well known that it was difficult to prevent the spread of the pernicious rumours to which Ellenborough had referred in the House of Lords.[29] On 17 June, when Ellenborough made a third attempt to break the parliamentary silence on the subject of the duchies by attacking Russell's decision to abandon the London Treaty, Derby advised the House against impairing Britain's diplomatic position by discussing the London Treaty while the conference was still in session.[30]

Thus did the government succeed in deferring parliamentary censure until after the failure of the London conference. But its own conduct in Parliament from February to June was most unsatisfactory. Its evasive replies served merely to excite resistance and suspicion, and to leave the field to the enemy who invariably got the better of the small exchanges. The government's attitude was too defensive and sometimes even too feeble. This was especially true in the House of Lords where Russell was consistently put to flight by Derby, Ellenborough, and Grey. Palmerston handled the Commons with much tact, but in his absence the liberals occasionally ran aground when Gladstone and Layard were left to reply to delicate questions. In both Houses a deep-seated *malaise* persisted throughout the session and the conservative reaction to the ministerial explanations of 27 June could easily have been foretold.

By the end of June there was such widespread disappointment over Britain's role in the Schleswig-Holstein tragedy that both the Lords and the Commons tended to treat the government's declarations with scepticism. Indeed both Palmerston and Russell were guarded and subdued. Palmerston was particularly sober and limited himself primarily to a factual outline,[31] while Russell was slightly more profuse with his explanations and denials.[32] Wisely adhering to their strongest line of defence, they both glossed over the unpleasant *dénouement* that had led to the crisis and concentrated instead on the existing state of things. Their message was simple: Britain can now do no more, but she retains her liberty of action should conditions take a radical turn. Both men reviewed the details of the conference very briefly and attributed its collapse, not to British vacillation, but to German ruthlessness and Danish obstinacy.

Well though they had spoken, the liberal leaders could not avoid the jibes of the opposition. Derby[33] and Disraeli attacked the whole principle of the London conference,[34] and blamed its failure on British mistakes. They argued that Britain had been unable to preserve the peace mainly because her influence had waned. They declined to initiate a debate at that moment but gave notice that the government's policy in the Danish crisis would be censured as soon as Parliament had been presented with all the details.

On 4 July the long-threatened motion of censure was introduced in the House of Commons. Accepted by the government as a challenge to its authority, the motion took precedence over all other business. It involved the right of the liberals to remain in office, or their obligation to resign in case of defeat. The motion therefore created a sensational stir both in Parliament and in the country. The motion itself was broad, general, and all-embracing: '... To express to Her Majesty our great regret that, while the course pursued by Her Majesty's Government has failed to maintain their avowed policy of upholding the integrity and independence of Denmark, it has lowered the just influence of this country in the counsels of Europe, and thereby diminished the securities for peace.' The resolution was not confined to specific details. Rather it complained loosely of dissatisfaction with the diplomacy of the liberals.

Disraeli introduced this motion of censure and ridiculed the whole liberal treatment of the Danish question. He argued that Russell's failure in the duchies was due chiefly to his blunders in Poland. By concentrating mainly on Russell's dealings with France, Disraeli contended that Britain persisted in alienating herself from Napoleon III every time she needed French assistance for a European object. He then emphasized the folly of threatening the Germans at a time when French support was problematical. He also charged the government with holding out material promises to Denmark at a moment when Britain could not possibly fulfil them. He did not think that Britain should even have meddled with the federal execution in any case, for that was a purely local matter between the Diet and the king of Denmark. Britain's persistent and undue meddling had resulted in that absurd conference which 'like a carnival, ... was an affair of masks and mystification.' Disraeli was not surprised that the conference failed. Russell needed allies to make it successful, but he had completely isolated himself from the rest of Europe by an incredible sequence of indiscretions. This was Disraeli's basic grievance.[35]

Gladstone immediately drew to the attention of the House that Disraeli had confined himself to a general assault upon the government but had recommended no program of his own. He easily proved that the conservative leader had not correctly analysed Anglo-French relations during the crisis, and he asked the conservatives for the concrete and conclusive proof upon which they had based their claim that British influence had waned. He countered Disraeli's accusations in connection with British threats and promises by declaring that Denmark had failed to follow any advice at all until it was too late. He strongly defended the cabinet's decision to remain at peace rather than embark on 'Quixotic enterprises' for questionable objectives. As for the motion itself, Gladstone could only remark that 'never will you find ... such a sterile, *jejeune* affair as this proposed to this House of Commons.'

Gladstone countered Disraeli's opening gambit with considerable skill but the sitting really belonged to Lord Stanley who hit directly at the root of the matter. The liberals were complaining that they could not understand the resolution. 'It means,' Stanley explained, 'that we think that you have blundered these foreign negotiations from beginning to end; and that we intend to call upon the House to say so.' The government should not ask the conservatives to avow a policy, for this was clearly not the responsibility of the opposition. Even so, Stanley thought that it would have been better for the liberals to follow the example of the French emperor. Stanley declared that Britain's influence had obviously waned since she had fallen hopelessly into discredit. For this decline her foreign policy was entirely responsible. It was the purpose of the resolution to have the opinion of the House on that point, and not to censure the government for having maintained peace. The motion, said Stanley, was neither warlike nor pacific; it was simply an announcement of keen and justifiable discontent. The statement that such a measure involved the degradation of the country was not to be borne, for that would deny any opposition the right to denounce all disgraceful lines of conduct which had sullied the national honour. Stanley thought that the results of recent British diplomacy were dreadful in the extreme: 'France alienated, Germany insulted, Denmark abandoned, Poland encouraged and left to perish.'

The motion was vigorously supported by General Peel who thought that if Russell had been bent on peace from the start he should have followed the line of non-intervention. He ridiculed the government for foolishly trying to pursue simultaneously a warlike and a peaceful program. The resultant war of words, Peel lamented, had been neither safe nor honourable.

Once again it was Newdegate who alluded to British interests in the Baltic. On this occasion he demonstrated a keener sympathy for the Danes and recommended a more warlike policy. He alone seemed willing to pay the price of prestige and honour, and his exhortations to lead the neutral powers in a more offensive stand against Germany were made in vain. The members of the opposition who hitherto had been so sympathetic to the Danish cause now began to deny the existence of a sufficient British motive or interest in the Baltic. By this time the strong pro-Danish sentiments of February had evaporated.

On the other side, the strongest pro-German speech was delivered by Kinglake, the liberal historian, who asserted that Britain had not incurred any obligations towards Denmark. Even if she had, he declared, the injudicious policy of the Danes must have absolved her from that responsibility. Kinglake made the very sound point that, far from encouraging Denmark, Britain had always urged forebearance. Since British advice had seldom made any impact on the Danish mind, he could only blame the Danes for their misfortunes.

On the whole, the speeches of 4 July were all too English in tone.[36] None of the speakers managed to see the Schleswig-Holstein question in its broader, European, context. There was a general tendency to exaggerate the wisdom of Napoleon's policy which was not clearly understood by the majority of those who praised it. Members on both sides of the House criticized both the Germans and the Danes, and neglected the basic merits of the Schleswig-Holstein case. Their major concern was the extent to which Britain was genuinely committed to help

Denmark. Both sides wanted peace. The liberals, therefore, accused the conservatives of seeking war, while the latter charged the government with drifting listlessly into hostilities. The House of Commons particularly desired to avert the recurrence of those circumstances which had given rise to the Crimean War, and its aversion to violence of any kind could not now be mistaken. Only on this point was there any semblance of unanimity. The keynote of the sitting was a rather insular emphasis on non-intervention despite the obvious disruption of the continental balance. Otherwise the debate of 4 July produced a bewildering confusion of ideas.

The government fared worse on 5 July than it had done on the previous night, for even some of those speakers who were eager to defeat the motion still attacked Russell's foreign policy. It is doubtful whether the liberals could have gained much pleasure or profit from the speeches of Cobden, Horsman, and Roebuck, all of whom – while expressing their determination to support the ministry – denounced the entire policy which the government had pursued in the Danish affair.

Cobden, the leader of the Manchester School, concentrated mainly on the economic aspect of the question and emphasized the commercial disadvantages which must result from Anglo-German war. He made a useful contribution to the debate by denouncing the pernicious doctrine of nationality and demonstrating the real evils inherent in a program of indiscriminate interference. Cobden impaired his argument, however, by carrying his case for non-intervention to almost impractical limits.

The liberal Horsman made a curious speech. He acknowledged the validity of the conservative criticisms and proceeded to argue that the blame for the current crisis was equally to be distributed. The opposition, he observed, had offered no useful guidance. In his opinion the failure in Schleswig-Holstein was a national rather than an exclusively liberal one. The liberals had done merely what the public and Parliament had desired. He recalled the violent pro-Danish temper which had pervaded British opinion in the previous winter and had made a British withdrawal from the affair impossible before April. Horsman reminded the House that its members had often remonstrated against the policies of Germany. To blame Russell now for being pro-Danish and protesting against German aggression was to view the question in retrospect. He could not sympathise therefore with vague resolutions which offered no advice for the present and little security for the future.

Roebuck severely criticized the Germans and denounced the doctrine of nationality. Regarding the duchies as standing in the same relation to Denmark as Ireland to England, he denied the Germans the right to interfere in Schleswig-

Holstein. He condemned with equal violence the irresolute policy of the government, Cobden's impractical notions of non-intervention, and the insipid motion of the conservatives. Roebuck admitted that the government had made many errors but he preferred the present ministers to those who would fain succeed them. The critics of the government, he noticed, had produced no evidence of their own ability to remedy the situation which they were now deploring.

There was a greater variety in the debate of 5 July, and a fuller treatment was given to many aspects which had been neglected on the opening night. The Schleswig-Holstein question was placed squarely within the circumstances of the moment and was discussed in its economic and military context. The debate dealt as much with what should now be done as with what had already passed. The opposition shifted its ground to enlarge the area of criticism.[37] Butler-Johnstone denounced the entire government as a body, and Liddell referred to failures other than the fiasco on the duchies. In doing so, the conservatives weakened their position, but the government took no advantage of this opening. The fact is that too many liberals were themselves unduly critical of Russell's foreign policy. Even Forster acknowledged that Britain's influence in Europe had suffered as a result of excessive meddling in affairs which did not directly concern the British people.

There was much confusion over the extent of British obligations, but again the majority advocated peace. The speakers were even more indifferent to Danish suffering than those who had criticized Denmark on 4 July. Cecil regretted the ungenerous remarks about the gallant Danes but circumstances had forced him to modify his own language. He was markedly less belligerent now than in the previous months.

The government received its most telling blows on 7 July. Only two speakers gave any support to the liberal cause. Layard, however, defended it with astonishing vigour and produced what was clearly the best liberal speech in the whole debate. He combined and reconciled all the various arguments that had thus far been made against the motion and marshalled them into a coherent synthesis. He dissected the main contentions of the opposition and refuted them individually. He concluded by reminding the House that the government had frequently been compelled to interfere in Schleswig-Holstein, as much by public opinion as by parliamentary pressure. He asked the conservatives to recollect that it was their own emotional outbursts during the Polish revolt that had almost led to war and he warned the House against probable conservative impolicies in areas remote from the Baltic. But on this day Layard was supported only by the attorney-general, and by him only feebly.

The remaining speakers on 7 July denounced the government with varying degrees of violence. The conservative Cavendish-Bentinck failed to see how Britain could use the most intemperate language, and even threaten war, while assiduously reducing her armaments to the point where they were hardly adequate during a time of peace. Lord John Manners assailed the futile policy of bombast which had made Britain the laughing stock of Europe. Gathorne-Hardy, another conservative, despised that meddling which had not only failed to maintain peace but had deprived Britain of all her alliances. Even the liberal Sir Francis Goldsmid much regretted the Schleswig-Holstein policy of the government although he could not vote for such paltry resolutions. Cogan, another liberal, noticed that the government had meddled and muddled with equal incompetence far and wide. The conservative Peacocke expressed the opinion that too long a continuance in office had ennervated the liberals and that their policy in the duchies was the most obvious symptom of this.[38]

By 8 July the topic was exhausted. The motion of censure had become a simple question of party-politics. Parliament was now being asked to consider whether it was expedient to set up a new administration on the basis of a vague motion which made specific reference only to Denmark but demanded the rejection of the whole liberal program. Would it not have been more fitting to separate the idea of Russell's bungling in the Baltic from a general confidence in the government's performance as a whole? This was the question implicitly asked by a number of malcontent liberals and which illuminated the basic weakness of the conservative motion. No one could doubt that Russell had failed in Schleswig-Holstein but there were independents as well as liberals who felt that the ministry had acquitted itself well in other fields.

When Palmerston spoke on the 8th he aimed directly at the main weakness of the resolution. He made no serious attempt to defend the government's policy in the duchies. He confined himself instead to general remarks on the economic position of Britain, her general prosperity under the liberal administration, her decreasing debts, her increasing trade, her triumphs in China, and the improvement of Indian commerce. He boasted of a British peace which his cabinet had secured and maintained in spite of all temptations. He could not agree, in the light of all these things, that there was any validity in the absurd motion proposed by the opposition.[39] But he lacked his usual verve, and Gladstone indeed described his effort as 'unequivocally weak in the mental and bodily sense.'[40] The Schleswig-Holstein problem had thus reduced the jaunty Palmerston to a Richard Cobden in miniature: a most curious spectacle indeed.

The result of the division, uncertain to the last, was close. The government, though unquestionably out-debated, was rescued by a majority of eighteen. The liberals had done far better than they had expected.[41] The immediate result of the vote itself was not, however, the most significant aspect of the great debate. One dominant factor stood out from the beginning: the House of Commons had become ultra-pacific. Of all the speakers, only Newdegate distinguished himself by advocating the use of force in the current contingency. In July even the hitherto bellicose Cecil showed no enthusiasm for war. Both sides endeavoured to strengthen their cause by stigmatizing each other as the 'war-party.' Both parties apparently sensed that the public passion for active measures had abated. Bernal Osborne could well ask: 'Now what has become of that great section – the war-party? ... Everyone is for peace ... I think, therefore, the House is now about to listen to the dictates of common sense and to preserve that peace which the country has determined to maintain.' There still prevailed that overwhelming sense of futility, that helplessness in a situation wherein flagrant injustice was being committed without the likelihood of punishment. But the Commons emphasized the disadvantages of meddling unduly in European affairs. Liberals and conservatives alike now reflected that it had merely led to universal mistrust. As Osborne remarked, 'The time has gone by for enacting in this way the bluster of Bobadil without the chivalry of Quixote.'[42]

The motion of censure in the House of Lords on 8 July was somewhat anticlimactic since the subject had already been exhausted by the Commons. As expected, the conservatives triumphed, but the margin of their victory was only nine votes. The liberals did better than they had anticipated not only because Derby and Ellenborough were regrettably absent but because a number of lords, like Clanricarde, failed to support the resolution although they rejected Russell's policy in Schleswig-Holstein. The result was thus a moral triumph for the government, which nevertheless suffered the mortification of hearing its foreign policy maligned by friend as well as foe.

Led by Malmesbury who proposed the motion, the opposition repeated the arguments already put forward in the House of Commons. It insisted that Russell had made too many promises to Denmark and too many threats to Germany, and condemned his whole Schleswig-Holstein policy as weak and inconsistent. The liberal Lord Grey supported the resolution and restated Disraeli's contention that Russell had made problems for himself in Denmark by floundering in Poland.

The liberals put up an inept defence. Russell was diffuse and evasive, choosing to deal mainly with abstract principles like freedom, right, justice, and obligations. Wodehouse, while blaming European behaviour for the failure of the London conference, produced a mere paraphrase of the colourless speech he had delivered on 11 April. The essence of the liberal strategy indeed was to attribute the failures of British diplomacy to the immoral conduct of the European powers. It was, therefore, a simple matter for Carnarvon, as well as Grey, to point out that Europe's failure to co-operate with Britain was the inevitable result of Russell's blunders in the previous year. The opposition also held that Russell had compounded his errors by continuing his foolish policy of swagger after it was clear that he could obtain no assistance from France or Russia. Argyll gave the government its best defence by claiming that it was the conservatives themselves who had encouraged Denmark to be adamant. He defied them to show clearly at which point in the crisis the government had gone wrong. Britain, he remarked, could not have interfered effectively in the winter, and the circumstances after April did not favour her single-handed intervention. But it was nonsense to say that Britain should have remained silent from the start when, in actual fact, she had been invited on all sides to settle the dispute. Argyll spoke extremely well, but the liberals weakened their own case by trying too desperately to deny that British prestige had suffered from the recent events. This argument could not be sustained in the face of such contrary evidence.

The House of Lords, like the Commons, came out strongly on the side of peace on 8 July.[43] The warlike opinions they had expressed earlier were coolly retracted. Posing now as the staunch advocates of peace, the conservatives were amazed that the liberals should denounce them as war-mongers. For, as Carnarvon asked, how could Russell accuse them of belligerence when, even at that stage, the House was not yet sure that the government wanted peace? In any case, as it appeared to the opposition, the peace won by the liberals had been dishonourably achieved *in spite of* the foreign secretary. In the final analysis the Lords, like the Commons, blamed Russell not so much for maintaining peace as for failing to uphold the national honour while doing so.

The liberal policy was after all vindicated by Parliament, but it was over the press that the government really scored its overwhelming triumph. Apart from rabid conservative publications like the *Morning Herald*, the *Standard*, the *Press*, the *Quarterly Review*, and *Blackwood's Magazine*, the British press gave wholehearted support to Palmerston. It admitted that Britain had failed in Schleswig-Holstein but denied that this was enough to justify a political upheaval.

The bulk of the British press unsparingly denounced the motion of censure, which was seen as a selfish attempt to unseat the government rather than an honest effort to remedy the situation. *The Times*, indeed, condemned Disraeli's resolution, on 29 June, as a 'leaf out of Bismarck's book, somewhat crumpled and soiled.' Most of the British newspapers assailed the conservatives, not for taking Russell to task over his undoubted errors in the duchies, but for their failure to produce a recognizable alternative of their own. As the *Economist* declared on 9 July, while the policy of the liberals 'has been such as to puzzle all men,' that of the conservatives 'has never yet been explained.' On the whole, the press was delighted to see that the government had preserved peace and that Parliament had voted solidly against war, but it was left with the feeling that Britain had somehow brought a needless humiliation upon herself. It regarded the collapse of Russell's diplomacy in Schleswig-Holstein as a clear sign that Britain should alter her entire diplomatic pattern and strategy, appreciate the limits of her continental influence, and withdraw from active participation in European affairs. This message was perhaps delivered most articulately on 16 July by the *Illustrated London News*:

We are a great naval, not a land power. We can only play a secondary part in enterprises which require vast military forces. Henceforth, it may be hoped, our Foreign Office will confine itself to its proper role, and construct its system of policy upon a mature consideration of what the British nation is really concerned in and qualified to undertake. In that case, the bitter lesson we have learnt will be unspeakably profitable.

The *Illustrated London News*, like the Manchester meeting of 11 February, called upon the government to devote its major energies to the solution of social and economic problems at home. The British press, in fact, demanded the abandonment of the traditional diplomacy of interference which had brought the country to grief.

So great indeed was this public reaction against the methods of Palmerstonian diplomacy that Britain not only withdrew from the Danish dispute, but cultivated thereafter the Gladstonian habit of treating European affairs with a certain cautious detachment. In the fifty years which followed the Schleswig-Holstein fiasco, only once (during the Balkan crisis of 1877-8) did she revert to the jingoism of the earlier era. Palmerstonian tactics no longer appealed to the British public, which henceforth gave hearty support to the Cobdenite doctrine of non-intervention. In this sense, it can be argued that public opinion was a contributory factor to the passive diplomacy of the Mancunians who held the centre of the stage immediately after Palmerston's death.

On the Danish question itself, however, British public opinion was too confused to wield an effective influence over Russell's policy. Englishmen were so puzzled by this riddle that, in this instance, they tended to resign themselves to the guidance of their political leaders. But the latter now found themselves at the crossroads as it were and knew not which direction to take in the conduct of foreign policy.

In the early 1860s British politicians were still trying to recover from the bitter experiences suffered in the Near East. The Crimean War had left them with the suspicion that it was, from a purely British standpoint, totally unproductive to participate actively in European struggles for essentially European objectives. The Victorians had emerged with nothing to show for their Crimean sacrifices, which succeeded only in magnifying the psychological and political barriers between themselves and Russia. This isolation from Russia created diplomatic problems for which the Victorians found no solution at all. It actually increased their dependence upon the unreliable French who still remained basically their most dangerous rivals. A sensible British foreign policy after 1856 therefore became almost impossible: for her to uphold her dignity, be it in Italy, Mexico, Syria, Poland, or Denmark, Britain had to co-operate more closely with France than she was prepared to do. The net result, in all cases, was the same: her political leaders, after much bitter debate among themselves, decided to do nothing of material consequence. Their mistrust of Napoleon III, heightened by his diplomacy during the Austro-Italian War of 1859–60, prevented them from solidifying the so-called western alliance which alone could have saved Britain from diplomatic embarrassment in the Polish and Danish crises. Unable to work in concert with France or Russia, Britain had to look to her own material resources and these were painfully inadequate in the early 1860s. Although the Crimean War and the Indian Mutiny had exposed the serious shortcomings of the British army, Gladstone's budgets (to Palmerston's dismay) consistently placed more stress on strict economy than on military reconstruction. It was not feasible, therefore, for Britain to contemplate single-handed interference on the continent, particularly when she was also concerned about possible American complications.

Non-intervention had thus become the pattern of British diplomatic behaviour prior to the Schleswig-Holstein crisis. But it differed fundamentally from Cobdenite or Gladstonian forms of pacifism in that it was incongruously accompanied by Palmerstonian swagger. This curious program was not yet based on a general belief in the principle of non-interference. Still less was it based on a deliberate governmental determination to follow the dictates of public opinion. It was rather the result of the constant failure of mid-Victorian political leaders to agree among themselves on matters diplomatic. Vacillation was the inevitable consequence of ministerial and parliamentary discord. These disagreements often sprang from increasing knowledge rather than from continuing ignorance. The Foreign Office, which had generally provided leadership on foreign problems, now found that more British politicians were becoming increasingly better informed on external affairs. This was due chiefly to the phenomenal newspaper boom which followed the removal of the stamp and paper duties in the mid-century and to the speeding up of the dissemination of news with the introduction of the telegraphic system.

This journalistic explosion undoubtedly made the British Parliament, as well as the general public, more and more conscious of foreign developments. Parliamentary and public opinion became increasingly important factors in the conduct of British foreign policy as the century progressed. But it still cannot be argued that Parliament played a prominent role in the Danish crisis. The many debates on Schleswig-Holstein during the session of 1864 proved only that the British Parliament was just as divided as the cabinet.

9
Conclusion

In spite of the overwhelming evidence to support the contrary view, the liberals spent four nights in the House of Commons and one in the House of Lords trying desperately to prove that Britain's influence had not suffered grievous harm as a result of the Schleswig-Holstein conflict. But nothing that they were then capable of saying could ever have convinced the British Parliament and public that there was not a good deal of truth in the conservative motion. It was patently clear that Britain had not emerged unscathed from the Dano-German dispute. It was painfully obvious that the national honour had been sullied by a number of European slights which themselves bore ample testimony to Britain's moral weakness in international politics at that stage. Her influence had waned to such an extent that she could no longer exert any appreciable pressure upon the policies of any European state. During the Schleswig-Holstein crisis her words of warning were flouted openly not only by the Diet as a body but also by some of the minor German states individually. Austria and Prussia deliberately rejected every fair British proposal during the Schleswig-Holstein war. France and Russia refused to follow Britain in her attempts to foist a reasonable compromise upon the antagonists. Even Denmark regularly declined to accept her conciliatory advice. In the end the Danes became impatient at Britain's feebleness of spirit and struck out boldly on their own, during the London conference, when Russell meekly gave up the neutral propositions of 28 May 1864.

These European attitudes heralded the decline of Britain in Europe. Her diplomatic strength on the continent had depended to a large extent on her moral influence, and this had been wielded most effectively when she could persuade a continental power with adequate military resources to act in concert with her.

Her failure in the Schleswig-Holstein question was based largely upon her inability to find a reliable ally of this type. It was this diplomatic weakness which led to the ruin of the London conference. This conference was created and inspired mainly by British exertions. It was, in a real sense, a British interest. It represented the final arrow in Russell's diplomatic quiver. Its failure was unquestionably a British disaster, especially since it illuminated the helplessness of Britain to control the affairs of Europe in a moment of awkward isolation.

The failure of the conference left Britain with little choice but to resign herself to a policy of withdrawal from the Schleswig-Holstein quarrel. This British decision at the end of June was the climax of a long sequence of British retreats. She had for twelve years tenaciously adhered to the London Treaty and now she was compelled, in May 1864, to retreat from that stand. When the arrangement of 1852 was given up by the majority of European states it meant that the whole base of Britain's diplomacy in the duchies was shattered in one blow. Earlier she had been forced to retreat from the position she had taken with respect to the terms of the Dano-German armistice. Later she was forced to abandon the Schlei-Dannevirke line when the Germans rejected it. She had also to retreat from the policy of mediation when France and Russia refused to help her impose it upon the obstinate belligerents.

These defeats during the London conference crowned a program of failure which Britain had pursued since 1848. The only significant triumph gained by British diplomacy in Schleswig-Holstein was the ill-fated treaty of 1852 and this was, at best, a Pyrrhic victory. For the London Treaty tended to complicate rather than solve the riddle of the Elbe duchies. It undoubtedly increased the problems in the way of Britain's diplomacy, for it left her with the task (admittedly shared by the rest of Europe) of enforcing allegiance to an unpopular settlement abhorred in equal measure by Germany and Denmark. The essence of British diplomacy thereafter was to recommend moderation and urge both sides to honour their engagements.

Britain, however, failed to induce Denmark to adhere to the letter and spirit of the London Treaty. She failed to persuade the Danish government to deal generously with its German subjects in Schleswig and Holstein or to satisfy the reasonable claims of the Estates in the two duchies. Thus Britain failed to prevent the crisis of the mid-1850s. Thereupon she devoted her major energies to hindering a federal investigation in Holstein. But she was signally unsuccessful in forestalling the Schleswig-Holstein discussions in the Diet. Moreover she was not able to prevent the Diet from decreeing its order for federal execution, and ultimately she could not avert the occupation of Holstein. In defiance of her advice Denmark allowed the patent of March 1863 to remain in force until it was superseded by the November Constitution, the sanction of which Britain likewise failed to postpone. The direct negotiations between Denmark and the two great German powers collapsed because neither side could be urged to accept British advice. Finally Austria and Prussia invaded Schleswig despite the admonitions of the British government. The Diet, recalcitrant to the last, proclaimed in favour of the Augustenburg pretensions although Russell had often warned it of the serious consequences which could ensue from such a course. From beginning to end, Britain's efforts to solve the Schleswig-Holstein problem during 1852–64 were conspicuously futile.

These failures in Schleswig-Holstein were due in great measure to the general attitude of Britain herself. She was far too Danophile in the early stages to see the problem objectively. This obvious prejudice encouraged the Danes to believe that, in spite of British advice, they could obtain British support for their Eiderdanish designs. Britain strengthened these Danish hopes by trying so hard to thwart federal jurisdiction in Holstein. Britain did not deny the Diet's right to discuss Holstein's grievances, yet she spent six years feverishly trying to avert such a discussion at Frankfurt. Had she pursued an apparently more impartial course in the early 1850s she might possibly have succeeded in moderating the truculent attitude of the Danes. Once Denmark had provoked the Diet to adopt an aggressive policy, the Schleswig-Holstein problem could no longer be handled effectively by British statesmen.

At the climax of the crisis Britain was far less able to speak with authority because her foreign policy during 1859–63 had weakened her international position. She had quarrelled with Russia over the Polish question at a time when the wounds of the Crimean War had not yet healed. Russia in the meantime had drawn closer to Prussia. Consequently Britain could not persuade the Russian government to join in any European concert for the express purpose of coercing Germany. Nor could she obtain French support for this object since her own diplomacy had destroyed the western alliance. France had joined with Britain in settling the Chinese dispute and the Syrian affair,[1] but Britain had not been equally co-operative. She opposed the Franco-Italian aggressions against Austria in 1859,[2] denounced the French seizure of Nice and Savoy, abandoned France in the Mexican adventure,[3] left her in the lurch in the quarrel with Russia over Poland, and then rejected her congress proposal at the end of 1863. These manifestations of anti-French feeling naturally forced Napoleon III to adopt a more sceptical attitude towards the Anglo-French concert. He was therefore reluctant in 1864 to help Russell put a better face on the Danish affair. As Clarendon remarked to Cowley, 'to speak honestly, I cannot much blame his dislike of the Earl who has given him many a *mauvais quart d'heure* though I really believe without intention.'[4] Clarendon considered that Russell had 'for five years put him [Napoleon III] through a course of snubs and slights that must have nearly tried his patience.' In these circumstances Napoleon was not unhappy to witness the diplomatic indignities which Russell was now forced to endure.

The indifference of Russia and the ambivalence of France forced Britain to depend upon her own material resources. But these were avowedly insufficient. Britain could not seriously contemplate a single-handed war with all Germany at a time when Anglo-American relations were very uncertain. Britain could not provide enough troops to defend Denmark in Schleswig and Jutland against what might conceivably have been a united German front. In actual fact, one of the main causes of her restraint in the Danish as well as the Polish question was the necessity of keeping a small army in Canada to patrol the American border in case of emergency.[5] The Crimean War and the Indian mutiny had also served to illuminate the serious weaknesses of the British military machine. For these reasons Britain could not afford to provoke a continental war in which, as Palmerston remarked, she might ultimately have to contend with some 300,000 German soldiers.[6] As Palmerston and Russell must have known, there were only 219,000 (including officers) in the British army in 1864, and of these 82,000 were stationed in India.[7]

One of the main reasons then for the weakness of Britain's policy in the Schleswig-Holstein crisis was her awareness of her military shortcomings. The feeble program also had its roots in deeper and more fertile soil. It was the outgrowth of internal confusion. The deep divisions of British opinion on the merits of the Schleswig-Holstein case prevented the government from formulating a definitive program at any stage. The main trouble was that the British public had never studied the history of the question, and the majority of Englishmen upheld the validity of the Danish pretensions merely through ignorance and prejudice. But the minority who delved more deeply into the subject maintained that the German claims were more reasonable. The result was British bewilderment and discord.

Nowhere was this discord more blatant or more far-reaching in its consequences than in the counsels of the British ministers themselves. The cabinet remained divided and bemused throughout the crisis. As a result Russell could never deal firmly with either the Germans or the Danes. Unable to pursue the Palmerstonian line, which he preferred, and reluctant to support the *laissez-faire* attitude of the Mancunians in the cabinet, Russell vacillated between two very different strategies and ultimately chose the worst features of both. As the cabinet seldom came forward with concrete or practical substitutes for the proposals it rejected, it thus failed to offer constructive guidance to the foreign secretary and then compounded this dereliction of duty by refusing to accept his leadership. Britain was therefore caught without a recognizable or resolute policy while the Germans were violating the integrity of Denmark and disrupting the delicate

European balance. The British ministers all agreed that Germany was in the wrong in 1864, but they could not agree on the subject of active interference. The peace-party rejected the idea of giving material aid to the Danes so long as France and Russia could not be urged to do the same. In these circumstances Mancunianism consistently triumphed.

The success of Mancunianism was based on the fact that the ministers had no genuine desire for war and were concerned chiefly with the question of British material interests. This was particularly true of Granville, Grey, Villiers, and Wood. The policy of peace, for rather different reasons, also appealed to de Grey and Somerset. De Grey was alarmed by the unpreparedness of the British army. He was definitely pro-Danish, but his fear of British humiliation in the military field made him one of the staunchest promoters of peace.[8] Somerset opposed strong measures largely because he was too much alive to the obstacles in the way of effective naval action. Throughout the winter he tried hard to impress upon Palmerston and Russell the dangers inherent in a Baltic expedition. Convinced that the British navy could not be at its most effective in the Baltic, that a naval excursion to Copenhagen would give rise to Anglo-American complications, and that this would not in any case suffice to expel the Germans from Denmark, Somerset made every effort to discourage the idea of direct British intervention.[9] Argyll was vehemently anti-German in the winter, but by April had veered round to the side of non-intervention. Neither Granville nor Wood ever accepted the pro-German views of the court but their anxiety for the British welfare always made them eager to weigh the sacrifices involved in war against the doubtful gain that British honour might derive from hostilities. Gladstone was not primarily interested in the question of honour. His motivating impulse was the balancing of the national budget. At the very time when Russell was angling for French support to halt the German progress in Jutland, the chancellor of the exchequer was framing a stringent budget which provided for the reduction of armaments – a budget prepared entirely in anticipation of peace. Even the *Saturday Review*, which had advocated a policy of non-intervention from the start of the Danish crisis, could not but remark, on 20 February 1864, that Gladstone's budget was, in the circumstances of the day, a most astonishing program. Gladstone's determination to carry through his plans for financial reconstruction made him hostile to any measures that might create financial difficulties. This attitude, coupled with a genuine aversion to war, made him one of the most uncompromising participants in the ministerial rebellion against Palmerston and Russell. And, of course, from avowed or suspected Mancunians like Cardwell, Milner-Gibson, and Villiers, the foreign secretary could expect no help at all.

Against these powerful forces the war-party could not hope to prevail. The Lords Westbury and Stanley of Alderley consistently denounced the policy of ignoble peace, but their efforts were ultimately neutralized by the remarkable 'apostasy' of Palmerston who gravitated more and more towards the moderate camp after Parliament's refusal to encourage a warlike approach in February. Palmerston's conduct during the first six months of 1864 was noticeably ambivalent. Occasionally he struck an attitude of defiance such as he displayed in his memorable interview with Apponyi at the end of April, but he never seemed to have had any real desire to pursue a policy of violence. Even when he recommended stern action, he appeared to have done so on the conviction that he could preserve the peace simply by threatening war. His sound grasp of the obstacles which bedevilled the path of active interference made him shrink from giving Russell unstinted support. Indeed, even during the period of excitement which attended the collapse of the London conference, Clarendon found it possible to report that Palmerston had grown increasingly cautious since the waning of the warlike fervour of the House of Commons.[10] Palmerston's conversion rendered Russell's position in the cabinet almost untenable, and it was scarcely improved by the introduction of the pacific Clarendon into the ministry early in April. Clarendon was especially suspicious of France and he always thought that Britain should not commit herself to any serious undertaking in the Baltic while Napoleon III remained on the fence.[11]

It is remotely possible that, despite these ministerial differences, Russell might yet have succeeded in carrying his colleagues with him had it not been for the vigorous and persistent intervention of the court. The queen maintained a lively interest in the Schleswig-Holstein controversy because it directly involved her closest relatives. She was connected by birth and marriage to several of the German sovereigns as well as to the Glücksburg house. Furthermore, her devotion to the memory of the prince consort made her almost as German as she was British in her outlook. Naturally she attempted to reconcile her German and British prejudices. This made her equate and confound the national interests of her kingdom with those of a united Germany. As a result her main concern was to avoid Anglo-German hostilities at all cost.

In order to do this the queen needed to keep a firmer grip than usual over the Foreign Office, especially since it was obvious that the majority of her subjects were sympathetic to Denmark. In fact, the press, Parliament, and public were all so violently opposed to the German cause that the queen had every right to be uneasy. Russell gave her even more cause for alarm with his constant demands for an Anglo-French concert to resist the German progress in the duchies. The queen deplored this state of things because she was sincerely convinced that the German case, beyond any shadow of doubt, was the just one in the dispute. It pained her to see her own people treat the quarrel in such a partial and narrow-minded fashion. Her conscience as well as her heart dictated that everything should be done to prevent the well-meaning British from committing an act of wrong. Her self-appointed duty was to educate her cabinet and divert her ministers from the foolish path which their two old leaders seemed eager to follow.

There can now be no doubt that the queen stretched her constitutional prerogative to the limit in the performance of this duty. She refused to sanction despatches which gave any hint of Anglo-German antipathy. She frequently appealed to the cabinet to settle differences of opinion between the Foreign Office and the court, and then ruthlessly interfered to make sure that the cabinet emerged with the desired verdict. Behind the backs of Palmerston and Russell, she often corresponded with Granville and Wood, while consistently encouraging General Grey to use his influence to convert ministerial waverers. Grey was actually sent to 'lobby' the ministers during the cabinet meeting of 25 June.[12] The queen heartily sanctioned the ministerial rebellion against Palmerston and Russell, and went so far as to confide to Granville, on 14 February 1864, that she would persevere in her current attitude of hostility towards Russell's warlike proposals even if it meant the resignation of her foreign secretary.[13]

The queen's influence over British diplomacy in the Danish crisis cannot be exaggerated. It was not only considerable, it was predominant. The queen's opinions prevailed at almost every stage. She compelled Russell to retreat whenever he threatened to defy the court, and actually forced him to recall a number of despatches he had initially sent without her express approval. British ambassadors were sometimes embarrassed by having to convey the countermanding message after they had already followed their 'unauthorized' instructions. This lack of harmony at the centre of the diplomatic network inevitably undermined the authority with which British envoys spoke. The queen, however, was prepared to make any sacrifice to avoid an Anglo-German war, which she regarded as the greatest of all possible calamities.

While it is true that Russell was hindered by the court from pursuing the methods of his choice in dealing with the Schleswig-Holstein crisis, there is no evidence that the queen resorted to pressures other than consultative in her endeavour to preserve peace. She made no improper threats to the leaders of the cabinet. She tried in the main to influence them by force of argument. Her arguments failed to convince the majority of the ministers who remained opposed to her German sentiments, but she realized that the peace-party and the court could unite on the common ground of hostility to Anglo-German war. She used this circumstance to the greatest advantage. Her success lay essentially in the strengthening of the pacific groups in the country. She sought to instil in the opposition, as well as in the government, the urgent necessity of a policy of peace. Indirectly she compelled obedience from the cabinet by inspiring the liberals with the fear that she might call upon the tories to replace them if they should prove themselves unruly. She did so by keeping in close contact with the leaders of the opposition as well as with the ministerial rebels. She actually succeeded in January 1864 in extracting a promise from Derby that he would not make the Danish crisis a party-question during the parliamentary session of that year. As Derby himself had no clear-cut program, he proved an easy convert to the queen's cause.[14]

While it is beyond dispute that the queen went to great lengths to keep the peace-party intact, to inspire and embolden it, and generally speaking to dictate British policy in the duchies over Russell's head, it is also true that the peace-party was not altogether passive in this matter. Royal interference, in fact, was actively encouraged by the pacific ministers who sought the queen's support as zealously as she sought theirs. The court and the peace-party needed each other's assistance since they were both anxious to thwart the aggressive measures so often contemplated by the foreign secretary. On one occasion, at least, Palmerston and Russell expressed irritation with the conduct of Gladstone whom they suspected of encouraging the queen to defend the contentions of the peace-party after an indecisive cabinet meeting.[15] In short, the alliance between the queen and the ministerial 'rebels' was by no means one-sided.

It is obvious that the pacific faction was sufficiently strong to have made it difficult for Russell to pursue an independent course – even had the queen behaved otherwise. But it is equally clear that, if the queen had been warlike, nothing would have prevented Russell from pursuing the strongest line from the beginning of the crisis. A number of his despatches threatening war might never have come before the cabinet at all, had the queen not objected to them and demanded a ministerial review. Had there been harmony between the royal opinions and those of Russell, the cabinet might eventually have been led into the Dano-German war. It is only when these possibilities are considered that the enormous influence of the queen over British diplomacy in this crisis can be measured effectively.

On the whole, the alliance between the cabinet and the court was advantageous to both. It enabled the queen to exert the royal will more assertively than she was normally able to do, while it permitted the other ministers to supervise Russell's Schleswig-Holstein policy in such a way as to deprive him of virtually all control over that question. Indeed the cabinet came to assume a strange kind of importance during the Danish crisis. It became, so to speak, the final court of appeal since the ministerial verdict was so often sought both by the queen and the Foreign Office. In assessing the importance of the cabinet's role in this affair, it is necessary only to speculate what might have been the result had the ministers chosen to accept Russell's leadership rather than the queen's.

It is difficult to understand why Russell submitted to royal and ministerial dictation in this crisis and accepted full responsibility for a policy with which he obviously did not always agree. It seems as though he should definitely have re-signed in January 1864 as he had more than once threatened to do. Perhaps he refrained because, like so many of his contemporaries, he really could not decide which course was best. This fundamental uncertainty must have prevented him from feeling strongly enough on the subject to dissociate himself from the passive program recommended by the Mancunians. Had he been convinced of the intrinsic justice of a stronger policy, he was by nature too sensitive to have endured the rebuffs of his colleagues for so long. It is reasonable to argue therefore that the supremacy of the crown and the peace-party over British policy in Schleswig-Holstein was due partly to Russell's own vacillation and uncertainty.

Russell had made such a serious effort to study the facts of this case that it is unfair to say, as so many historians have said, that his lack of resolution was caused by lack of knowledge. Apart possibly from Cecil and Morier, he knew more indeed about the Dano-German dispute than any other Englishman of that age. But in formulating a Schleswig-Holstein program he seemed baffled by the astonishing contrariety of advice which was tendered all at once. Not only was his cabinet divided, but so too was his diplomatic staff. British ministers abroad tended to see the question from different angles, and their conflicting reports appear to have puzzled rather than enlightened the Foreign Office.

Ambassadorial influence, like any other, defies exact measurement. When envoys are united they can play a vital role in the execution of a diplomatic plan. Unfortunately for Russell, however, harmony was not the keynote in ambassadorial opinion in the case of Schleswig-Holstein, and so his task was rendered more difficult. Nor was he helped much by the attitude of the queen who disregarded all those reports that expressed opinions at variance with her own. The queen, for instance, mildly rebuked Cowley on one occasion for attempting to encourage a renewal of the Anglo-French concert,[16] and she deplored the warlike tone of some of Napier's despatches.[17] Russell, on the other hand, thought it necessary to take more seriously the considered views of Britain's leading diplomats.

The British ambassadors were agreed on the whole upon only one idea. They all felt that the British policy in the duchies was tarnishing Britain's image on the continent. The manner in which British admonitions were ignored by the minor German states was a source of considerable shame and alarm. Small states as well as great powers were snubbing Britain with impunity, and the impression which the Polish revolt had created was now being confirmed by the Dano-German struggle. Britain was regarded universally as an arrogant but cowardly nation. This touched her ambassadors to the quick and the majority of them pleaded for some token of defiance, some suggestion of power, that would demolish once and for all this most pernicious delusion. They were ashamed of Britain's feebleness of spirit in the face of German swagger. This was their only common ground; otherwise they tended to take sides.

The majority of Britain's diplomats gave moral support to Denmark. This was especially true of Paget, her ambassador in Copenhagen, who had become increasingly pro-Danish although he had been a keen critic of Danish misrule in the duchies in his earlier days in Denmark. He had tried hard to persuade the Danes to follow Russell's moderate and prudent counsel, and he was quite jubilant when, under Christian ix, the Danish government began to relent. It pained him to see that the new spirit of Danish conciliation was doomed to meet only with the most inadmissible demands on the other side. He urged Russell to abandon the weak policy which had only emboldened the Germans. He called unequivocally for a British policy of war.[18] So too did Buchanan who had once been attached to the British legation in Denmark. He was violently pro-Danish and continued to use menacing language in Berlin even after it had become clear that Britain would do nothing to restrain Austria and Prussia. For this he was mildly rebuked by Russell early in July.[19] Buchanan became so emotional upon the subject that Anglo-Prussian relations were strained to the limit. The crown princess of Prussia, Queen Victoria's eldest daughter, complained that Buchanan was actually doing more harm than good in Berlin.[20] To ease the tension the government transferred him to St Petersburg. He remained convinced that a strong line from the start would have kept the Germans in check. Identical advice was offered by Napier, the British minister in St Petersburg, although he was not as fanatically pro-Danish as Paget or Buchanan. His call to action was based upon a sincere desire to improve Anglo-Russian relations. The fact is that he had fallen under the influence of Gorchakov whose grandiose scheme of a quadruple alliance to impede the progress of France was being imperilled by the Austro-Prussian aggressions in Jutland. Napier felt that Britain could repair the damage done by the Crimean War and the Polish revolt by showing some firmness in Schleswig-Holstein. Such a program, he thought, would win Gorchakov's co-operation.[21] Malet, the British representative at Frankfurt, likewise called for more powerful measures to restore British prestige in central Europe. He felt that the whole of Germany was impelled by an insane outburst of national fervour which was certainly dangerous to European equilibrium. Malet thought that a resolute British approach was necessary to restrain the Germans.[22]

There were pro-German ministers also. In Hanover, Howard had never ceased to complain of Danish tyranny in the duchies, while Morier was as ardently German as the Prussian court itself. Equally partisan in their views on the dispute were Ward (now the British consul at Hamburg) and Sir Joseph Crowe, the British consul-general at Leipzig in the 1860s. In fact, these two representatives had become so intolerably pro-German that Palmerston was moved to urge Russell to remind them that they were agents of the British crown.[23] It was in accordance with this suggestion that Russell sent this acrid note to Ward early in 1864: 'It is my duty to remind you that you are serving under the British Crown and not under any of the German states, and that your Reports of what is going on in Holstein and Lauenburg ought to be marked by an impartial attention to facts, and not written in the spirit of a partisan ...'[24] In spite of this reminder Ward still thought that the British dilemma was of her own making. Had she discouraged Denmark from the start, the Germans would never have been driven to extremes.

In the middle of these two schools stood Bloomfield in Vienna, Cowley in Paris, and Loftus at Munich. They saw the problem from the British point of view and felt assured that Britain could wield a greater influence by showing clearly that she was in earnest. So long as she encouraged the suggestion that she would confine her activity to words, she could produce no effect upon the German mind. Cowley deviated eventually to the path of peace and repeatedly warned Russell that the French emperor was not to be trusted. In a word, Cowley was governed by that morbid fear of France which had been the traditional impulse behind British diplomacy since the days of Louis XIV. From early in February 1864 Cowley's primary aim was to thwart the aspirations of Napoleon III, whom he suspected of plotting to derive huge benefits from a policy of nonintervention in the duchies. The merits of the German or Danish case became secondary in Cowley's calculations. He was outraged by the German aggressions not so much because he considered them impolite and unjust as because he suspected that Bismarck's unusual boldness was mainly the offspring of Franco-Prussian intrigue.

In the long run Cowley's advice was accepted. It was accepted not only because a host of external factors conspired to render active interference inexpedient but because it made sense to the British intellect of that day. By alerting Britain to the ulterior aims of Napoleon III Cowley struck the most pleasant chord to British ears. His reminder of the Rhenish peril was a notion around which most mid-Victorians were eager to unite. It had, in fact, been the guiding principle of British diplomacy in Schleswig-Holstein as elsewhere. Russell had wished to revive the western alliance as much to teach the Germans a good lesson as to prevent the French from taking undue advantage of the prevailing chaos. This was the main concern of the peace-party as well as the court. The queen and the majority of the cabinet agreed that an Anglo-German war would produce just the opportunity for which Napoleon had long been waiting. Even Russell admitted in the end that he was 'very glad that we have not given in to the temptation of a war between France and Germany. The French, if they get an inch, will certainly take an ell.'[25] Palmerston, too, was disturbed by such a prospect, and this was one of the major reasons for his constant desertion of Russell after

January 1864. His whole attitude towards the Schleswig-Holstein problem was warped by the tendency to overestimate the power of Napoleon and belittle that of Bismarck. As late as 26 December 1863 he still thought that 'the French would walk over [the Prussian army] and get without difficulty to Berlin ...'[26] With this outmoded view of Prussian military strength, it is not surprising that Palmerston appreciated Cowley's advice.

Cowley's suggestion that Britain should withdraw from the Dano-German quarrel and preserve her freedom of action was favoured also by the British Parliament. But Parliament emerged with this solution only by being able, in July 1864, to see the whole Schleswig-Holstein question in retrospect. It did not volunteer this advice when its guidance was sought by Palmerston and Russell in February. It accepted this program only after it had been announced by the cabinet at the end of June. This should not have surprised so astute a politician as Palmerston who ought clearly to have observed, during his long career, that Parliament had tended to be a critic rather than a formulator of policy. British policy in the final analysis had to be the work of the cabinet. The mid-Victorian Parliament was seldom anxious to debate a foreign or colonial issue unless it happened to involve directly the fate of the administration, which was rare, or the declaration of war, which was no more frequent. It was in the Foreign Office that questions of war and peace had generally been decided. Parliament had not made the decision to participate in the Crimean War, nor had it voted on the declaration of Palmerston's wars with China. The journalistic revolution of the mid-century had already begun to inspire a keener awareness of foreign issues, but it was too much to expect Parliament to produce a blue-print for the cabinet's guidance on the Danish question.

The British Parliament, as a matter of fact, assembled on 4 February 1864 to hear what the government was planning to do. It was as baffled as most Englishmen. Even Milner-Gibson, a member of the cabinet, had publicly confessed only a few days before that he knew very little about the Schleswig-Holstein question.[27] The average member of the House of Commons must undoubtedly have known even less. This lack of specific knowledge was made manifest by the general nature of remarks on the Danish crisis which were uttered spasmodically during the early weeks of the session. Parliament was groping in the dark. This made it extremely difficult for Palmerston to interpret its attitude. He had hoped for some parliamentary signal but nothing of any substance was vouchsafed him. He could only conclude, somewhat uncertainly, that there was no genuine desire for war although both Houses were predominantly pro-Danish.

Palmerston's difficulty in gauging the parliamentary temper was due to the same kind of vagueness and doubt that had hampered the resolution of the cabinet. Parliament was evidently divided and confused. Party-lines became blurred on the Danish question since no party knew quite where it stood. Among the liberals, the Manchester faction, led by Cobden and Bright, cared little for British honour but were interested mainly in the preservation of peace. Forster considered British prestige as only secondary and objected to the subordination of British interests to a 'fanciful chivalry,' although he did not accept the extreme pacifism of the Mancunian radicals. Kinglake subordinated everything to a fear of France, while Grant Duff was pro-German.[28] Osborne was interested chiefly in repudiating the London Treaty which he regarded as the cause of the recent strife. These men typified five distinct classes of liberals, all of whom were hesitant to give material support to Denmark. There was a sixth segment, led by Goschen, who wanted to warn the Germans that there was a limit to British patience. These groups outnumbered the Palmerstonians, led by Russell and Westbury, who were anxious to fight for Denmark. On the whole the liberals seemed pro-Danish enough, but the majority of them were committed to a peaceful policy. A restless minority, however, felt that though peace was a boon much to be sought after by the British nation it should not be purchased at too high a price.[29] The majority of the liberals realized that Britain's prestige was suffering as a result of her timidity, and they concluded that Britain should either interfere with an effect in keeping with her dignity and greatness, or meddle less in continental affairs.

The conservatives were also disorganized. Unlike the younger tories, Derby and Disraeli wanted peace. Derby was willing to criticize Russell's diplomacy but he did not want to commit himself before the collapse of the London conference. He even warned Disraeli on 12 May 1864 about being 'less guarded than is your wont.'[30] Disraeli himself was too fearful of France to contemplate with equanimity a British war on Denmark's account.[31] Sir Stafford Northcote was also pacific,[32] while Malmesbury seems to have had no clear-cut views on the subject. But Cecil, Carnarvon, and Manners were belligerent. Cecil thought that the British obligations to Denmark required British intervention as a duty.[33] Carnarvon wished to declare war against the Germans to avert a dangerous Prussian hegemony in the Baltic.[34] Manners advised forestalling the liberals by advocating war and thus gaining a measure of popular support for the tories.[35] The majority of the conservatives were pro-Danish, but Lord Bath was not.[36] In these circumstances the opposition failed to unite or come forward with any concrete suggestions. The tories waited on the course of events and finally appealed to providence by framing a very general and optimistic motion. Discordant to the last, they even disagreed over this tactic: the Lords Bath, Buccleuch, Stanhope, and Winchester all objected to the idea of moving such a resolution in the House of Lords.[37]

Parliament therefore failed to be of any service to Palmerston and Russell during the Schleswig-Holstein crisis. It made no material recommendations although it frequently condemned the government's diplomacy. It was clear that Parliament did not like Russell's program; equally clearly, Parliament was incapable of producing an alternative. In the end it attacked the policy of 'meddle and muddle' but voted to retain the ministry. Thus its influence over British policy in Schleswig-Holstein was not considerable. Its excitement in 1863 had encouraged the government to adopt a pro-Danish stand, but it is likely that Russell would have pursued such a line in any case. Parliament's pacifism in the spring and summer of 1864 merely strengthened the cabinet in its determination to remain at peace. Had Parliament been more warlike in February and March, it is possible that Palmerston and Russell would have dealt more firmly with their timid colleagues, although it is doubtful how far they would have been able to carry the court with them. On the whole Parliament's influence over British policy in the duchies was indirect. Its coolness towards a warlike policy gave strength to those ministers who had advocated non-intervention. It cannot, however, be argued that parliamentary pressure forced the cabinet to withdraw from the dispute at the end of June. The most that can be said is that the pro-Danish bias of Parliament encouraged Britain to play an active part in the controversy during the 1850s and early 1860s and to treat the question in too partisan a manner. It was partly a result of this parliamentary attitude that forced Russell to abandon his 'Coburg' proposals in 1862.

Parliament's bewilderment in 1864 reflected the general feeling of the British public. Only a small minority of Englishmen knew what the Dano-German quarrel involved. The majority supported Denmark out of a peculiar and instinctive contempt for things German, but the whole country seemed uncertain as to the nature and extent of British obligations. Britain's function in a controversy that was European in essence and origin was then a subject of much public debate. Some Englishmen felt that the national honour demanded war; others imagined that the national interests required peace.

The underlying feeling of anti-Germanism was expressed in a variety of ways. Pro-Danish letters were written to the press, the public became noticeably more restless after each new German victory, and funds were launched for the relief of the Danish sick and wounded. The managing committee of the Danish Soldiers' and Sailors' Sick and Wounded Relief Fund collected £9,423 between 24 February and 10 May 1864.[38] No similar committees operated on behalf of the Germans although the cause of the Schleswig-Holstein liberals, who wanted to free themselves from Danish control, was not much different from that of the Poles to whom the British gave moral support in their struggle against Russian oppression. Apart, however, from this obvious and common sympathy for Denmark the British public emerged with a wilderness of half-formed and obscure ideas. Britain was so confounded by the Elbe riddle that even her knowledgeable citizens had no solution to offer. Some of them actually added to the confusion by changing their minds from time to time.

This last group is exemplified by John Thadeus Delane, the famous editor of *The Times*, who knew more about current affairs than many of his contemporaries. He wielded perhaps a greater influence over British policy than anyone outside the cabinet and the court. Yet his knowledge of the Danish question at the end of 1863 was surprisingly sparse. He seemed to know so little of the critical events of that year that he spoke of the Dano-German war on 19 November as being suddenly imminent.[39] He was clearly unaware of those crucial issues which had been threatening to result in an open breach since 1857. He instinctively assumed that the Danes were being bullied by the Germans, and felt that Britain should adhere to the London Treaty and protect this settlement, if necessary by sending a squadron to Kiel. He was still warlike at the beginning of the year when he greatly regretted that Palmerston's absence from the cabinet meeting of 2 January 1864 had permitted the ineffective counsels of the peace-party to prevail.[40] After studying the problem carefully, however, Delane veered round to the side of peace and repeatedly denounced the idea of actively participating in the Baltic struggle. He became more and more neutral as the war progressed, and it is unfortunate that he chose to examine the issue only after it had reached the highest point of crisis, for it is possible that his earlier belligerence (which was manifested also in *The Times*) encouraged the Danes to be more obstinate than they might otherwise have been.

While Delane changed his stand and recanted too late, there is no evidence that John Ruskin, the famous author and critic, ever did the same. Ruskin remained hostile to the Germans and deplored the attitude of British statesmen who spoke so glibly but did so little while Denmark was being overrun. He was particularly disappointed in Gladstone and Kinglake, who could be so sensitive to Italian suffering but could not be moved by the plight of the Danes. In a strong letter to the *Morning Post* on 7 July 1864, he advised Gladstone to pay a visit to Alsen as he had once done to Naples. Ruskin failed to see how it was possible for Britain to abandon Denmark and still maintain her honour and her dignity.[41]

Ruskin, however, was vigorously opposed by John Stuart Mill, who praised British policy not only in Schleswig-Holstein but also in Poland. He argued that Britain could not remain silent even though she did not intend to fight. He thought that she was acting nobly by remonstrating against flagrant injustices even when they did not affect her own material interests. Mill, who wrote to the

Daily News in this vein on 1 July 1864, gave inspiration to Lord Brougham who repeated the same argument when addressing the Social Science Association on the following day.[42] Brougham declared that the British policy was honest if not chivalrous, and it seemed to him and to Mill that Britain had taken a significant step in the direction of social progress by resorting to moral protest rather than the sword. Mill did not retract these opinions. As late as 1865, he insisted on making a sharp distinction between what was expedient and what was right. He wrote:

It is not, however, a necessary consequence that because a thing might rightfully be done, it is always expedient to do it. I would not have voted for a war in behalf either of Poland or of Denmark, because on any probable view of consequences I should have expected more evil than good from our doing what, nevertheless, if done, would not have been, in my opinion, any violation of international duty.[43]

Mill, like Brougham and Ruskin, was pro-Danish, although unlike Ruskin he was pacific. Also pacific was Richard Monckton Milnes, the first Lord Houghton who, however, was pro-German. He was strongly opposed to the 'fatuous' London Treaty and greatly alarmed by the nature of British public opinion which, in his view, had been distorted by the Anglo-Danish marriage-alliance. He considered Russell's policy in the duchies quite praiseworthy as the foreign secretary had 'acted with singular moderation and good sense,' in view of the dynastic relationship and the general British attitude. Houghton was relieved when the cabinet decided to remain at peace, for he had feared that popular excitement might have induced the government to fight against Germany.[44]

These examples illuminate the chaotic nature of British public opinion on the Danish crisis. So perplexing indeed was the Schleswig-Holstein question that it divided even closely-knit families. The outstanding example was the royal family itself. The queen and her eldest daughter, both of whom had had German husbands, remained uncompromisingly pro-German throughout. But the Prince of Wales, recently married to a Danish princess, took the Danish side. As late as 1877, the future Edward VII was still pleading vainly for the right of self-determination which Bismarck had promised (but subsequently denied) the inhabitants of north Schleswig.[45] The prince was heartily supported by the queen's cousin, George, duke of Cambridge, who was deeply moved by Denmark's plight. Cambridge regarded the whole war as unnecessary and he feared that the Danish monarchy would be totally destroyed by the ruthless Germans.[46]

The Bulwer-Lyttons were also divided over the issue. Edward Bulwer, the first Lord Lytton, who is now remembered less for his political than for his literary achievements, was wholly opposed to the idea of a British war in support of Denmark. He thought that Britain was too weak to interfere effectively and that, in any case, the Danes had been much too stubborn and wrong-headed. He was not really pro-German but was hostile to the London Treaty and hoped that the inhabitants of the duchies would be consulted so that a durable solution could be found.[47] These opinions were markedly different from those of Bulwer's son, who was then attached to the British embassy at Copenhagen and was passionately pro-Danish.

Similarly divided over Schleswig-Holstein were the members of the Paget family. While Sir Augustus sympathized with Denmark, his wife, Lady Walburga, herself of German extraction, was anti-Danish.[48]

These discordant opinions could not but be reflected in the British press which attempted no detailed analysis until it was too late. The crisis, therefore, took the press by surprise at the end of 1863. Even so prominent a paper as the *Manchester Guardian*, suddenly alerted by the German threat of federal execution, still persisted in regarding the matter as a trifle as late as 4 December. The *Daily News*, no better informed (despite its close association with Russell), complacently stated on 14 October that it was 'difficult to believe, however, that the Diet will persist in incurring this tremendous responsibility on such trivial grounds.' The *Observer* coolly remarked on 25 October that 'we can never believe that so rash a step will be taken by the German Powers.' Most of the British journalists misunderstood the gravity of the situation even after the Diet had voted for the occupation of Holstein.

The rapidity with which events occurred after October 1863 jolted the press out of its languid indifference. The majority of the papers forthwith echoed the public reaction by assuming impulsively that the Germans were wrong, and clamouring for a strong British policy to prevent the dismemberment of Denmark. When the editors began to explore the roots of the quarrel, however, they gradually came to realize that the Danes were not altogether guiltless in the affair. But they still argued amongst themselves over the nature and extent of British obligations and whether the national honour demanded a more heroic program. This confusion of journalistic thought prevailed until the beginning of July 1864, after which the editors resigned themselves to the ministerial decision of 25 June and the parliamentary verdict of 8 July. They were left with the distinct impression that British prestige had been undermined, but this was counterbalanced by the enormous sense of relief that attended the resolution to avoid the horrors of war.

It cannot truthfully be said that Russell's policy in the Danish crisis was dictated by press and public opinion. The mid-Victorians were too much baffled by this problem to offer Russell any useful or constructive advice. The most that one can claim is that A.J.P. Taylor probably exaggerated the influence of Cobdenism in 1864,[49] and that public opinion played only a minor role in shaping British policy in the duchies. All that now seems clear is that the British people, despite the belligerence of a vocal minority, did not wish to join the Dano-German fray in the spring of 1864 when it had already become obvious that brute force and colossal sacrifice would be required to expel the Germans from Danish soil.

Direct pressure from the press and the public was not in fact significant. The British public failed to unite or to give articulate expression to any definitive principles. Like Parliament, it tended to look instead to the Foreign Office and the cabinet for effective leadership on a foreign issue that it did not altogether comprehend. This general bewilderment, both within and outside the British Parliament, thus permitted the queen and a handful of her ministers to exert more influence on Britain's Schleswig-Holstein policy than has previously been supposed. The public was obviously concerned about Denmark's plight but could not decide whether British interests demanded active interference. The Victorians wanted to defend the weak against the powerful, and to take the side of right against wrong, but the Schleswig-Holstein quarrel was too complex to permit them to categorize the protagonists in a meaningful way. Denmark had committed too many mistakes and illegalities to be considered worthy of unqualified British support. The public, moreover, mistrusted the French more than it despised the Germans, and there was always the underlying fear that an Anglo-German war would be of profit only to Napoleon III. Decisions therefore were not easily reached and the British people eventually resigned themselves to the guidance of their political leaders.

British public opinion, then, was influential in the Schleswig-Holstein crisis only in so far as it gave little countenance to the designs of the war-party, especially after the Germans had become entrenched in Schleswig and Jutland, and thus afforded moral support to the Manchester faction which seemed ultimately to exert the greatest influence over the cabinet. In the final analysis, the British public acquiesced in the ministerial decision to withdraw from the Dano-German conflict; it did not compel the government to adopt a policy of peace.

The reluctance of the British people, particularly in the midlands and the north of England, to give constant and vocal support to a Palmerstonian approach (as they had done just before the Crimean War) disappointed Russell, who felt that a passive policy would only encourage the Germans. In the end, the conflict between Cobdenite and Palmerstonian attitudes at home prevented Russell from pursuing any definite policy at all. Left without a program or an ally, Britain's influence had become almost negligible by the time the London conference had been deliberately ruined by the other powers.

For Palmerston's ministry the Dano-German quarrel produced but a single consolation. In Britain it helped to keep the conservatives in disarray and thus allowed the liberals to prolong that supremacy in British politics which they had enjoyed since the repeal of the corn laws and were destined to maintain until 1874. The great debate of 1864 was a decisive victory for the liberals chiefly because of the opposition's inability to produce an alternative to the government's policy in the duchies. The margin of triumph was only eighteen votes, but this was due to the hostility of the Irish Catholics who were still sulking over Russell's desertion of Poland. The liberals drew a surprising degree of support from England, Scotland, and Wales. Only eighteen liberals voted against the government and, with the exception of Colonel Greville, they were all Catholics. The government, in fact, claimed a majority of sixty-four in England, Scotland, and Wales. Six conservatives even voted against Disraeli's motion.[50] The failure of the July resolution left the opposition even more disarranged than before, and its embarrassment was complete when, in the following year, the electorate endorsed the parliamentary vote of confidence. Ironically, it was Russell's failure in Schleswig-Holstein which had provoked that parliamentary vote, and although the members disavowed his diplomacy they expressed satisfaction with the rest of the government's work.

In Europe, however, there was no such consolation to relieve the total and abject gloom. The fiasco not only affected Britain's immediate reputation on the continent but compelled her to overhaul her entire diplomatic strategy. The absolute collapse of the Palmerstonian system of interference, which had suffered such irreparable set-backs during 1863-4, led at once to its abandonment. Earlier in the nineteenth century Britain had been able to meddle frequently and effectively in European affairs, chiefly because she had nearly always found a military power willing to support her point of view. But the Schleswig-Holstein question demonstrated clearly the fundamental weakness of Britain's position in Europe. It proved, more conclusively than had hitherto been done, how impotent she really was without a continental ally.

Had Britain been discreet enough to accept this revelation philosophically she might perhaps have weathered the Schleswig-Holstein storm, but she emphasized her lack of power by imprudently using a superfluity of powerful words. It is true that her course in the winter of 1863-4 was difficult to navigate; quite clearly there were very few directions it could have taken safely. The exigencies of the moment definitely required a circumspect approach similar to the one adopted by Napoleon and Gorchakov. Britain was not any more responsible for upholding the London Treaty than the rest of Europe. She did not even sincerely believe that the arrangement was satisfactory. Palmerston, Delane, and Ellenborough expressed themselves in favour of it, but Russell himself had been ready to abandon it since 1859.[51] Throughout the early 1860s he had made several proposals which called for a drastic revision of the settlement of 1852. His eventual decision to stand by the fateful treaty when many European states wanted to give it up was doubly lacking in prudence. He compounded this error by arrogantly demanding allegiance to the London Treaty in defiance of a series of German snubs. But the failure of British policy in Schleswig-Holstein was not the result of any single act, either of omission or commission, on Russell's part. It sprang from a long series of miscalculations dating back to 1848. Had Britain dealt less cavalierly with the aspirations of the national liberals in Schleswig-Holstein, she would not have left the Germans with the means of interfering provocatively in the internal affairs of the Danish monarchy. Alternatively, had Britain compelled the Danes to fulfil their engagements of 1851-2 the Diet could have found no pretext for occupying Holstein. The seeds of the crisis, in short, were planted prior to 1859. Even so, Russell's personal contribution to the British disaster in the Baltic was immense. Lacking a concrete strategy at all points, he indiscreetly created additional problems for himself by impatiently offering too many simultaneous proposals during the peak of the crisis.

The major weakness of British diplomacy in the duchies lay in the fact that it had been governed more by emotion than by logic. It had been dictated primarily by a morbid fear of France and Russia, an irrational sympathy for Denmark and Poland, a remarkable contempt for all members of the Germanic Confederation, and a general mistrust of the whole constellation of European states. When formulating a program, British statesmen had to cater to these well-known prejudices while trying at the same time to protect British material interests. The Danish crisis, however, provided a most difficult dilemma. For how could Britain protect her commercial interests in the north of Europe without providing opportunities for the tsar and Napoleon whom she most feared? She could not honestly claim that she had no material interests in that area, since the Baltic ports accounted for more than ten per cent of the total value of British export trade during the period 1848-63 and approximately thirteen per cent of her import trade during the same span. Indeed, in 1864 Britain imported from the Baltic goods to the value of almost £30,000,000 in spite of the difficulties created by the war.[52]

It could not be denied that British commercial interests were deeply involved in the Dano-German struggles of 1863-4. Thus it was necessary to decide whether the economic losses likely to accrue from German triumphs were greater than the sacrifices involved in a full-fledged war to uphold the integrity of Denmark. The irony of the whole situation was that, in the upshot, the German victories did no visible damage to British trade and shipping in the Baltic. The value of British imports and exports to and from that region continued to increase even after Denmark had been shorn of Holstein, Lauenburg, and Schleswig. But this had nothing whatever to do with the eventual British decision to hold her peace. This resolution was based in no small measure on the fact that the mid-Victorians had developed a profound aversion to war as a method of diplomacy. They had come to regard war as the very last resort, to be considered only when all other methods had been exhausted. In the Schleswig-Holstein case, war was even more distasteful to Britain since it meant fighting beside a restless and suspect Bonaparte. The majority of Englishmen ultimately felt that German encroachment on the Eider was a lesser evil than French expansion on the Rhine. Throughout the nineteenth century Britain was haunted by that *fantôme du Rhin* which induced her, in 1864, to make two vital errors of judgment: an exaggerated estimate of Napoleon's power and the belittlement of Prussian potential.

When Bismarck, and not Napoleon, emerged with all the prizes from the Dano-German war, all the foundations of mid-Victorian diplomacy were shattered. Britain had failed to see that the Crimean War had seriously altered the European circumstances upon which the Treaty of London had been based. That arrangement depended upon Anglo-Russian co-operation, but the Crimean War had destroyed this alliance and no substitute could be organized in its place. Britain's failure to revive a European concert to preserve the continental balance finally convinced her of the folly of interfering in Europe for strictly European objects. The Schleswig-Holstein *débacle* created a tremendous impact upon her proud and sensitive spirit. Britain withdrew thereafter into her shell and voluntarily pursued a policy of relative isolation. Only once during the next fifty years, in the Near Eastern crisis of 1877–8, did she briefly revert to the jingoism of the earlier era. The Schleswig-Holstein question thus marked the end of Palmerstonianism as a method of British diplomacy and heralded the advent of a new age dominated by the Gladstonian slogan of 'peace, retrenchment, and reform.'

Notes

CHAPTER 1

1 For information on Bell, I am indebted to Professor Steefel who says that Bell was actually born in Hamilton, Ontario, and was naturalized in the United States in 1919.
2 A.J.P. Taylor, *The Struggle for Mastery in Europe, 1848-1918* (Oxford, 1954), pp. 153-4; and *The Trouble Makers: Dissent over Foreign Policy 1792-1939* (London, 1957), pp. 64-7
3 For more details on these schools and on this whole subject generally, see K.A.P. Sandiford, 'British Historians and the Schleswig-Holstein Crisis,' *Canadian Journal of History* (December 1974), IX, 293-309
4 *Britain in World Affairs* (London, 1961), p. 181. See also W.N. Molesworth, *History of England after 1830* (London, 1873), p. 322.
5 A. Hassall, *History of British Foreign Policy* (London, 1912), pp.

277-82; G. Saintsbury, *The Earl of Derby* (London, 1906), p. 135; C. Whibley, *Lord John Manners and his Friends* (London, 1925), p. 131
6 For example, J. Morley, *Life of Gladstone* (London, 1903), II, 118; and G.M. Trevelyan, *Life of John Bright* (London, 1913), pp. 333-4
7 L.D. Steefel, *The Schleswig-Holstein Question* (Harvard, 1932), pp. 45-7, 61, 147
8 K.A.P. Sandiford, 'The British Cabinet and the Schleswig-Holstein Crisis, 1863-4,' *History* (October 1973), LVIII, 360-83
9 Taylor, *The Trouble Makers*, pp. 62 ff
10 Count K.F. Vitzthum, *St. Petersburg and London, 1852-64* (London, 1887), pp. 255-375
11 Brand to Palmerston, 10 June 1864, Palmerston MSS (Historical Manuscripts Commission, London)
12 A. Aspinall, *Politics and the Press, 1780-1850* (Harvester Press reprint, 1973), pp. 2-4

13 *The Times: The Tradition Estab-lished* (London, 1939), II, 337–43

14 W. Hindle, *The Morning Post, 1772–1937: Portrait of a Newspaper* (London, 1937), pp. 179–202; also R. Lucas, *Lord Glenesk and the Morning Post* (London, 1910), pp. 126, 193

15 J. Ridley, *Lord Palmerston* (London, 1970), pp. 114, 413. See also the *Globe*, 1 January 1903.

16 Ridley, p. 114

17 Ibid., p. 527. See also *The Times: Tradition*, II, 354.

18 Lord E. Burnham, *Peterborough Court: The Story of the Daily Tele-graph* (London, 1955), pp. 15–20; also H.W. Massingham, *The London Daily Press* (London, 1892), pp. 94–9

19 *The Times: Tradition*, II, 338

20 Massingham, p. 43

21 W.E. Mosse, *Rise and Fall of the Crimean System 1855–71* (London, 1963), p. 4

22 W.D. Jones, *Lord Derby and Victo-rian Conservatism* (Oxford, 1956), p. 215

23 M. Pinto-Duschinsky, *Political Thought of Lord Salisbury, 1854–68* (London, 1967), passim

CHAPTER 2

1 K. Bourne, *The Foreign Policy of Victorian England 1830-1902* (Oxford, 1970), p. 67; A.J.P. Tay-lor, *The Struggle for Mastery in Europe 1848-1918* (Oxford, 1954), p. 12

2 Hansard, *Parliamentary Debates*, 3rd series, CLXXIV, 1342

3 S.M. Toyne, *The Scandinavians in History* (London, 1948), p. 253

4 A.W. Ward, *Germany: 1815-90* (Cambridge, 1917), II, 105

5 Ibid.

6 Ibid., pp. 105–6; Toyne, pp. 201–2; J. Stefansson, *Denmark and Sweden, with Iceland and Finland* (London, 1916), p. 98

7 Ward, II, 106

8 Ibid., p. 107

9 H. Westergaard, *Economic Develop-ments in Denmark Before and Dur-ing the War* (Oxford, 1922), p. 2

10 Ward, II, 108–9

11 Toyne, p. 257

12 M.T. Florinsky, *Russia: A History and an Interpretation* (New York, 1961), pp. 856–7

13 Taylor, p. 16

14 H.C.F. Bell, *Lord Palmerston* (London, 1936), II, 3

15 Ibid., p. 9. See also Evelyn Ashley, *Life and Correspondence of Vis-count Palmerston* (London, 1879), II, 171.

16 *Parliamentary Debates*, XCVIII, 522

17 Bell, II, 10

18 The queen to Palmerston, 17 April 1848, *Letters of Queen Victoria*, first series (London, 1907), II, 202; also Palmerston to the queen, 18 April 1848, ibid., p. 203

19 *Parliamentary Debates*, XCVIII, 524–6

20 Ibid., p. 605. See also H. Hjelholt, *British Mediation in the Danish-German Conflict, 1848-50* (Copen-hagen, 1965–6), I, 85–8

21 Ibid., I, 124–99 and II, 89–240

22 The queen to Palmerston, 21 June 1849, *QVL*, II, 264–5

23 Palmerston to Wynn, 19 February 1850, *Correspondence Respecting the Affairs of Denmark, 1850–53* (Papers presented to Parliament, LXV, 1864), no. 1

24 Wynn to Palmerston, 19 February 1850, ibid., no. 2

25 Bloomfield to Palmerston, 8 March 1850, ibid., no. 13

26 Augustenburg to Palmerston, 27 May 1850, ibid., no. 18

27 The queen to Palmerston, 22 June 1850, *QVL*, II, 295–6

28 Bunsen to Palmerston, 3 and 4 July 1850, *Correspondence ... Denmark, 1850–53*, nos. 26–7

29 Protocol of London Conference, 4 July 1850, ibid., no. 28

30 A.W. Ward and G.P. Gooch (eds.), *Cambridge History of British Foreign Policy: 1815–66* (Cambridge, 1923), II, 529

31 Magenis to Palmerston, 20 August 1850, *Correspondence ... Denmark, 1850–53*, no. 65

32 Bloomfield to Palmerston, 3 September 1850, ibid., no. 77. Early in 1851, however, Russia withdrew her opposition to the Glücksburg choice. See Bloomfield to Palmerston, 4 February 1851, ibid., no. 85; and the same to the same, 29 April 1851, ibid., no. 98.

33 Bloomfield to Palmerston, 6 June 1851, ibid., no. 108

34 Cowley to Palmerston, 16 September 1851, ibid., no. 150

35 Palmerston to Wynn, 23 September 1851, ibid., no. 157; also Palmerston to Bloomfield, 25 September 1851, ibid., no. 159

36 Bloomfield to Palmerston, 25 September 1851, ibid., no. 164

37 Cowley to Palmerston, 21 October 1851, ibid., no. 186; also Hodges to Palmerston, 14 November 1851, ibid., no. 200

38 Ward and Gooch, *Cambridge History of British Foreign Policy*, II, 535

39 Malmesbury to Bloomfield, 18 March 1852, Earl of Malmesbury, *Memoirs of an Ex-minister* (London, 1884), I, 332

40 Heinrich von Sybel, *The Founding of the German Empire*, translated by M.L. Perrin (New York, 1891), III, 82

41 Palmerston to Wynn, 25 October 1851, *Correspondence ... Denmark, 1850–53*, no. 187; the same to the same, 14 November 1851, ibid., no. 199

42 Blühme to Bille, 8 February 1852, ibid., no. 226 (enclosure no. 2); also Wynn to Granville, 5 February 1852, ibid., no. 225

43 The third duchy (in addition to Schleswig and Holstein) was Lauenburg which, as a result of the Vienna settlement, had been governed by Denmark since 1815.

44 Ward, II, 117–8

45 See *Correspondence between Austria, Prussia and Denmark, 1851–2* (Papers presented to Parliament, LXIII, 1864).

46 Malmesbury to Westmoreland, 20 April 1852, Malmesbury, I, 330
47 Bloomfield to Malmesbury, 30 April and 3 May 1852, *Correspondence ... Denmark, 1850-53*, nos. 288, 291
48 Sybel, III, 89
49 Baroness F. Bunsen (ed.), *Memoirs of Baron Bunsen* (London, 1869), II, 186
50 Sybel, III, 89
51 Palmerston to Bloomfield, 19 May 1848, Bell, II, 9. See also Hjelholt, I, 219.
52 F. Eyck, *The Prince Consort* (London, 1959), p. 104
53 The queen to Palmerston, 16 October 1850, *QVL*, II, 323
54 Memorandum by Prince Albert, 8 August 1850, cited in Eyck, p. 145
55 *Abstract Tables, nos. 1 & 4: Real Values of the Total Imports and Exports of Merchandise* (Papers presented to Parliament, LXVIII, 1866). Much lower figures appear in B.R. Mitchell and Phyllis Deane, *Abstract of British Historical Statistics* (Cambridge, 1971), p. 315. But here also the pattern is the same. Whereas the 'computed values' of British 'imports and re-exports' to and from North and North-eastern Europe totalled £31.2 million in 1860, for instance, they had risen to £35.6 in 1865. Indeed, the figure for 1870 is given here as £47.8. As all the statistics quoted by Mitchell and Deane (pp. 315-17) show a steady increase from 1848 until the outbreak of war in 1914, the conclusion seems to be that British commerce was hardly affected by the political upheavals which took place from time to time in other parts of the world.

CHAPTER 3

1 Wynn to Malmesbury, October-December 1852, nos. 35, 43-4, 53, FO 97/131
2 Malmesbury to Wynn, 14 December 1852, no. 25, draft, ibid.
3 Wynn to Malmesbury, 23 December 1852, no. 53, ibid.
4 The same to the same, November-December 1852, nos. 42, 46, 52, ibid.
5 Malmesbury to Bille, 21 October 1852, draft, ibid.
6 Milbanke to Malmesbury, 1 December 1852, no. 65, ibid.
7 Milbanke to Russell, 22 January 1853; and Wynn to Russell, 22 January 1853, nos. 6-7, FO 97/132
8 Russell to Milbanke, 18 January 1853, no. 1, draft, ibid.
9 Clarendon to Prince Frederick of Holstein, 12 March 1853, ibid. See also Aberdeen-Augustenburg correspondence, March 1853, ibid.
10 Wynn to Clarendon, 11 May 1853, no. 34, FO 97/133
11 Memorandum by Clarendon, 25 May 1853, ibid.
12 Wynn to Clarendon, 7 June 1853, no. 39, ibid.; also Bloomfield to Clarendon, 20 May 1853, no. 195, ibid.

13 Buchanan to Clarendon, 26 July 1853, no. 27, confidential, ibid.

14 Ward, *Germany: 1815-90*, II, 122

15 The Danish legislature created by the constitution of 5 June 1849

16 Wynn to Clarendon, 23 March 1853, no. 21, FO 97/132

17 Steefel, *Schleswig-Holstein Question*, p. 15; Ward, II, 122–3

18 Steefel, p. 16

19 W.E. Mosse, *The European Powers and the German Question, 1848-71* (Cambridge, 1958), pp. 55–9

20 See, e.g., Buchanan to Clarendon, 1 February 1856, no. 20, FO 97/135

21 Hodges to Clarendon, 12 January 1856, ibid.

22 Ward to Clarendon, 10 July 1856, no. 20, ibid.

23 Buchanan to Clarendon, 1 February 1856, no. 20, ibid.

24 Malet to Clarendon, 4 and 28 July 1856, nos. 51, 61, ibid.

25 Clarendon to Buchanan, 11 March 1857, no. 65, draft, FO 97/137

26 Ward, II, 127

27 Buchanan to Clarendon, 30 June 1856, no. 144, FO 97/135

28 Clarendon to Buchanan, 11 October 1856, no. 106, draft, FO 97/136. See also Bloomfield to Clarendon, 11 September 1856, no. 374, ibid.; and Clarendon to Buchanan, 26 June 1856, no. 57, draft, FO 97/135.

29 Malet to Clarendon, 26 November 1856, no. 81, confidential, FO 97/136

30 Clarendon to Seymour, 31 March 1857, no. 200, draft, FO 97/137

31 Mosse, p. 76

32 Cowley to Clarendon, 2 April 1857, no. 520, FO 97/137; also Wodehouse to Clarendon, 15 April 1857, no. 176, FO 97/138

33 Bloomfield to Clarendon, 4 April 1857, no. 179, FO 97/137

34 Clarendon to Orme, 15 and 29 April 1857, nos. 21, 29, drafts, FO 97/138

35 Orme to Clarendon, 2 April 1857, no. 17, FO 97/137; Seymour to Clarendon, 6 July 1857, telegram, FO 97/140

36 Ward to Clarendon, 28 May 1857, secret and confidential, no. 13, FO 97/138

37 Clarendon to Orme, 9 June 1857, no. 47, draft, FO 97/139

38 Clarendon to Jerningham, 20 May 1857, no. 29, draft, FO 97/138

39 Orme to Clarendon, 23 June 1857, telegram, FO 97/139

40 Buchanan to Clarendon, 4 August 1857, no. 184, FO 97/141

41 The same to the same, 26 July 1857, no. 168, ibid.

42 Steefel, pp. 20–1

43 Buchanan to Clarendon, 15 September 1857, no. 234, FO 97/142

44 Bloomfield to Clarendon, 18 September 1857, no. 216, ibid.

45 Buchanan to Clarendon, 2 December 1857, no. 312, FO 97/143

46 Cowley to Clarendon, 4 October 1857, no. 1380, FO 97/142

47 Clarendon to Bloomfield, 25 November 1857, no. 449, draft, FO 97/143

48 Clarendon to Seymour, 2 December 1857, no. 809, draft, ibid.

49 Clarendon to Crampton, 24 February 1858, FO 97/144

50 Steefel, pp. 21-2

51 Sybel, *Founding of the German Empire*, III, 107; see also Edwards to Clarendon, 16 January 1858, and Malet to Clarendon, 12 February 1858, nos. 5-6, FO 97/144.

52 Elliot to Malmesbury, 27 April 1858, no. 7, confidential, FO 97/146; and Buchanan to Clarendon, 23 February 1858, no. 61, FO 97/145

53 Elliot to Malmesbury, 1 June 1858, no. 17, confidential, FO 97/146; and Malet to Malmesbury, 27 April 1858, no. 49, FO 97/145

54 Elliot to Malmesbury, 1 June 1858, no. 17, confidential, FO 97/146

55 Malmesbury to Elliot, 23 June 1858, no. 13, draft, ibid.

56 Elliot to Malmesbury, 28 June and 5 July 1858, nos. 35, 39, FO 97/147

57 Sybel, III, 107-8

58 Elliot to Malmesbury, 14 July 1858, no. 48, FO 97/147

59 Ibid.

60 Malmesbury to Elliot, no. 20, to Loftus, no. 136, and to Paget, no. 104, 21 July 1858, drafts, ibid.

61 Malet to Malmesbury, 13 August 1858, no. 93, FO 97/148; also Sybel, III, 108

62 Elliot to Malmesbury, 28 July 1858, no. 55, FO 97/148; and the same to the same, 7 November 1858, no. 108, FO 97/150

63 Ibid.

64 Malet to Malmesbury, 9 November 1858, no. 126, ibid.

65 Malmesbury to Elliot, 13 November 1858, no. 50, draft, ibid.

66 Forbes to Malmesbury, 16 November 1858, no. 50, ibid.

67 Ward to Malmesbury, 17 November 1858, no. 22, ibid.

68 Elliot to Malmesbury, 22 December 1858, no. 132, ibid.

69 Steefel, pp. 30-1

70 Malmesbury to Elliot, 2 December 1858, no. 58, draft, FO 97/150

71 Elliot to Malmesbury, 6 January 1859, no. 2, FO 97/151

72 Malmesbury to Bloomfield, 29 December 1858, no. 225, draft, FO 97/150

73 Malmesbury to Hodges et al., 16 February 1859, no. 2, draft, FO 97/151

74 Malmesbury to Elliot, 12 January 1859, no. 2, draft, ibid.

75 Elliot to Malmesbury, 14 March 1859, no. 39, FO 97/152

76 Ward, II, 128

77 For a more detailed discussion of the expansion of the Foreign Office staff and the extension of the permanent under-secretary's authority, see V. Cromwell and Z.S. Steiner, 'The Foreign Office before 1914: a study in resistance,' in G. Sutherland (ed.), *Studies in the Growth of Nineteenth Century Government* (London, 1972), pp. 167-94; R.A. Jones, *The Nineteenth Century Foreign Office: An Administrative History* (London, 1971), passim; and Z.S. Steiner, *The Foreign Office and Foreign Policy 1898-1914* (Cambridge, 1969), pp. 6-8.

78 Sir H. Maxwell, *The Life and Letters of George William Frederick, Fourth Earl of Clarendon* (London, 1913), II, 135–6

CHAPTER 4

1 Malet to Russell, 11 August 1859, no. 45, FO 97/153
2 Ward, *Germany*, II, 128–9
3 Russell to Paget, 3 July 1859, no. 2, draft, FO 97/152
4 Paget to Russell, 3 August 1859, no. 13, FO 97/153
5 Steefel, *Schleswig-Holstein Question*, pp. 30–2
6 Malet to Russell, March 1860, *Correspondence respecting the Affairs of the Duchies of Schleswig and Holstein, 1860–61* (Papers presented to Parliament, LXV, 1861), nos. 4–7
7 Bille to Russell, 25 March 1860, ibid., no. 10
8 Paget to Russell, 27 March 1860, ibid., no. 11
9 Russell to Paget, 11 April 1860, ibid., no. 12
10 Paget to Russell, 24 April 1860, ibid., nos. 14, 15
11 Russell to Paget, 27 June 1860, ibid., no. 33
12 Paget to Russell, 3 July 1860, ibid., no. 36; see also no. 39
13 Sybel, *Founding of the German Empire*, III, 111
14 Hamilton to Russell, 27 July 1860, no. 9, FO 30/192
15 Steefel, p. 34
16 Russell to Paget, 2 August 1860, *Correspondence, 1860–61*, no. 45

17 Steefel, p. 34
18 Howard to Russell, 10 November 1860, *Correspondence, 1860–61*, no. 69
19 Schleinitz to Bernstorff, 8 November 1860, ibid., no. 70
20 Russell to Lowther et al., 8 December 1860, ibid., no. 82
21 Steefel, pp. 34–5
22 Ibid., p. 37
23 Russell to Jerningham, 19 April 1861, *Correspondence respecting the Affairs of Holstein, Lauenburg and Schleswig, 1861–63* (Papers presented to Parliament, LXXIV, 1863), no. 42
24 Steefel, p. 35
25 Paget to Russell, 3 March 1861, no. 42, FO 22/284
26 Steefel, p. 35
27 Russell to Loftus, 19 April 1861, *Correspondence, 1861–63*, no. 40
28 Russell to Cowley et al., 19 April 1861, ibid., no. 41; cited also Steefel, p. 38
29 *Correspondence, 1861–63*, nos. 56–61
30 Steefel, p. 39
31 Paget to Russell, 22 August 1861, *Correspondence, 1861–63*, no. 119
32 Sybel, III, 111–2
33 Ibid., p. 113
34 Paget to Russell, 3 April 1862, *Correspondence, 1861–63*, no. 224
35 Russell to Cowley, Napier and Jerningham, 7 and 16 April 1862, ibid., nos. 226, 235
36 Ibid., nos. 229, 241, 242
37 Russell to Fane, et al., 24 September 1862, ibid., no. 274
38 Steefel, p. 45

39 R. Wemyss, *Memoirs and Letters of Sir Robert Morier* (London, 1911), I, 388–9

40 Paget to Russell, 22 February 1861, no. 35 (enclosure), FO 22/284

41 Mosse, *European Powers*, pp. 108–9

42 *Correspondence, 1861–63*, nos. 275, 278, 283–4, 292–5, 300, 310; see also Paget to Russell, 14 November 1862, most confidential, FO 22/294.

43 The *Examiner*, 1 November 1862, and 6 December 1862

44 *Saturday Review*, 24 January 1863, XV, no. 378, pp. 107–8

45 Malmesbury, *Memoirs*, II, 285–8

46 Wemyss, I, 389

47 Steefel, p. 46

48 Russell to Paget, 21 January 1863, *Correspondence, 1861–63*, no. 332

49 Memorandum by Russell, 21 January 1863, ibid., no. 333 (enclosure)

50 The Danish legislature established by the Constitution of 1855

51 Ward, II, 131

52 Steefel, p. 60

53 R.H. Lord, 'Bismarck and Russia in 1863,' *American Historical Review* (October 1923–July 1924), XXIX, 40

54 Steefel, pp. 57–8

55 Ward, II, 132–3

56 Paget to Russell, 29 April 1863, *Denmark and Germany: Correspondence respecting the Affairs of Holstein, Lauenburg and Schleswig* (Papers presented to Parliament, LXIV, no. 2, 1864), no. 49

57 Hansard, *Parliamentary Debates*, third series, CLXX, 1738–65

58 Ibid., col. 1755

59 Russell to the queen, 17 May 1863, *Letters of Queen Victoria*, second series, I, 84–5 (hereafter quoted as *QVL*)

60 Russell to Paget, 22 April 1863, *Denmark & Germany, 2, 1864*, no. 36

61 Paget to Russell, 30 April 1863, no. 105, confidential, FO 22/301

62 Hall's reply to Berlin and Vienna, 16 May 1863, *Denmark & Germany, 2, 1864*, no. 61; also Buchanan to Russell, 23 May 1863, ibid., no. 64

63 Russell to Bloomfield, 27 May 1863, ibid., no. 65

64 Corbett to Russell, 10 July 1863, ibid., no. 88

65 Russell to Malet, 9 June 1863, no. 27, draft, FO 30/205; Russell to Corbett, 24 June 1863, no. 4, draft, ibid.

66 Wemyss, I, 391

67 *Parliamentary Debates*, CLXXII, 1249–52

68 Russell to Bloomfield, 31 July 1863, no. 163, confidential, FO 7/648; cited also in Mosse, p. 152

69 Bloomfield to Russell, 6 and 13 August 1863, *Denmark & Germany, 2, 1864*, nos. 107, 110

70 Steefel, pp. 62–8

71 Russell to Palmerston, 13 August 1863, Palmerston MSS (Historical Manuscripts Commission, London)

72 Palmerston to the queen, 11 August 1863, *QVL*, I, 103–4

73 Russell to Lowther, 31 August 1863, *Denmark & Germany, 2, 1864*, no. 117

74 Bismarck to Katte, 11 September 1863, ibid., no. 123
75 E. Eyck, *Bismarck and the German Empire* (London, 1948), pp. 75-6
76 Russell to Palmerston, 4 September 1863, Palmerston MSS (HMC, London)
77 Russell to Grey, 16 September 1863, *Denmark & Germany, 2, 1864*, no. 125
78 Mosse, pp. 126-8
79 Grey to Russell, 18 September 1863, *Denmark & Germany, 2, 1864*, no. 126
80 Mosse, pp. 109, 145
81 Ibid., pp. 153-4
82 Steefel, pp. 69-71
83 Ward, II, 143
84 Russell to Bloomfield and Buchanan, 30 September 1863, *Denmark & Germany, 3, 1864*, no. 140; also no. 139, ibid.; cited in Steefel, p. 85
85 Howard to Russell, 28 October 1863, *Denmark & Germany, 3, 1864*, no. 198
86 Paget to Russell, 14 October 1863, and Russell to Paget, 13 October 1863, ibid., nos. 159, 165
87 XXXVI, no. 1841, p. 2593

CHAPTER 5

1 Steefel, *Schleswig-Holstein Question*, pp. 71-4
2 Sybel, *Founding of the German Empire*, III, 172
3 Steefel, pp. 77-8
4 *Denmark & Germany, 3, 1864*, no. 236
5 Paget to Russell, 23 November 1863, telegram, ibid., no. 251
6 The same to the same, 29 October 1863, ibid., no. 203
7 Buchanan to Russell, 5 November 1863, ibid., no. 219
8 13 November 1863, ibid., no. 224
9 Mosse, *European Powers*, p. 138
10 The queen to the king of the Belgians, 12 November 1863, *QVL*, I, 114
11 Russell to Palmerston, 6 November 1863, Palmerston MSS (HMC, London)
12 Palmerston to Russell, 8, 12, and 18 November 1863, Russell Papers, PRO 30/22/22; Cowley to Russell, 8 November 1863, private, copy, Cowley Papers, FO 519/231; Hammond to Russell, undated, Hammond Papers, FO 391/7
13 Russell to Cowley, 25 November 1863, no. 1226, draft, FO 27/1483. The same to the same, 12 November 1863, no. 1192, draft, FO 27/1482
14 The queen to Russell, 16 November 1863, *QVL*, I, 114-15
15 General Grey to Russell, 18 November 1863, ibid., p. 115
16 The queen to the king of the Belgians, 19 November 1863, ibid., p. 116
17 Palmerston to Russell, 16 November 1863, Russell Papers, PRO 30/22/22
18 *Denmark & Germany, 3, 1864*, no. 237
19 Paget to Russell, 20 November 1863, no. 265, FO 22/304
20 Ward, *Germany*, II, 139; Steefel, pp. 79-80

21 Palmerston to the queen, 19 November 1863, *QVL*, I, 118

22 General Grey to Russell, 20 November 1863, ibid., pp. 118-20

23 *Denmark & Germany, 3, 1864*, no. 274

24 Russell to Bloomfield and Buchanan, 23 November 1863, ibid., no. 275

25 Palmerston to Russell, 21 November 1863, Russell Papers, PRO 30/22/22

26 Russell to Murray et al., 21 November 1863, no. 22, draft, FO 68/126

27 Loftus to Russell, 23 November 1863, no. 106, FO 9/160

28 Clarendon to Cowley, 26 November 1863, Cowley Papers, FO 519/179

29 Hammond to Cowley, 19 and 21 November 1863, ibid., FO 519/191

30 Clarendon to Cowley, 24 November 1863, ibid., FO 519/179

31 The *Standard*, 19 November 1863

32 Napier to Russell, 24 November 1863, nos. 721, 724, confidential, FO 65/639; Russell to Bloomfield et al., 26 November 1863, *Denmark & Germany, 3, 1864*, no. 292; also Steefel, pp. 135-6; and Mosse, p. 155

33 Steefel, p. 135

34 Mosse, pp. 132-8

35 Ibid., p. 145; C.W. Clark, *Franz Joseph and Bismarck Before 1866* (Harvard, 1934), pp. 21-48

36 Steefel, p. 101; Sybel, III, 202-3; Ward, II, 143-6

37 W.E. Mosse, 'Queen Victoria and her Ministers in the Schleswig-Holstein Crisis, 1863-64,' *English Historical Review* (April 1963), LXXVIII, 266; the queen to Russell, 24 November 1863, *QVL*, I, 121-2; Russell to the queen, 25 November 1863, ibid.

38 Mosse, *European Powers*, p. 157

39 The queen to Russell, 2 December 1863, *QVL*, I, 125-6

40 Bell, *Palmerston*, II, 216-19; D. Beales, *England and Italy 1859-60* (London, 1961), pp. 93-9; K. Bourne, *The Foreign Policy of Victorian England 1830-1902* (Oxford, 1970), pp. 89-92, 101, 109; D. Southgate, *The Most English Minister: Policies and Politics of Palmerston* (London, 1966), pp. 456-8

41 Palmerston to the queen, 3 December 1863, *QVL*, I, 127-9

42 Wood to General Grey, 3 December 1863, ibid., pp. 126-7

43 Mosse, *European Powers*, p. 155; Steefel, pp. 135-6

44 Palmerston to Russell, 29 November 1863, Russell Papers, PRO 30/22/22; Mosse, *European Powers*, p. 156, fn. 1; Russell to Palmerston, 26 November 1863, Palmerston MSS (HMC London)

45 Memoranda by Wood, de Grey, Argyll, Grey, Granville, Gladstone, Palmerston, and Westbury, 7 December 1863, Russell Papers, PRO 30/22/27

46 Instructions to Wodehouse, 8 December 1863, copy sent by Hammond to Cowley, 20 December 1863 (enclosure), Cowley Papers, FO 519/191; Russell to Wodehouse, 9 December 1863, no. 4, confidential, FO 22/306

47 Wodehouse to Russell, 12 December 1863, no. 3, FO 22/306
48 The same to the same, 16 and 21 December 1863, *Denmark & Germany, 4, 1864*, nos. 451, 507
49 Russell to Buchanan et al., 8 December 1863, draft, no. 198, FO 64/537
50 Russell to Bloomfield and Buchanan, no. 207, telegram, ibid.
51 Russell to Malet, 14 December 1863, *Denmark & Germany, 4, 1864*, no. 429
52 Russell to Buchanan, 21 December 1863, no. 212, telegram, FO 64/537
53 Russell to Malet, 26 December 1863, no. 68, draft, FO 30/205
54 Ward to Russell, 27 December 1863, *Denmark & Germany, 4, 1864*, no. 544
55 Hall to Bille, 24 December 1863, ibid., no. 545
56 Russell to Buchanan and Malet, 31 December 1863, ibid., nos. 554, 579
57 Palmerston to Russell, 26 December 1863; see also the same to the same, 10, 13, 18, and 21 December 1863, Russell Papers, PRO 30/22/14G
58 Argyll to Russell, 12 and 31 December 1863, Russell Papers, PRO 30/22/26; Argyll to Gladstone, 30 December 1863, Gladstone Papers, ADD MSS, 44099, fols. 259–62
59 Clarendon to Hammond, 20, 23, and 27 December 1863, Hammond Papers, FO 391/4
60 Hammond to Cowley, 23 December 1863, Cowley Papers, FO 519/191
61 See *The Times*, 11 and 12 December 1863

62 The queen to Russell, 24 December 1863, *QVL*, I, 131–2; Russell to the queen, 26 December 1863, ibid., p. 132

CHAPTER 6

1 Clark, *Franz Joseph and Bismarck*, pp. 55–61
2 Ibid., pp. 62–4; Sybel, *Founding of the German Empire*, III, 198 ff.
3 Russell to Malet et al., *Denmark & Germany, 4, 1864*, no. 579
4 Russell to Palmerston, 28 and 31 December 1863, Palmerston MSS (Historical Manuscripts Commission, London)
5 J. Morley, *Life of Gladstone* (London, 1903), II, 116
6 Mosse, *European Powers and the German Question*, p. 161
7 Palmerston to Russell, 1 & 3 January 1864, Russell Papers, PRO 30/22/15A
8 The queen to Russell, 1 January 1864, *QVL*, I, 138–40
9 General Grey to Russell, 3 January 1864, Russell Papers, PRO 30/22/15A
10 Palmerston to the queen, 4 January 1864, and the queen to Palmerston, 5 January 1864, *QVL*, I, 140–2
11 *Denmark & Germany, 4, 1864*, nos. 608, 614; Phipps to Russell, 5 January 1864, Russell Papers, PRO 30/22/15A; Russell to the queen, 7 January 1864, Mosse, p. 161
12 *Denmark & Germany, 4, 1864*, nos. 615, 620
13 Phipps to the queen, 7 January 1864, *QVL*, I, 142. See also Rus-

sell's memorandum, 7 January 1864, Russell Papers, PRO 30/22/27

14 Mosse, pp. 161-2

15 Ibid.

16 The queen to Palmerston, 8 January 1864, *QVL*, I, 144; Palmerston to the queen, 8 January 1864, ibid., p. 145

17 Palmerston to Russell, 29 December 1863, Russell Papers, PRO 30/22/14G

18 Russell to Palmerston, 8 January 1864, Palmerston MSS (HMC, London)

19 Mosse, p. 162

20 Bloomfield to Russell, 7 January 1864, private, Russell Papers, PRO 30/22/43

21 Malet to Russell, 8 and 9 January 1864, nos. 11 and 12, FO 30/213

22 Mosse, p. 162, fn. 5

23 Napier to Russell, 11 January 1864, no. 23, telegram, and 33, FO 65/657

24 Russell to Palmerston, 10 January 1864, Palmerston MSS (HMC, London)

25 Granville to Phipps, 12 January 1864, *QVL*, I, 150; Mosse, pp. 162-3

26 Cowley to Russell, 15 January 1864, no. 99, FO 27/1523

27 Napier to Russell, 15 January 1864, no. 43, FO 65/657

28 Mosse, pp. 145-9; Clark, p. 47

29 Palmerston to Russell, 7 & 16 January 1864, Russell Papers, PRO 30/22/15A

30 *Denmark & Germany, 4, 1864*, no. 741

31 Ibid., no. 742

32 Russell to Cowley and Napier, 22 January 1864; ibid., no. 773

33 Ibid., no. 815

34 Buchanan to Russell, 24 January 1864; ibid., no. 820; Mosse, p. 169

35 Russell to Cowley, 30 January 1864, ibid., no. 843

36 Russell to Bloomfield and Buchanan, 16, 18, & 20 January 1864; ibid., nos. 715, 743, 758

37 Bismarck to Bernstorff, 24 January 1864; ibid., no. 834

38 Ibid., nos. 880-1

39 The queen to Granville, 27 January 1864; Lord E. Fitzmaurice, *Life of the Second Earl Granville* (London, 1905), I, 456-7

40 Russell to Palmerston, 27 January 1864; Palmerston MSS (HMC, London)

41 Memoranda by Stanley of Alderley, Westbury, Wood, and Somerset, 27 January 1864, Russell Papers, PRO 30/22/27

42 Fitzmaurice, I, 457-8; W.D. Jones, *Lord Derby and Victorian Conservatism* (Oxford, 1956), pp. 279-80; the queen to Palmerston, 2 February 1864, *QVL*, I, 154

43 Hansard, *Parliamentary Debates*, 3rd series, CLXXIII, 107-11, 22-41

44 Lord R. Grosvenor, House of Commons, 4 February 1864; ibid., col. 78

45 For a summary of European press reaction to the royal address, see the *Manchester Guardian*, 9 February 1864.

46 Ibid., 9 January 1864

47 Ibid., 27 and 30 January 1864

48 Ibid., 21 January 1864

49 Ibid., 27 January 1864

50 Ibid., 30 January 1864

51 Ibid., 29 January 1864

52 *The Times*, 12 January 1864

53 Ibid., 2 February 1864

54 Ibid., 3 February 1864

55 *Manchester Guardian*, 12 February 1864

56 Russell to Palmerston, 6 February 1864, Palmerston MSS (HMC, London)

57 The same to the same, 13 February 1864, ibid.; cited also in Steefel, *Schleswig-Holstein Question*, pp. 175-6

58 Palmerston to Russell, 13 February 1864, Russell Papers, PRO 30/22/15A. The whole letter is published in Steefel, pp. 176-7.

59 Fitzmaurice, I, 458-9

60 Granville to General Grey, 13 February 1864, *QVL*, I, 157

61 Russell to Paget, 19 February 1864, *Denmark & Germany, 5, 1864*, no. 987. See also Mosse, p. 178.

62 Russell to Palmerston, 15 February 1864, Palmerston MSS (HMC, London)

63 Steefel, p. 201; Clark, pp. 67-8; Sybel, III, 293-5. See also Ward, *Germany: 1815-90*, II, 162-5.

64 *Denmark & Germany, 5, 1864*, no. 998. See also no. 997.

65 Somerset to the queen, 21 February 1864, *QVL*, I, 160

66 Palmerston to Russell, 20 February 1864, Russell Papers, PRO 30/22/15A

67 Palmerston to Somerset, 20 February 1864, E. Ashley, *Life and Correspondence of Palmerston*, II, 431-2

68 Phipps to Somerset, 22 February 1864, *QVL*, I, 160-1

69 Somerset to Palmerston, 22 February 1864, Palmerston MSS (HMC, London); Somerset to Russell, 10, 11, & 15 January 1864, Russell Papers, PRO 30/22/26

70 Mosse, pp. 180-3

71 The queen to Russell, 22 February 1864, *QVL*, I, 161

72 Russell to the queen, 22 February 1864, Mosse, p. 182

73 Palmerston to the queen, 22 February 1864, *QVL*, I, 161-6

74 Mosse, p. 184

75 Memorandum by General Grey, 25 February 1864, *QVL*, I, 167

76 Russell to Cowley and Napier, 24 February 1864, no. 65, telegram, FO 65/655; cited also in Mosse, p. 184

77 Cowley to Russell, 22 February 1864, no. 289, FO 27/1526; Mosse, pp. 184-5

78 Buchanan to Russell, 24 March 1864, no. 312, FO 64/559

79 Steefel, p. 204

80 Palmerston to Russell, 18 April 1864, Russell Papers, PRO 30/22/15B; cited in Walpole, *Life of Lord John Russell* (London, 1891), II, 404-5

81 Russell to the queen, 18 April 1864, *QVL*, I, 173; and the queen to Russell, 19 April 1864, ibid., p. 174

82 Mosse, 'QV and her Ministers,' *EHR*, LXXVIII, 275

83 Memorandum by Russell, 27 April 1864; and Palmerston to Russell, 27 April 1864, Russell Papers, PRO 30/22/52

84 Palmerston to Russell, 1 May 1864, ibid., PRO 30/22/15B

85 Fitzmaurice, I, 463–4
86 Ibid., p. 465; Mosse, *EHR*, LXXVIII, 277
87 Sybel, III, 326
88 Buchanan to Russell, 4 and 7 April 1864, nos. 353 & 358, FO 64/559
89 *Manchester Guardian*, 11 March 1864

CHAPTER 7

1 Steefel, *Schleswig-Holstein Question*, pp. 207–8; Mosse, *European Powers and the German Question*, pp. 189–90
2 Russell to Cowley, 4 April 1864, no. 342, draft, FO 27/1518
3 The same to the same, 9 April 1864, no. 356, draft, ibid.; Cowley to Russell, 5 April 1864, private, copy, Cowley Papers, FO 519/231
4 Russell to Clarendon, 12 April 1864, Clarendon MSS (Bodleian Library, Oxford); cited also in Mosse, p. 188
5 Palmerston to Russell, 13 April 1864, Clarendon MSS (Bodleian Library, Oxford); Mosse, p. 188
6 Clarendon to Hammond, 9 and 10 April 1864, Hammond Papers, FO 391/4
7 Clarendon to Russell, 14 and 15 April 1864, Russell Papers, PRO 30/22/26. See also Mosse, pp. 188-9; and Steefel, pp. 205-6.
8 Protocols of sessions of 25 April, and 4, 9, & 12 May 1864, *Denmark & Germany, 1864*
9 Mosse, p. 194
10 F.O. Memorandum, confidential, 18 May 1864, Russell Papers, PRO 30/22/52

11 Clarendon to Russell, 20 May 1864, ibid., PRO 30/22/26; Clarendon to Hammond, 16 May 1864, Hammond Papers, FO 391/4; General Grey to Clarendon, 19 May 1864, *QVL*, I, 193
12 Protocols of sessions of 28 May and 2 June 1864, *Denmark & Germany, 1864*
13 The queen to the king of Prussia, 28 May 1864, *QVL*, I, 203–4
14 The king of Prussia to the queen, 4 June 1864, ibid., pp. 212–14
15 Mosse, p. 197
16 Ibid., p. 202; Morley, *Life of Gladstone*, II, 118
17 Russell to the queen, 12 June 1864, *QVL*, I, 215–16
18 The queen to Russell, 12 June 1864; and Wood to Granville, 13 June 1864, ibid., pp. 216–17
19 Granville to the queen, 15 June 1864, Mosse, p. 203
20 Memorandum by Russell, 8 June 1864, Russell Papers, PRO 30/22/52
21 Russell to Palmerston, 10 June 1864, Palmerston MSS (HMC, London)
22 Russell to the queen, 13 June 1864, Russell Papers, PRO 30/22/15C
23 Palmerston to Russell, 5 June 1864, ibid.
24 Fitzmaurice, *Life of Granville*, I, 470–1
25 Memoranda by Russell, Wood, and Villiers, 18 June 1864, Russell Papers, PRO 30/22/52
26 Russell to Palmerston, 21 June 1864, Palmerston MSS (HMC, London)

27 Cowley to Clarendon, 20 June 1864, Clarendon MSS (Bodleian Library, Oxford); cited also in Mosse, p. 205
28 The queen to Russell, 23 June 1864, *QVL*, I, 226-7
29 Palmerston to Russell, 17 & 21 June 1864, Russell Papers, PRO 30/22/15C
30 Extract from the queen's journal, 21 June 1864, *QVL*, I, 223-4
31 Memorandum by Russell, 24 June 1864, Russell Papers, PRO 30/22/52
32 Wood to General Grey, 24 June 1864, *QVL*, I, 228-9
33 Mosse, p. 206
34 Memoranda by Gladstone, 24-5 June 1864, Gladstone Papers, ADD. MSS., 44753, fols. 116-22
35 Memorandum by Russell, 25 June 1864, Russell Papers, PRO 30/22/27
36 Mosse, p. 206, fn. 6. See also Gladstone Papers, ADD. MSS., 44753, fol. 119.
37 General Grey to the queen, 25 June 1864, *QVL*, I, 230
38 The queen to Russell, 25 June 1864, ibid., pp. 230-1
39 The queen to Clarendon, 25 June 1864, ibid., pp. 231-2
40 Clarendon to Cowley, 8, 15, and 25 June 1864, Cowley Papers, FO 519/179
41 Brand to Palmerston, 10 June 1864, Palmerston MSS (HMC, London)
42 Palmerston to Russell, 11 June 1864, ibid.
43 Clarendon to Cowley, 25 June 1864, Cowley Papers, FO 519/179

44 Clark, *Franz Joseph and Bismarck*, p. 88; Ward, *Germany*, II, 185-9
45 Monrad to Bille, 28 June 1864, and Russell to Paget, 6 July 1864, *Denmark & Germany, 7, 1864*, nos. 1-2
46 Russell to Paget, 21 July 1864, no. 170, draft, FO 22/312
47 Paget to Russell, 21 July 1864, private, Russell Papers, PRO 30/22/51; the same to the same, 3 August 1864, no. 312, FO 22/317
48 Palmerston to Russell, 8 August 1864, Russell Papers, PRO 30/22/15C
49 The same to the same, 16 August 1864, ibid.; Russell to Lowther, 20 August 1864, no. 9, draft, FO 64/554
50 General Grey to Granville, 25 August 1864, Fitzmaurice, I, 476
51 Russell to Paget, 24 August, 30 September, and 19 October 1864, nos. 177, 196, and 208, drafts, FO 22/312

CHAPTER 8

1 Lady G. Cecil, *Life of Lord Robert, Marquis of Salisbury* (London, 1921), I, 306-14
2 W.F. Monypenny and G.E. Buckle, *The Life of Benjamin Disraeli* (London, 1916-20), IV, 343-4
3 W.D. Jones, *Lord Derby and Victorian Conservatism*, pp. 279-80
4 Hansard, *Parliamentary Debates*, 3rd series, CLXXIII, 302-9
5 Ibid., cols. 550-60
6 Ibid., cols. 1061-2
7 Ibid., cols. 1158-60

8 Ibid., cols. 217–18

9 Ibid., cols. 324–33

10 Ibid., cols. 861–86

11 Clarendon to Cowley, 27 February 1864, Cowley Papers, FO 519/179

12 *Parliamentary Debates*, CLXXIII, 1260–77

13 Ibid., col. 858

14 Ibid., cols. 1068–70

15 Ibid., cols. 1251–2

16 Ibid., CLXXIV, 533–4

17 Shaftesbury, 7 April 1864, ibid., cols. 531–2; Malmesbury, 19 April 1864, ibid., col. 1276

18 Ibid., cols. 1418–19

19 Ibid., col. 294

20 Ibid., col. 533

21 Ibid., cols. 696–719

22 Ibid., cols. 729–30

23 Ibid., cols. 722–85

24 Ibid., cols. 1292–1315

25 Ibid., cols. 1315–72

26 Ibid., CLXXV, 437–40

27 Ellenborough, 26 May 1864, ibid., cols. 606–10

28 Ibid., cols. 610–15

29 The queen to Derby, 28 May 1864, *QVL*, I, 199–200; Russell to the queen, 31 May 1864, ibid., pp. 208–9

30 *Parliamentary Debates*, CLXXV, 1917–28

31 Ibid., CLXXVI, 337–51

32 Ibid., cols. 302–24

33 Ibid., cols. 324–31

34 Ibid., cols. 351–5

35 Ibid., cols. 709–51

36 Ibid., cols. 709–817

37 Ibid., cols. 827–931

38 Ibid., cols. 952–1071

39 Ibid., cols. 1272–87

40 Morley, *Gladstone*, II, 120

41 See, e.g., Clarendon to Cowley, 9 July 1864, Cowley Papers, FO 519/179.

42 *Parliamentary Debates*, CLXXVI, 1198–1220

43 Ibid., cols. 1076–1190

CHAPTER 9

1 R.W. Seton-Watson, *Britain in Europe, 1789–1914* (Cambridge, 1955), p. 421

2 Ibid., p. 402; Beales, *England and Italy*, pp. 37–61

3 Seton-Watson, p. 422; Bourne, *Foreign Policy of Victorian England*, pp. 89–90, 98–105

4 Clarendon to Cowley, 15 and 29 June 1864, Cowley Papers, FO 519/179

5 W.C.B. Tunstall, 'Imperial Defence, 1815–70,' *The Cambridge History of the British Empire* (Cambridge, 1961), II, 833; see also Sir J.W. Fortescue, *A History of the British Army* (London, 1930), XIII, 522.

6 Palmerston to Russell, 13 February 1864, Russell Papers, PRO 30/22/15A

7 *Army Estimates* (Papers presented to Parliament, XXXII, 1863; and XXXV, 1864). Slightly higher figures are given by Fortescue, XIII, 532–3.

8 L. Wolf, *Life of the First Marquis of Ripon* (London, 1921), I, 204 ff.

9 Somerset to Russell, 10, 11, and 15 January 1864, Russell Papers, PRO

30/22/26; Somerset to Palmerston, 22 February 1864, Palmerston MSS (Historical Manuscripts Commission, London)

10 Clarendon to Cowley, 25 June 1864, Cowley Papers, FO 519/179

11 See, e.g., the same to the same, 6 February 1864, ibid.

12 Mosse, *European Powers and the German Question*, p. 206

13 Fitzmaurice, *Life of Granville*, I, 460

14 Jones, *Lord Derby and Victorian Conservatism*, p. 279

15 Palmerston to Russell, 19 February 1864, Russell Papers, PRO 30/22/23

16 The queen to Russell, 23 June 1864, *QVL*, I, 226-7

17 Phipps to Russell, 12 January 1864, Russell Papers, PRO 30/22/15A

18 Paget to Russell, 3 February 1864, private, ibid., PRO 30/22/51

19 Russell to Buchanan, 6 July 1864, no. 218, draft, FO 64/554

20 The crown princess of Prussia to Queen Victoria, 26 May 1864, *QVL*, I, 204-6

21 Napier to Russell, 11 January 1864, private, Russell Papers, PRO 30/22/84; the same to the same, 1 March 1864, no. 137, FO 65/658; the same to the same, 25 May 1864, no. 271, most confidential, FO 65/659

22 Malet to Russell, 9 and 11 January 1864, nos. 12 and 19, confidential, FO 30/213

23 Palmerston to Russell, 30 December 1863, Russell Papers, PRO 30/22/14G

24 Russell to Ward, 9 January 1864, no. 1, draft, FO 33/185

25 Russell to Cowley, 9 July 1864, private, Cowley Papers, FO 519/200

26 Palmerston to Russell, Russell Papers, PRO 30/22/14G

27 *The Times*, 21 January 1864

28 Sir M.E. Grant Duff, *Out of the Past* (London, 1903), II, 118-19

29 For an interesting summary of the divisions among the liberals, see the *Spectator*, 6 February 1864, XXXVII, no. 1858, p. 146.

30 Jones, p. 280

31 Monypenny and Buckle, *Life of Disraeli*, IV, 343-4

32 A. Lang, *Life and Letters of Sir Stafford Northcote* (London, 1890), I, 208 ff.

33 Lady G. Cecil, *Life of Salisbury*, I, 306-14

34 A.H. Hardinge, *The Fourth Earl of Carnarvon* (Oxford, 1925), pp. 248-55

35 C. Whibley, *Lord John Manners and his Friends* (London, 1925), II, 130-1

36 Malmesbury, *Memoirs of an Ex-minister*, II, 318

37 Ibid., p. 327

38 *The Times*, 11 May 1864

39 A.I. Dasent, *John Thadeus Delane* (New York, 1908), II, 77

40 Ibid., pp. 79, 96, 113

41 E.T. Cook and A. Wedderburn, *The Complete Works of John Ruskin* (London, 1905) XVIII, 545-9

42 See the *Manchester Guardian*, 4 July 1864.

43 Mill to Beal, 19 April 1865, H.S.R. Elliott, *The Letters of John Stuart Mill* (London, 1910), II, 24

44 T. Wemyss Reid, *The Life, Letters and Friendships of Richard Monckton Milnes, the First Lord Houghton* (London, 1890), II, 123-6

45 Sir S. Lee, *King Edward VII* (London, 1925), I, 148, 214, 260-1

46 E. Sheppard, *George, Duke of Cambridge* (London, 1906), pp. 248-51

47 Earl Lytton, *Life of Edward Bulwer, First Lord Lytton* (London, 1913), II, 357-8

48 Lady W. Paget, *Embassies of Other Days* (London, 1923), I, 179-80

49 In *The Trouble Makers: Dissent over Foreign Policy, 1792-1939* (London, 1957), pp. 64-7

50 For a shrewd analysis of the politics involved in the great debate, see an article entitled 'The Vote of Censure' in *The Times*, 12 July 1864.

51 Russell to Paget, 28 December 1859, no. 25, draft, FO 97/153

52 *Abstract Tables, nos. 1, 4, 5 and 7: Real Value of British Imports and Exports* (Papers presented to Parliament, LI, 1854-5; XXVIII, 1859; LVII, 1864; LXVIII, 1866; LVIII, 1868-9)

Bibliography

PUBLIC DOCUMENTS AND MANUSCRIPT SOURCES

FOREIGN OFFICE PAPERS

FO 7/586-674 Drafts and official correspondence between Great Britain and Austria, 1860-4

FO 9/143-165 Drafts and official correspondence between Great Britain and Bavaria, 1860-4

FO 22/278-325 Drafts and official correspondence between Great Britain and Denmark, 1860-4

FO 27/1322-1537 Drafts and official correspondence between Great Britain and France, 1860-4

FO 30/190-215 Drafts and official correspondence between Great Britain and the German confederation, 1860-4

FO 33/165-186 Drafts and official correspondence between Great Britain and Hamburg, 1860-4

FO 34/116-146 Drafts and official correspondence between Great Britain and Hanover, 1860-4

FO 64/487-566 Drafts and official correspondence between Great Britain and Prussia, 1860-4

FO 65/549-663 Drafts and official correspondence between Great Britain and Russia, 1860-4

FO 68/112-133 Drafts and official correspondence between Great Britain and Saxony, 1860-4

FO 97/120-153 Supplement of drafts and official correspondence relating to the Schleswig-Holstein question, 1851-9

FO 97/154–155 Drafts and rough drafts of the protocols of the sessions of the London conference, 1864

PAPERS PRESENTED TO PARLIAMENT
Correspondence respecting the Affairs of Denmark, 1850–53, LXV, 1864
Correspondence between Austria, Prussia and Denmark, 1851-2, LXIII, 1864
Accessions to the Treaty of London of May 8, 1852, relative to the Succession to the Danish Crown, LXV, 1864
Correspondence respecting the Affairs of the Duchies of Holstein, Lauenburg and Schleswig, 1858, LXV, 1864
The Reports of Consul Ward and Vice-consul Reinals on Holstein and Schleswig LXV, 1864
Correspondence respecting the Affairs of the Duchies of Schleswig and Holstein 1860–61, LXV, 1861
Correspondence respecting the Affairs of Holstein, Lauenburg and Schleswig, 1861–63, LXXIV, 1863
Denmark and Germany (No. 1): Correspondence respecting the Maintenance of the Integrity of the Danish Monarchy, LXIV, 1864
Denmark and Germany (Nos. 2,3,4,): Correspondence respecting the Affairs of Holstein, Lauenburg and Schleswig, 1863–64, LXIV, 1864
Denmark and Germany (Nos. 5,6,7): Correspondence respecting the Affairs of Holstein, Lauenburg and Schleswig, 1864, LXV, 1864
Protocols of the London Conference, 1864, LXV, 1864
Correspondence respecting the Affairs of Holstein, Lauenburg and Schleswig, 1864, LVII, 1865
Army and Navy Estimates, 1861-4: XXXVI, XXXVIII, 1861; XXXII, XXXIV, 1862; XXXII, XXXV, 1863; XXXV, XXXVII, 1864
Abstract Tables, nos. 1,4,5,7: Real Values of the Total Imports and Exports of Merchandise, LI, 1854-5; XXVIII, 1859; LVII, 1864; LXVIII, 1866; LVIII, 1868-9

PARLIAMENTARY DEBATES
Hansard, *Parliamentary Debates*, third series, XCVII-CXV; CLXIX-CLXXVI

PRIVATE CORRESPONDENCE
Bloomfield Papers, FO 356/16–20 (Public Record Office, London)
Cardwell Papers, PRO 30/48/41–5 (Public Record Office, London)
Clarendon Manuscripts (Bodleian Library, Oxford)
Cowley Papers, FO 519/171–231 (Public Record Office, London)

Gladstone Papers (British Museum, London)
Granville Papers, PRO 30/29/18-31 (Public Record Office, London)
Halifax Papers (British Museum, London)
Hammond Papers, FO 391/1-8 (Public Record Office, London)
Iddesleigh Papers (British Museum, London)
Layard Papers (British Museum, London)
Palmerston Manuscripts (Historical Manuscripts Commission, London)
Ripon Papers (British Museum, London)
Russell Papers, PRO 30/22/14-114 (Public Record Office, London)

GUIDES TO PUBLIC DOCUMENTS
Brooke, J. (ed.), *The Prime Ministers' Papers, 1801-1902* (London, 1968)
Ford, P. &G. *Select List of British Parliamentary Papers, 1833-1899*
 (London, 1953)
- *A Guide to Parliamentary Papers* (London, 1955)
Jones, V.H. *A Catalogue of British Parliamentary Papers, 1801-1900*
 (London, 1901)
PRO Handbook, *The Records of the Foreign Office, 1782-1939* (London,
 1969)
Temperley, H.W.V. & Penson, L.M. *Foundations of British Foreign Policy,
 1792-1902* (London, 1938)
- *A Century of Diplomatic Blue Books, 1814-1914* (London, 1939)

NEWSPAPERS AND PERIODICALS

DAILY NEWSPAPERS
[Files consulted for the period January 1862 to December 1864]
Daily News
Daily Telegraph
Dublin Daily Express
Glasgow Herald
Globe
Liverpool Mercury
Manchester Guardian
Morning Herald
Morning Post
Standard
The Times

WEEKLY PUBLICATIONS
[Dates in brackets indicate the files consulted]
Economist (1863–4)
Examiner (1862–4)
Illustrated London News (1860–5)
Observer (1863–4)
Punch (1860–4)
Saturday Review (1863–4)
Spectator (1863–4)

MONTHLY MAGAZINES
Blackwood's Edinburgh Magazine (1863–5)
Gentlemen's Magazine and Historical Review (1863–4)

QUARTERLY REVIEWS
Eclectic Review (1860–70)
Edinburgh Review (1860–70)
Fortnightly Review (1860–5)
Quarterly Review (1860–70)
Westminster Review (1860–5)

MISCELLANEOUS
Annual Register of Events (1850–65)
Aspinall, A. 'The Circulation of Newspapers in the Early Nineteenth Century,' *Review of English Studies*, XXII (1946)
Ayerst, D. *Guardian: Biography of a Newspaper* (London, 1971)
Burnham, Lord E. *Peterborough Court: The Story of the Daily Telegraph* (London, 1955)
Ellegard, A. 'Public Opinion and the Press: Reactions to Darwinism,' *Journal of the History of Ideas*, XIX (1958)
Escott, T.H.S. *Masters of English Journalism* (London, 1911)
Fox-Bourne, H.R. *English Newspapers* (London, 1887)
Grant, A.J. *The Newspaper Press* (London, 1871–3)
Graves, C.L. *Mr. Punch's History of Modern England* (London, 1921)
Hindle, W. *The Morning Post, 1772–1937: Portrait of a Newspaper* (London, 1937)
MacCalmont, F.H. *Parliamentary Poll Book* (London, 1879)
Massingham, H.W. *The London Daily Press* (London, 1892)
Newspaper Press Directory, 1864 (Mitchell & Co., London)
Price, R.C.G. *A History of Punch* (London, 1957)
Read, D. 'North of England Newspapers (*c.*1700–*c.*1900) and their Value to Historians,' *Proceedings of the Leeds Philosophical and Literary Society*, VIII (1957)

The Times: A Newspaper History 1785-1935 (London, 1935)
The Times: The Tradition Established (London, 1939)
Thomas, W.B. *Story of the Spectator 1829-1928* (London, 1928)
Wadsworth, A.P. 'Newspaper Circulations, 1800-1954,' *Manchester Statistical Society* (March, 1955)

AUTOBIOGRAPHIES, BIOGRAPHIES, LETTERS, AND MEMOIRS

Argyll, Dowager Duchess (Ed.) *Autobiography and Memoirs of Douglas, Eighth Duke of Argyll* (London, 1906)
Aronson, T. *Queen Victoria and the Bonapartes* (London, 1972)
Ashley, Hon. E. *The Life and Correspondence of Henry John Temple, Viscount Palmerston* (London, 1879)
Ausubel, H. *John Bright: Victorian Reformer* (New York, 1966)
Balfour, Lady B. (Ed.) *Personal and Literary Letters of Robert, First Earl of Lytton* (London, 1906)
Bell, H.C.F. *Lord Palmerston* (London, 1936)
Benson, E.F. *Queen Victoria* (London, 1935)
Beust, Count F.F. *Memoirs* (London, 1887)
Bismarch, Otto von. *Reflections and Reminiscences* (Trans., London, 1898)
Blake, R. *Disraeli* (London, 1966)
Bloomfield, Baroness G. *Reminiscences of Court and Diplomatic Life* (London, 1883)
Buckle, G.E. (Ed.) *Letters of Queen Victoria, 1862-78*; second series (London, 1926)
Bunsen, Baroness F. (Ed.) *Memoirs of Baron Bunsen* (London, 1869)
Cavendish, F.W.H. *Society, Politics and Diplomacy, 1820-64* (London, 1913)
Cecil, A. *British Foreign Secretaries, 1807-1916* (London, 1927)
- *Queen Victoria and her Prime Ministers* (London 1953)
Cecil, Lady G. *Life of Lord Robert, Marquis of Salisbury* (London, 1921)
Childers, Lt-Col. S. *Life and Correspondence of the Rt. Hon. H.C.E. Childers* (London, 1901)
Colson, P. *Lord Goschen and his Friends* (London, 1946)
Concise Dictionary of National Biography to 1930
Connell, B. *Regina v. Palmerston, 1837-65* (London, 1962)
Cook, Sir E. *Delane of "The Times"* (London, 1915)
Cook, E.T. & Wedderburn, A. *The Complete Works of John Ruskin* (London, 1903-12)
Cooper, T. (Ed.) *Men of the Time* (London, 1875)
Crowe, Sir J.A. *Reminiscences of Thirty Five Years of My Life* (London, 1895)

Dasent, A.I. *John Thadeus Delane* (New York, 1908)
Dawson, W.H. *Richard Cobden and Foreign Policy* (New York, 1927)
Dictionary of National Biography
Elliott, H.S.R. *The Letters of John Stuart Mill* (London, 1910)
Escott, T.H.S. *Great Victorians* (London, 1916)
Esher, Lord & Benson, A.C. *Letters of Queen Victoria*; first series (London, 1907)
Eyck, E. *Gladstone*, trans. B. Miall (London, 1938)
- *Bismarck after Fifty Years* (London, 1948)
- *Bismarck and the German Empire* (London, 1958)
Eyck, F. *The Prince Consort* (London, 1959)
Fitzmaurice, Lord E. *The Life of the Second Earl Granville* (London, 1905)
Gooch, G.P. *Later Correspondence of Lord John Russell, 1840-78*
    (London, 1925)
Grant Duff, Sir M.E. *Studies in European Politics* (London, 1866)
- *Notes from a Diary* (London, 1897)
- *Out of the Past* (London, 1903)
Guedalla, P. *Palmerston* (London, 1926)
- *Gladstone and Palmerston, 1853-65* (London, 1928)
- *The Queen and Mr. Gladstone* (London, 1933)
Hammond, J.L. *Gladstone and the Irish Nation* (London, 1938)
Hammond, J.L. & Foot, M.R.D. *Gladstone and Liberalism* (London, 1952)
Hardinge, A.H. *The Fourth Earl of Carnarvon* (Oxford, 1925)
Hobson, J.A. *Richard Cobden - The International Man* (New York, 1919)
Jagow, Dr K. *Letters of the Prince Consort 1831-61* (London, 1938)
Jeans, W. *Parliamentary Reminiscences* (London, 1912)
Jones, W.D. *Lord Derby and Victorian Conservatism* (Oxford, 1956)
Kennedy, A.L. *Salisbury, 1830-1903* (London, 1953)
Knaplund, P. *Gladstone's Foreign Policy* (New York, 1935)
Lang, A. *Life, Letters and Diaries of Sir Stafford Northcote, First Earl of
    Iddesleigh* (London, 1890)
Layard, A.H. *Autobiography and Letters* (London, 1903)
Leader, R.E. (Ed.) *Life and Letters of J.A. Roebuck* (London, 1897)
Lee, Sir S. *Queen Victoria: A Biography* (London, 1904)
- *King Edward VII* (London, 1925)
Loftus, Lord A. *Diplomatic Reminiscences, 1862-79* (London, 1894)
Longford, E. *Victoria R.I.* (London, 1964)
Lucas, R. *Lord Glenesk and the "Morning Post"* (London, 1910)
Lytton, Earl B. *The Life of Edward Bulwer, the First Lord Lytton* (London,
    1913)
Magnus, P. *Gladstone* (London, 1954)

- *King Edward VII* (London, 1964)

Malmesbury, Earl. *Memoirs of an Ex-minister* (London, 1884)

Marriott, Sir J.A.R. *Queen Victoria and her Ministers* (London, 1933)

Martin, B.K. *The Triumph of Lord Palmerston* (London, 1924)

Martin, Sir T. *Life of the Prince Consort* (London, 1875-80)

Maxwell, Sir H. *Life and Letters of George William Frederick, Fourth Earl of Clarendon* (London, 1913)

Monypenny, W.F. & Buckle, G.E. *The Life of Benjamin Disraeli* (London, 1916-20)

Morley, J.E. *Life of Cobden* (London, 1881)

- *Life of Gladstone* (London, 1903)

O'Brien, R.B. *John Bright: A Monograph* (London, 1910)

Paget, Lady W. *Embassies of Other Days* (London, 1923)

Pemberton, W.B. *Lord Palmerston* (London, 1954)

Pflanze, O. *Bismarck and the Development of Germany, 1815-71* (Princeton, 1963)

Pinto-Duschinsky, M. *The Political Thought of Lord Salisbury, 1854-68* (London, 1967)

Prest, J. *Lord John Russell* (London 1972)

Raymond, E.T. *Disraeli: Alien Patriot* (New York, 1925)

Read, D. *Cobden and Bright: A Victorian Political Partnership* (London, 1967)

Redesdale, Lord. *Memories* (London, 1915)

Reid, S.J. *Lord John Russell* (London, 1895)

Ridley, J. *Lord Palmerston* (London, 1970)

Ringhoffer, Dr K. *The Bernstorff Papers* (London, 1908)

Russell, Earl J. *Selections from Speeches and Despatches* (London, 1870)

- *Recollections and Suggestions, 1813-73* (London, 1875)

Saintsbury, G. *The Earl of Derby* (London, 1906)

Selborne, Lord. *Memorials of Roundell-Palmer* (London, 1896-8)

Sheppard, E. *George, Duke of Cambridge* (London, 1906)

Southgate, D. *The Most English Minister: Policies and Politics of Palmerston* (London, 1966)

St Aubyn, G. *The Royal George: Life of the Duke of Cambridge, 1819-1904* (London, 1963)

Strachey, L. *Queen Victoria* (New York, 1921)

Taylor, A.J.P. *Bismarck* (London, 1955)

Tilby, A.W. *Lord John Russell* (London, 1930)

Tingsten, H. *Victoria and the Victorians* (London, 1972)

Trevelyan, G.M. *Life of John Bright* (London, 1913)

Villiers, G. *A Vanished Victorian* (London, 1938)

Vitzthum, Count K.F. *St. Petersburg and London, 1852-64* (London, 1887)
Walpole, Sir S. *The Life of Lord John Russell* (London, 1891)
Ward, T.H. (Ed.) *Men of the Reign* (London, 1885)
Waterfield, G. *Layard of Nineveh* (London, 1963)
Wellesley, F.A. *The Paris Embassy during the Second Empire* (London, 1928)
Wemyss, Mrs R. *Memoirs and Letters of Sir Robert Morier from 1826 to 1876* (London, 1911)
Wemyss Reid, Sir T. *The Life of the Rt. Hon. W.E. Forster* (London, 1888)
Whibley, C. *Lord John Manners and his Friends* (London, 1925)
Whitton, P.E. *Moltke* (London, 1921)
Wiegler, P. *Wilhelm I: His Life and Times* (Boston, 1929)
Wolf, L. *Life of the First Marquess of Ripon* (London, 1921)

OTHER SECONDARY SOURCES

Arnaud, R. *The Second Republic and Napoleon III* (London, 1930)
Aspinall, A. *Politics and the Press, 1780-1850* (London, 1949)
Bartlett, C.J. (Ed.) *Britain Pre-Eminent: Studies in British World Influence in the Nineteenth Century* (London, 1969)
Beales, D.E.D. *England and Italy 1859-60* (London, 1961)
Binkley, R.C. *Realism and Nationalism 1852-71* (New York, 1935)
Bond, B. (Ed.) *Victorian Military Campaigns* (London, 1967)
- 'Prelude to the Cardwell Reforms, 1856-68,' *Journal of the Royal United Service Institution* (1961)
Bourne, K. *Foreign Policy of Victorian England 1830-1902* (Oxford, 1970)
Bourne, K. & Watt, D.C. (Eds.) *Studies in International History* (London, 1967)
Briggs, A. *The Age of Improvement, 1784-1867* (London, 1959)
Bright, J.F. *History of England, 1837-80* (London, 1902)
Bury, J.P. *France, 1814-1940* (London, 1949)
Carr, W. *Schleswig-Holstein, 1815-48* (Manchester, 1963)
Case, L.M. *French Opinion on War and Diplomacy during the Second Empire* (Philadelphia, 1954)
Clark, C.W. *Franz Joseph and Bismarck before 1866* (Harvard, 1934)
Danstrup, J. *A History of Denmark* (Copenhagen, 1949)
Egerton, H.E. *British Foreign Policy in Europe* (London, 1918)
Evans, R.J. *The Victorian Age, 1815-1914* (London, 1950)
Farrer, J.A. *The Monarchy in Politics* (London, 1917)
Flenley, R. *Modern German History* (London, 1959)
Florinsky, M.T. *Russia: A History and an Interpretation* (New York, 1961)

Fortescue, Sir J.W. *A History of the British Army, XIII: 1852-70* (London, 1930)

Gooch, G.P. & Masterman, J.H.B. *A Century of British Foreign Policy* (London, 1917)

Görlitz, W. *The Prussian General Staff, 1657-1945* (London, 1953)

Gosch, C.A. *Denmark and Germany since 1815* (London, 1862)

Guedalla, P. *The Second Empire* (London, 1922)

Hardie, F. *The Political Influence of Queen Victoria, 1861-1901* (London, 1935)

Hassall, A. *A History of British Foreign Policy* (London, 1912)

Headlam-Morley, Sir J. *Studies in Diplomatic History* (London, 1930)

Hjelholt, H. *British Mediation in the Danish-German Conflict, 1848-50* (Copenhagen, 1965-6)

Imlah, A.H. *Economic Elements in the Pax Britannica* (Harvard, 1958)

Jelavich, B. *A Century of Russian Foreign Policy, 1814-1914* (New York, 1964)

Jones, R.A. *A Nineteenth Century Foreign Office: An Administrative History* (London, 1971)

Kissinger, H. *A World Restored* (Cambridge, 1957)

Kohn, H. *The Mind of Germany* (London, 1961)

Kraehe, E.E. 'Austria and the Problem of Reform in the German Confederation, 1851-63,' *American Historical Review*, LVI, (1951)

Lauring, P. *A History of the Kingdom of Denmark* (Copenhagen, 1960)

Lord, R.H. 'Bismarck and Russia in 1863,' *American Historical Review*, XXIX, 1924

Luvaas, J. *The Education of an Army: British Military Thought, 1815-1940* (Chicago, 1964)

Marriott, Sir J.A.R. *England since Waterloo* (London, 1927)

Mazour, A.G. 'Russia and Prussia during the Schleswig-Holstein Crisis,' *Journal of Central European Affairs* (1941)

McCarthy, J. *A History of our own Times* (London, 1887)

Millman, R. *British Foreign Policy and the Coming of the Franco-Prussian War* (Oxford, 1965)

Mitchell, B.R. & Deane, P. *Abstract of British Historical Statistics* (Cambridge, 1971)

Molesworth, W.N. *A History of England after 1830* (London, 1873)

Mosse, W.E. *The European Powers and the German Question, 1848-71* (Cambridge, 1958)

- *The Rise and Fall of the Crimean System, 1855-71* (London, 1963)

- 'England and the Polish Insurrection of 1863,' *English Historical Review*, LXXI (1956)

- 'Public Opinion and Foreign Policy, 1870,' *Historical Journal*, VI (1963)
- 'Queen Victoria and her Ministers in the Schleswig-Holstein Crisis, 1863-64,' *English Historical Review*, LXXVIII (1963)
The New Cambridge Modern History, X, Zenith of European Power: 1830-70 (Cambridge University Press, 1971)
Ollivier, E. *L'Empire Libéral* (Paris, 1903)
Otté, E.C. *Scandinavian History* (London, 1874)
Parris, H. *Constitutional Bureaucracy* (London, 1969)
Paul, H. *A History of Modern England* (London, 1904)
Petrie, Sir C. *The Victorians* (London, 1960)
Pinson, K.S. *Modern Germany* (New York, 1954)
Platt, D.C.M. *Finance, Trade and Politics: British Foreign Policy 1815-1914* (London, 1968)
Ramsay, A.A.W. *Idealism and Foreign Policy* (London, 1925)
Raymond, D.N. *British Policy and Opinion during the Franco-Prussian War* (New York, 1921)
Read, D. *Press and People, 1790-1850* (London, 1961)
Seton-Watson, R.W. *Britain in Europe, 1789-1914* (Cambridge, 1937)
Sheppard, E.W. *A Short History of the British Army* (London, 1926)
Sontag, R.J. *Germany and England: Background of Conflict, 1848-94* (New York, 1938)
Southgate, D. *The Passing of the Whigs 1832-1886* (London, 1962)
Steefel, L.D. *The Schleswig-Holstein Question* (Harvard, 1932)
Stefansson, J. *Denmark and Sweden, with Iceland and Finland* (London, 1916)
Steiner, Z.S. *The Foreign Office and Foreign Policy, 1898-1914* (Cambridge, 1969)
Strang, Lord. *Britain in World Affairs* (London, 1961)
Sutherland, G. (Ed.) *Studies in the Growth of Nineteenth Century Government* (London, 1972)
Sybel, H. *The Founding of the German Empire*, trans. M.L. Perrin (New York, 1891)
Taylor, A.J.P. *The Struggle for Mastery in Europe, 1848-1918* (London, 1954)
- *The Trouble-Makers: Dissent over Foreign Policy, 1792-1939* (London, 1957)
Toyne, S.M. *The Scandinavians in History* (London, 1948)
Trevelyan, G.M. *British History in the Nineteenth Century and After* (London, 1937)
Tunstall, W.C.B. 'Imperial Defence, 1815-70,' *The Cambridge History of the British Empire*, chap. XXII, vol. II (1961)
Twiss, T. *On the Relations of the Duchies of Schleswig and Holstein to the Crown of Denmark* (London, 1848)

Vincent, J.R. *The Formation of the Liberal Party, 1857-68* (London, 1966)
Walpole, Sir S. *The History of Twenty Five Years* (London, 1904)
Ward, A.W. *Germany, 1815-90* (Cambridge, 1917)
- 'The Schleswig-Holstein Question, 1852-66,' *The Cambridge History of British Foreign Policy*, chap. XIII, vol. II (1922)
Westergaard, H. *Economic Developments in Denmark before and during the War* (Oxford, 1922)
Wood, A.C. *Nineteenth Century Britain, 1815-1914* (London, 1960)
Woodward, E.L. *War and Peace in Europe, 1815-70* (London, 1931)
- *The Age of Reform: 1815-70* (Oxford, 1962)
Young, G.M. (Ed.) *Early Victorian England, 1830-65* (London, 1934)

Index